Uruguay

WORLD BIBLIOGRAPHICAL SERIES

General Editors:

Robert G. Neville (Executive Editor)

John J. Horton   Ian Wallace

Hans H. Wellisch   Ralph Lee Woodward, Jr.

John J. Horton is Deputy Librarian of the University of Bradford and currently Chairman of its Academic Board of Studies in Social Sciences. He has maintained a longstanding interest in the discipline of area studies and its associated bibliographical problems, with special reference to European Studies. In particular he has published in the field of Icelandic and of Yugoslav studies, including the two relevant volumes in the World Bibliographical Series.

Ian Wallace is Professor of Modern Languages at Loughborough University of Technology. A graduate of Oxford in French and German, he also studied in Tübingen, Heidelberg and Lausanne before taking teaching posts at universities in the USA, Scotland and England. He specializes in East German affairs, especially literature and culture, on which he has published numerous articles and books. In 1979 he founded the journal *GDR Monitor*, which he continues to edit.

Hans H. Wellisch is Professor emeritus at the College of Library and Information Services, University of Maryland. He was President of the American Society of Indexers and was a member of the International Federation for Documentation. He is the author of numerous articles and several books on indexing and abstracting, and has published *The Conversion of Scripts* and *Indexing and Abstracting: an International Bibliography*. He also contributes frequently to *Journal of the American Society for Information Science*, *The Indexer* and other professional journals.

Ralph Lee Woodward, Jr. is Chairman of the Department of History at Tulane University, New Orleans, where he has been Professor of History since 1970. He is the author of *Central America, a Nation Divided*, 2nd ed. (1985), as well as several monographs and more than sixty scholarly articles on modern Latin America. He has also compiled volumes in the World Bibliographical Series on *Belize* (1980), *Nicaragua* (1983), and *El Salvador* (1988). Dr. Woodward edited the Central American section of the *Research Guide to Central America and the Caribbean* (1985) and is currently editor of the Central American history section of the *Handbook of Latin American Studies*.

VOLUME 102

Uruguay

Henry Finch

with the assistance of
Alicia Casas de Barrán
Compilers

CLIO PRESS
OXFORD, ENGLAND · SANTA BARBARA, CALIFORNIA
DENVER, COLORADO

British Library Cataloguing in Publication Data

Finch, M.H.J. (Martin Henry John), *1941–*
Uruguay. – (World bibliographical series ; v. 102)
1. Uruguay. Bibliographies
I. Title II. Series
016.9895

ISBN 1–85109–098–3

Clio Press Ltd.,
55 St. Thomas' Street,
Oxford OX1 1JG, England.

ABC–Clio Information Services,
Riviera Campus, 2040 Alameda Padre Serra,
Santa Barbara, CA 93103, USA.

Designed by Bernard Crossland,
Typeset by Columns Design and Production Services, Reading, England.
Printed and bound in Great Britain by
Billing and Sons Ltd., Worcester.

THE WORLD BIBLIOGRAPHICAL SERIES

This series, which is principally designed for the English-speaker, will eventually cover every country in the world, each in a separate volume comprising annotated entries on works dealing with its history, geography, economy and politics; and with its people, their culture, customs, religion and social organization. Attention will also be paid to current living conditions – housing, education, newspapers, clothing, etc. – that are all too often ignored in standard bibliographies; and to those particular aspects relevant to individual countries. Each volume seeks to achieve, by use of careful selectivity and critical assessment of the literature, an expression of the country and an appreciation of its nature and national aspirations, to guide the reader towards an understanding of its importance. The keynote of the series is to provide, in a uniform format, an interpretation of each country that will express its culture, its place in the world, and the qualities and background that make it unique. The views expressed in individual volumes are not necessarily those of the publishers.

VOLUMES IN THE SERIES

To my parents
Hilda and Martin Finch

Contents

Contents

Contents

Introduction

Uruguay is a country which at first sight does not appear to require the use of superlatives or extremes of language for its description. Even where it does excel, this is often at the diminutive end of things, being the smallest of the original South American republics (about the size of the state of Missouri, or not much larger than England and Wales), with its population of three million growing at the lowest rate in Latin America (0.7 per cent per annum). Physically it is an understated land, having a beauty of its own but not one which (apart from its beaches) makes an obvious appeal to the average traveller. The climate is temperate, rather hot in summer, not too cold in winter. In social terms Uruguay is a middle-class country. It does not lack a wealthy élite, an urban proletariat and marginalized population, nor small farmers and casual labourers, but nonetheless it is a society which takes its character from the ranks of government employees, clerical workers, professionals and pensioners, in the capital city of Montevideo. The economy provides an intermediate level of average incomes (about US$ 2,700 in 1987), considerably higher than in the majority of other Latin American nations but equal to only the poorest of Western European countries. Politically, Uruguay has through most of the twentieth century made a virtue of compromise, rejecting extremes of left and right in favour of a negotiated 'middle way'. Internationally, the nation has neither the size nor strategic location to ensure an automatic audience for its views on world affairs. The history of the country is brief, since the indigenous population was very sparse and in colonial times the territory saw little settlement; neither Indian nor Spaniard has left an appreciable legacy of buildings or artefacts. A small black community has descended from the former slave population, but in general Uruguay lacks the racial and linguistic diversity which is characteristic of most other Latin American nations.

However, if the external appearance is in many respects modest or unremarkable, the reality of Uruguay is very different. Particularly in its social and political organization, the country has a singular record

Introduction

of achievement standing to its credit. In the early years of this century Uruguay embarked on a prolific period of social reform which earned for it the informal title 'Latin America's first welfare state'. Pensions funds and laws in defence of labour were a feature of the period, but so too was the separation of Church and State, protection for women (including liberal divorce legislation) and for natural children, the banning of cruel sports, and the abolition – permanently and uncontestedly – of capital punishment. It is worth pointing out that many of these reforms not only anticipated their implementation in notionally more 'advanced' countries, but in many cases have yet to be achieved in them.

Even more remarkable than these was the adoption of a new constitution in 1919 which introduced a collegiate executive (the *colegiado*) sharing power with the president of the country. It lasted until 1933 and then was reintroduced in modified form in 1952 for a further period of fifteen years. The distinctive culture of Uruguay has by no means been confined to its political institutions and social reforms, however. Uruguayan writers and artists have achieved recognition throughout Latin America and beyond. At a less exalted level, Uruguay has traditionally attached importance to education at all levels, and the rate of adult literacy exceeds 96 per cent. However, the admiration and respect which these achievements invite cannot conceal the fact that Uruguay's national progress has not been continuous and sustained.

History

The flourishing of the Uruguayan nation in the first three decades of the twentieth century, and its more recent decline in an extended period of economic stagnation followed by military dictatorship (1973-85) is a dramatic story. It becomes even more so when one considers the unpromising nature of the country's origins. The Banda Oriental del Uruguay (east bank of the River Uruguay) was a sparsely populated, rather remote province in colonial times. From the sixteenth to the early nineteenth centuries, the territory changed hands between the Spanish and Portuguese several times. In 1776 it became part of the newly created Viceroyalty of La Plata of the Spanish colonial system. Wild *criollo* cattle grazed on the rough pasture-land, but commercial exploitation of the cattle stocks was limited mainly to hides. Although the country has no mountain barriers, and indeed very little land above 300m, internal transport by ox-cart over the roadless terrain was costly and slow. Even Montevideo, with its natural harbour overlooked by the Cerro (hill) on the other side of the bay, was not founded until 1726.

The political process which resulted in the emergence of an independent nation was complex and lengthy. The role of Uruguay's national hero, José Gervasio Artigas, was crucial, yet ironically Artigas sought to achieve a federalist structure with the other territories of the River Plate, rather than the independent republic of Uruguay which his campaigns against the forces of colonial Spain, Brazil, and his enemies in Argentina, helped to bring about. Incursions from Brazil were by no means a novelty of the Independence period; access to the River Plate had long attracted the Portuguese authorities in Brazil, and indeed they were responsible for the foundation of modern Uruguay's oldest settlement, the town of Colonia facing Buenos Aires across the river. But Brazilian and Argentine adventurism, which frustrated Artigas' vision and forced him into exile in Paraguay in 1820, also attracted the attention of British diplomacy. After the brief capture and occupation of Montevideo in 1807, Britain had nursed no ambition for territorial gains in the region. However, successive attempts by Buenos Aires and Brazil to exert dominance threatened British trade to the River Plate. By 1826 the creation of an independent Uruguay as a buffer state between the two major regional powers was seen as a solution; in 1828 the República Oriental del Uruguay was born, in part through British diplomatic efforts; and in 1830 Uruguay had its first constitution. These circumstances of the nation's origins still resound. While Artigas is the national hero and the only figure all parties can accept as the authentic patriot, the role of an outside power in promoting nationhood for its own purposes – for a population then of about 60,000 – is remembered today when doubts are cast on the economic viability of the modern nation-state of Uruguay.

Independence did not free Uruguay from interventions by her neighbours. Nor were Uruguayans united in resisting them. On the contrary, when ex-President Fructuoso Rivera rebelled against his successor Manuel Oribe in 1836, the latter found an ally in Juan Manuel de Rosas, the dictator in Buenos Aires. The Guerra Grande (great war) which resulted ended only in 1851, following a nine-year siege of Montevideo by Oribe in which the city was defended by, amongst others, Giuseppe Garibaldi. Significant for the future of the country was the fact that Rivera's forces wore red to distinguish themselves from the white of Oribe. The distinction gave its name to the two principal political forces, Colorado and Blanco (or Nacional), which have continuously dominated political life to the present day. Oribe in particular remains a totem figure for the Blanco party, but needless to say the modern parties have nothing in common with these original forces.

Introduction

The end of the Guerra Grande found the pastoral industries depleted and trade through Montevideo much reduced, and peace did not bring to an end internal anarchy and external intervention. But Uruguay was on the eve of a crucial transformation, the spread of capitalism, as the country became closely integrated into the expanding international economy. Sheep-farming for wool was the first sector to experience the effects of rising international demand. Modernizing landowners (including an important nucleus of British and Irish immigrants) in the south and west began the import of pedigree livestock to improve yields, and erected wire fences to rationalize the use of their pastures. In 1863 Liebig's Extract of Meat factory began operations at Fray Bentos, and added a new exportable meat product (meat extract) to the primitive *tasajo* (dried salt beef) consumed only by the slave populations of Brazil and Cuba. While the traditional *caudillo* landowners, especially in the north of the country, continued to assert their political dominance and property rights through their own armed supporters, the modernizing group expelled unproductive population from their lands and increasingly looked to the central authority of the state for the defence of property. The process was accelerated by the introduction of the railway and the telegraph, by the availability of British loans to governments, and by a period of military government (1876-86). The transition was symbolically completed in 1904, when a Blanco army from the north under the *caudillo* Aparicio Saravia was defeated by the forces of the state under President José Batlle y Ordóñez. In the same year the first *frigorífico* (meat-freezing plant) opened, bringing new export trades and increased prosperity.

The presidencies of Batlle (1903-7, 1911-15) marked an extraordinary turning-point in the history of Uruguay. The civil violence of the nineteenth century was now replaced by a representative system of government which rapidly acquired fame as the most open and democratic in Latin America. The population had grown substantially, to about one million by the time of the census of 1908, as a result of large-scale immigration, especially from Mediterranean Europe in the final decades of the nineteenth century. These new citizens of Uruguay were absorbed into the ranks of the Colorado – or Blanco – parties, rather than forming their own groupings, because their interests were met by the labour and social welfare policies of the government. Peace prevailed between the two parties as the practice of co-participation, which in the nineteenth century had meant the division of the country into territorial zones of power, was redefined to give the minority (Blanco) party a share in the spoils of government office.

Although the products of the livestock sector continued to provide almost all Uruguay's export earnings, in the late nineteenth century the urban character of modern Uruguay began to take shape. A high proportion of the country's population had indeed always lived in Montevideo, partly because of the significant position of the port in River Plate trade which was due to the natural advantage of its harbour compared with the shallow waters of Buenos Aires. But even when the construction of the port of Buenos Aires diminished the role of Montevideo's commercial interests, new activities in the city – construction, export processing, railway workshops, the bureaucracy – ensured that Montevideo's economic vitality was not reduced. Immigrants arriving in Uruguay found rather little cultivable land available for colonization, but substantial economic opportunity instead in the urban sector of the economy. This was reflected in the first tariff legislation as early as 1875; protection was further increased in the 1880s, and factory industry producing for domestic consumers was well established by (and further promoted during) the presidencies of Batlle y Ordóñez.

The influence of Great Britain on the development of the Uruguayan economy was immense. The reasons had nothing to do with British involvement in the independence process. They related instead to the willingness of British investors to subscribe to the loan issues of the Uruguayan government, and to invest in the railways and other public utilities. As late as 1914 the entire railway system was British-owned (mostly by the Central Uruguay Railway, formed in 1876). Gas and water supply to Montevideo were other British monopolies, and there was British involvement in tramways and the telephone system. In meat-packing, on the other hand, although Liebig's Fray Bentos plant was converted to a *frigorífico* and sold as the 'Anglo' to Vestey's in 1924, the industry was dominated by the American Swift and Armour groups. The operation of the public utilities attracted extensive public criticism even before 1900, but resentment at the deficiencies of service was more sharply expressed thereafter, especially by Batlle himself. Nonetheless, although British influence in Uruguay was in evident decline by 1920, as British capital exports dried up and British export trades failed to match the diversity of manufactured goods offered by other industrial nations, Uruguay's growing dependence on the meat trade gave new leverage to London. The fact was that Britain was the only market for the premium export, chilled beef, and in the 1930s Uruguay was forced to make concessions to British trade and British interests in order to keep a share of the British market.

From 1919 until 1933 Uruguay was governed by an executive divided between a president and a nine-man presidential committee (*colegiado*). The Colorado party was the majority party – indeed, the

Introduction

only elections it has ever lost were those of 1958 and 1962 – and within the party the followers of Batlle (the *batllistas*) were dominant. The great period of innovative social reforms was over by 1920, but in the following decade the achievements of earlier times were consolidated, including a large public sector in the economy. However in 1929 Batlle died, and within months the full impact of the world depression began to be felt. The most important repercussion of the crisis was the *coup d'état* of President Gabriel Terra, on 31 March 1933. Backed by the landowners, who needed a free hand to negotiate their beef export quotas with Britain, Terra dissolved the collegiate constitution (substituting his own in 1934) and constructed a ruling alliance of his supporters among the Colorados with the followers of the Blanco leader, Luis Alberto de Herrera. Both parties were thus split, with the *batllista* wing of the Colorados as well as the Independent *nacionalistas* consigned to the wilderness. The régime made some half-hearted gestures towards Italian fascism and diplomatic relations were broken with republican Spain (1936) and the Soviet Union (1935), but by 1938, with the accession of Alfredo Baldomir to the presidency, there were signs that Uruguay was about to return to the main currents of its history. In 1941 Terra's constitution was set aside, and a new presidential constitution was instituted in 1943. The 1933 coup had been almost bloodless and the repression of the subsequent régime was generally mild; nonetheless the events of 1941-43 were greeted with widespread relief.

International developments of course had some bearing on internal changes. The support expressed for Britain and her allies in the First World War was even more manifest in the Second. This was demonstrated very early, in December 1939, in the Battle of the River Plate which ended in the scuttling of the German warship *Graf Spee*. In spite of earlier tensions arising from the operations of the bloc of British-owned companies there was no doubting Uruguay's pro-British sympathies. Moreover, the invasion of the Low Countries and other small European nations was a shock to Uruguay, itself small and vulnerable. The entry of the United States and the Soviet Union into the war further strengthened support for the Allies within the Colorado party, which has traditionally tended to enjoy close relations with the United States, and within the trade unions which were resurgent at this time. Uruguay broke off relations with the Axis powers following the Rio conference in 1942, and its pro-Allied posture (in contrast with that of Argentina) found support on all sides except among the neutralist *herrerista* Blancos.

The political reintegration of the *batllistas* at the start of the 1940s was an event of major importance, since it both reflected and emphasized the changing socio-economic structure of the country after the world depression. The main direction the economy would take had already been evident in the late 1930s as manufacturing industry producing for the domestic market grew, while traditional export markets for meat and wool remained depressed. The war artificially reversed these trends, but from 1947 until the mid-1950s industry expanded very rapidly indeed. Government policy promoted the expansion, by direct intervention to subsidize industry and penalize competing imports and by measures promoting income redistribution. To a limited extent such policies had been practised by Batlle y Ordóñez early in the century, but progressively from about 1941 onwards, and emphatically from 1947 when Luis Batlle (his nephew) became president, a new and more exaggerated version (known as *neo-batllismo*) was implemented. The hallmarks of it were the promotion of the interests of urban labour and urban capital under the supervision of a corporatist and interventionist state. Trade unions grew, but had to bargain with employers in wages councils (established in 1942) in which the state was the dominant participant. The public sector in the economy expanded as new industries were added, but it was also vastly increased when the railways, tramways and waterworks were disposed of in 1948 to the Uruguayan government, in exchange for wartime supplies of frozen meat, by their much-relieved British owners who received £12 million.

The postwar decade was a period of immense national self-satisfaction. In addition to the growth of manufacturing industry, the Korean War boosted commodity prices, the railways were nationally owned, the retirement pension system was effectively completed, and in 1950 the national football (soccer) team beat Brazil in Rio de Janeiro to win the World Cup. These were the days of *como el Uruguay no hay* ('there is nowhere else like Uruguay'). A new constitution in 1952 even reintroduced the collegiate system of government, in which all executive power was now concentrated in the *colegiado*. It was all much too good to last.

The fat years came to an end in 1956, when the process of industrial growth by import substitution came to an end. Uruguay's very small market size and relatively high per capita incomes could not sustain for long a development effort geared exclusively to the domestic market. The problems were compounded by the non-discriminatory measures used to promote industry, which resulted in a high-cost, inefficient industrial structure. From the early 1950s inflation had begun to accelerate, and government controls, particularly on trade and exchange, multiplied. As economic stagnation took hold in the late 1950s, the character of *neo-batllismo* shifted somewhat. The original *batllismo* had used redistributive devices

Introduction

during a period of export-led growth to promote the expansion of the urban sector; redistribution under *neo-batllismo* as the economic crisis deepened allowed the political élite to survive in the face of a steadily deteriorating economic situation by building up its electoral clienteles. The number of public employees increased hugely, as did retirement pensions; and access to both the bureaucracy and the pensions funds required the mediation of a politician.

The first expression of change as a result of the economic crisis was the defeat of the Colorados in the elections of 1958. The victorious coalition of Herrera's Blancos and a rural middle-class movement implemented in 1959 a stabilization package – the Monetary and Exchange Reform – with backing from the International Monetary Fund, designed to restore macro-economic equilibrium, reduce government intervention in the economy, and bring down the rate of inflation. It had little success. In the early 1960s the first economic plan was prepared by the Comisión de Inversiones y Desarrollo Económico. It proposed various structural reforms, but there was no political will to secure their implementation. The Blancos won a second term in 1962, but had no new initiatives to offer. Attention then turned to constitutional reform as a means of promoting change. The elections of 1966 returned the Colorados to office with a new constitution which restored the one-man presidency, and on the death of President Oscar Gestido within months of taking office, Jorge Pacheco Areco became president at the end of 1967.

Pacheco's term of office ran to 1972, and represented a severe radicalization of Uruguayan politics. Governing through the semi-permanent imposition of emergency security measures, Pacheco dispensed with traditional modes of political practice. Policy, such as the wage and price freeze of 1968, was to be imposed, not negotiated. Some newspapers were closed, trade union members in public services were placed under military discipline, and the first reports of the use of torture by security services were heard. Throughout the 1960s the economic and social situation had deteriorated. Unemployment increased, and in 1967 inflation exceeded 100 per cent for the first time. Frustration grew amongst intellectuals and the middle classes at the inability of the political system to generate positive proposals to arrest the process of national decline. It was sharpened by the growth of anti-imperialist sentiment throughout Latin America following the Cuban revolution at the start of the decade, and was expressed within Uruguay in the columns of the immensely significant weekly journal *Marcha*. However, it was the emergence of the guerrilla organization, the Movimiento de Liberación Nacional-Tupamaros (MLN-T), which both signified the decay of the institutional political process and accelerated its collapse. The

Tupamaros had originated amongst sugar-cane workers in the north-west of the country, but developed their organization as an urban guerrilla movement to such effect that the security forces could do little to counter their audacious operations, which intensified from 1968 onwards. Bank raids, mass escapes from jail, kidnappings and embarrassing disclosures humiliated the government and generated considerable if passive support for the Tupamaros. But the execution by them of a hostage in 1970, and other killings, contributed to the movement's downfall. In 1971 the army was given command of anti-subversive operations in place of the police, and by the following year the MLN-T was a defeated force.

Pacheco's bid for re-election in 1971 was unsuccessful, but his nominee, Juan María Bordaberry, another right-wing Colorado, was elected. His presidency proved to be a disaster for the country in every respect. Having eliminated the Tupamaros by the start of 1973, the armed forces were not disposed to withdraw in favour of civilian politicians whom they believed to be financially corrupt and tainted with the Marxism they detected on all sides. Bordaberry threw in his lot with the military and presided over the dissolution of the legislature, suppression of the trade unions, intervention of the university, and the total abnegation of human rights. Uruguay during the military dictatorship (1973-85) was a fearful place, not only because of the many who were killed, tortured or disappeared, but also because of the overwhelmingly oppressive nature of the régime. In the name of freedom the armed forces of Uruguay are believed to have achieved the highest ratio of political prisoners to total population of any country at that time. The number of emigrants to neighbouring countries, or further afield, for political or economic reasons was immense. Popular rejection of the régime was total but for many years incapable of expression. The most democratic and politically most articulate of Latin American nations had been silenced. Bordaberry's own inglorious role as puppet president ended in 1976 with military displeasure at his proposals to extend his own period of office and dispense with political parties. Forced by this to develop a political strategy and thus legitimate the régime, the military decided to purify the Blanco and Colorado parties by suppressing the political rights of the entire leaderships, and to set a timetable for the eventual establishment of a controlled civilian régime. The key to the process would be the promulgation of a new constitution prepared by the military and offered for popular approval in a plebiscite in 1980.

The economic strategy of the dictatorship was decided more promptly. Shortly before the coup in 1973, Bordaberry's economic team published Uruguay's second economic plan. Its character was

Introduction

very different from the document of the 1960s. The new plan was
neo-liberal in inspiration. It proposed to promote the profitability of
private capital, to enhance the role of market forces in the economy
as the basic agent of resource allocation, to restrict state interventionism,
and to develop new export activities. Tariff levels protecting
inefficient domestic industry would be lowered. Inflation (almost
back to three figures in 1973) would be controlled by wage and
money supply restrictions. Convinced or not by the logic of the plan,
the military had no alternative of their own, and it was therefore
adopted. The performance of the economy thereafter was in some
respects predictable – real wage rates sustained severe cuts, inflation
still exceeded 50 per cent four years later – but in others surprising
results were achieved. In spite of the daunting international context
following the oil price rise, the policy of reducing restrictions on
international trade had positive short-term effects. Benefiting from
subsidies on non-tradititional items (textiles, leather goods, rice,
citrus fruit, etc), Uruguay's exports grew strongly. Indeed the
economy as a whole recorded the first sustained increases in per
capita income (unequally distributed though they were) for twenty
years. The experience did not last. Alejandro Végh Villegas, Minister
of Economy and Finance, resigned in 1976. In 1978, in a misguided
attempt to use exchange rate policy to bring down the rate of
inflation, the real gains were sacrificed in a welter of cheap dollars to
the interests of a booming financial sector.

The collapse of the economic model at the beginning of the 1980s
and the country's massive international indebtedness had obvious
implications for the dictatorship's political plan. The profound
unpopularity of the régime was revealed in the 1980 plebiscite which
convincingly rejected the military's proposed new constitution.
Elections within the Blanco and Colorado parties in 1982 showed that
party factions representing continuity with the régime could expect
little support. The transition leading to elections in 1984 and the
restoration of civilian government in March 1985 was in the end a
negotiated process in which the military had to make important
concessions. Not only were both traditional parties (and all their
factions though not all their leaders) free to contest the elections, but
in addition the left-wing Frente Amplio coalition, formed originally
for the elections of 1971 on the basis of the Socialist, Communist, and
Christian Democrat parties together with former factions of the
traditional parties, was also rehabilitated (although its leader was
not). The elections, though not entirely free, were nonetheless
remarkably so. They represented, in the whole-hearted commitment
of the electorate to the principles of democracy and the rule of law, a

triumphant return to the traditional mainstream of Uruguay's political life.

A feature of redemocratization in Uruguay is that the institutional structures within which Uruguayan democracy functions have been merely restored in their pre-1973 condition, rather than renovated to meet the new and severe challenges that the country now faces. The voting system used is that of the double simultaneous vote (DSV). It gives rise to the joke, which is also literally true, that elections in Uruguay are so secret that even the voters do not know who they are voting for. Each party may run with more than one presidential candidate (in 1971 the Colorados had had five, in 1984 only two). Victory is then awarded to the most-voted candidate of the most-voted party, as if party primaries were being held simultaneously with the election itself. Colorado centrist or reformist voters might vote for their preferred candidate only to find (as they did in 1971) that their votes had been used to elect a right-wing Colorado president. The system results invariably in the election of a president who has a minority of the vote. President Julio María Sanguinetti of the centrist Colorado faction was elected in 1984 with 31 per cent of the poll, and has moreover faced an opposition majority in the legislature. The factionalism which DSV encourages inhibits any ideological coherence within the parties. It is very hard for most foreigners and for many Uruguayans to find any reason for the continued existence of the Colorado and Blanco parties (which together received 76 per cent of the poll in 1984, their lowest share in any election) other than their mutual opposition and a complex electoral and party legislation. Parties (or party factions) seem no more equipped now than they were before 1973 to develop policy strategies and alternatives. Personalism remains a potent force within the party hierarchies, and clientelism is far from dead.

In spite of the difficulties, the first four years of Uruguay's return to democracy were accomplished with much greater success than seemed probable in 1985, or than was evident in Brazil and Argentina during the same period. The economy achieved a satisfactory rate of growth of output, and exports grew rapidly. Unemployment fell somewhat, while real wages recovered a modest proportion of the huge decline sustained under the dictatorship. The inflationary process was controlled but not dominated. However there was some suspicion that the economic achievement was based on fragile foundations, and relations between the military and civilian groups continued to be uneasy. An immediate amnesty for all Tupamaros and political prisoners was agreed in 1985, but the government's decision not to bring criminal charges against members of the security forces for offences committed during the dictatorship proved to be deeply divisive. The majority Blanco faction was persuaded to support Sanguinetti in this measure even though its leader Wilson Ferreira Aldunate, an implacable critic of the military, was held in jail after his return from exile in 1984 and thus prevented from standing for the presidency. A popular movement in the country was however successful in collecting enough signatures to force a referendum on the issue of the indemnity for the armed forces, and this was expected to be held in April 1989. The military therefore remains an issue in Uruguayan politics, if much less dangerously than in Argentina.

Another major problem which will confront future Uruguayan governments concerns the choice of an economic strategy which will permit a sustainable process of economic growth (whether or not a solution is found to the foreign debt problem). Experience with the inward-looking strategy of import-substituting industrialization was not happy; it resulted in considerable inefficiency, and only an abbreviated period of growth. A continuation in some form of the current export-led strategy therefore seems probable. The key to its success will lie in the vitality of markets in Brazil and Argentina, and in further diversification of markets and exportable commodities. But Uruguay's traditional economic base, the livestock industry, is the source not only of exportable meat and wool but also of raw materials for the textile and leather industries which are important non-traditional export activities. So in spite of the urban character of contemporary Uruguay, its prosperity will still depend to a considerable extent on finding a solution to a long-term problem which is both economic and technical in character: how landowners are to be induced to improve the quality of their pastures (seeding, fertilizing, etc.) and thus increase the population of cattle and sheep and the level of supply of animal products.

Although this introduction has emphasized aspects of Uruguay's political and material progress, it would be a distortion (as the contents of this bibliography reveal) not to underline the richness of Uruguay's intellectual and cultural history during the twentieth century. Literature and painting in particular have flourished to a degree which is truly remarkable in a society which even now has only three million inhabitants. The stimulus of the larger public in Buenos Aires has served to break down the comparative isolation of Montevideo, and a period of residence on the other side of the River Plate has figured in the lives and careers of many figures in Uruguay's cultural history. But more important is the fact that near-universal literacy, the high value attached to education, relatively high per capita incomes, and a large urban dependent middle-class population, have generated an environment in Montevideo which has promoted the work of creative writers, and endowed it with far more than merely national or regional significance.

The Bibliography

In compiling this bibliography we have attempted to bring together published works which deal with all aspects of Uruguay. Because the intended readership will have English as its first (or a principal) language, the coverage of material in English is extensive. Not all of the works included are entirely worthy of praise, and we have been critical in the annotations where we believed it appropriate. A very few rather indifferent works have been included when the title, author, topic, institution or publisher might have misled the reader into believing that attempts to secure the book would be time or money well spent. We have selected works written in Spanish primarily with the intention of supplementing those available in English. The inclusion or omission of Spanish-language materials therefore has nothing to do with their merit *per se*, but should be seen in terms of the perceived weakness or strength of the English-language sources. Spanish is an easy language to learn to read, and we have assumed that anyone with a particular interest in some aspect of Uruguay will happily make the effort. Unless noted otherwise, the language of the work is the same as the language of the title.

Because of Uruguay's proximity and cultural similarity to Argentina, a number of works have been included which deal primarily with the neighbouring country and include Uruguay as an adjunct, or which treat the River Plate region as an undifferentiated whole. To have excluded such works on the grounds that Uruguay was not the principal subject would have seriously weakened the compilation. Where necessary, page or chapter references have been given to the relevant sections on Uruguay.

Most of the materials are recently published, but by no means all. In an extreme case we have included a seventeenth-century publication, since we found it freely available in a good provincial city library in England. Mere age does not make a work unavailable or out-of-date. Readers (like bibliography compilers) who find that certain works are not to be had locally can always resort to the excellent facilities of the inter-library loan scheme.

All the works included in this bibliography have been read, re-read or at the very least skimmed by one or other of the compilers, with

Introduction

just two exceptions. Our best efforts to secure these two were frustrated, but we know that they exist and we therefore felt justified in including them. Final responsibility for the selection of items, for writing the annotations (and the judgements therein) and for this introduction rests with the principal compiler. The role of the assistant compiler was primarily to evaluate the coverage of the English-language works and to advise on and help sift through materials published in Montevideo. For all errors and omissions we jointly apologize.

Acknowledgements

It is a pleasure to acknowledge the assistance of the staff of many libraries, especially of the Sydney Jones Library, University of Liverpool; the Institute of Latin American Studies Library, University of London (whose invaluable union catalogue of Latin American holdings in British libraries has been discontinued as an economy measure in the face of the damaging funding cuts imposed by government); the Liverpool Central Libraries; and the Biblioteca Nacional, Montevideo. In March 1988 the principal compiler accepted an invitation from the Director of the Biblioteca Nacional to lecture there on the making of this work.

Theses and Dissertations on Uruguay

Gayle Royce Avant. 'Planning and political influence: the Uruguayan case', PhD thesis, University of North Carolina, Chapel Hill, 1969.

Freda Perez Beberfall. 'Thematic continuity and changing emphases in the work of Mario Benedetti', PhD thesis, University of Wisconsin, Madison, 1974.

William Mark Berenson. 'Group politics in Uruguay: the development, political activity, and effectiveness of Uruguayan trade associations', PhD thesis, Vanderbilt University, 1975.

Robert Erle Biles. 'Patronage politics: electoral behavior in Uruguay', PhD thesis, Johns Hopkins University, 1972.

Elba Doris Birmingham-Pokorny. 'The theme of alienation in contemporary Spanish-American literature as exemplified by Juan Carlos Onetti', PhD thesis, University of Washington, 1986.

Daniel Winship Boller. 'Social service curricula in Uruguay: backgrounds and perceptions of curricula held by Uruguayan social service professionals', PhD thesis, University of Arizona, 1981.

Beverly Jean Buchert. 'The Tupamaros: anomalies of guerrilla war', PhD thesis, University of Kansas, 1979.

Robert Henderson Burton IV. 'Uruguay: a study in arrested economic development', PhD thesis, Louisiana State University, 1967.

Wm. Orrick Bullis. 'A history of the Southern Baptists in Uruguay', MA thesis, Baylor University, Waco, Texas, 1965.

Juan José Buttari. 'The wage structure in the manufacturing sectors of two developing economies: an analysis of Venezuela and Uruguay', PhD thesis, Georgetown University, 1973.

Graciana del Castillo. 'Balance of payments analysis: an econometric test of Uruguay', PhD thesis, Columbia University, 1986.

Kenneth Gilmore Coates. 'Export stagnation: the Uruguayan case, 1950-1974', PhD thesis, Stanford University, 1981.

Luis O. Coirolo. 'An econometric analysis of the beef-cattle industry of Uruguay', PhD thesis, Michigan State University, 1980.

Herman Edward Daly. 'Trade control and the Uruguayan economy', PhD thesis, Vanderbilt University, 1967.

Theses and Dissertations on Uruguay

John Frederick Deredita. 'Disintegration and dream: patterns in the fiction of Juan Carlos Onetti', PhD thesis, Yale University, 1972.

G. T. Downing. 'The life and works of Florencio Sánchez', MA thesis, University of Oklahoma, 1928.

Linda Kay Davis East. 'The imaginary voyage: evolution of the poetry of Delmira Agustini', PhD thesis, Stanford University, 1981.

Arthur William Feldman. 'The legal citizen of Uruguay: an historical analysis of respect deprivation', PhD thesis, United States International University, 1980.

Elizabeth Ann Finch. 'The politics of regional integration: a case-study of Uruguay's decision to join LAFTA', MA thesis, University of Liverpool, 1970.

David Ross Gerling. 'An application of the literary theories of Georg Lukacs to the prose of Enrique Amorim', PhD thesis, University of Arizona, 1975.

Charles G. Gillespie. 'Party strategies and redemocratization: theoretical and comparative perspectives on the Uruguayan case', PhD thesis, Yale University, 1987.

Luis Eduardo González. 'Political structures and the prospects for democracy in Uruguay', PhD thesis, Yale University, 1988.

Ulises Federico Graceras. 'Inter-generational cleavages and political behavior: a survey study of the 1971 presidential election in Uruguay', PhD thesis, Michigan State University, 1977.

Ernst Clark Griffin. 'Agricultural land use in Uruguay', PhD thesis, Michigan State University, 1972.

Frank Scott Helwig. 'Narrative techniques in the rural novels of Enrique Amorim', PhD thesis, University of Kansas, 1972.

Norman Stanford Holland Jr. 'The doll in the work of Felisberto Hernandez', PhD thesis, Johns Hopkins University, 1979.

Djelal Kadir II. 'The aesthetics of Juan Carlos Onetti's novel', PhD thesis, University of New Mexico, 1972.

Robert C. Klove. 'Pastoral and agricultural occupance in Uruguay', MS thesis, University of Chicago, 1937.

Hans Dieter Kurz. 'Uruguay: a case-study of economic stagnation', MA thesis, University of Texas, Austin, 1967.

Heinz Kusel. 'Joaquín Torres-García: a synthesis of twentieth century European painting and the Indoamerican heritage in the work of the Uruguayan painter, 1874-1949', MA thesis, Fresno State College, 1964.

Frederick Hart Langhorst. 'Three Latin Americans look at us: the United States as seen in the essays of José Martí, José Enrique Rodó, and José Vasconcelos', PhD thesis, Emory University, 1975.

Francisco J. Lasarte. 'Artistic trajectory and emergent meaning in the fiction of Felisberto Hernandez', PhD thesis, Princeton University, 1975.

John William McCarthy. 'Application of selected curriculum development criteria to curriculum development procedures described in government documents for secondary education in Ecuador and Uruguay', EdD thesis, University of Georgia, 1972.

Doris Brandenburg McLaughlin. 'From Batlle to Batlle: Uruguay in the late nineteenth century', PhD thesis, University of Michigan, 1973.

Philip Marcus McVey. 'Urban guerrilla warfare: the internal wars of Uruguay and Canada', MS thesis, California State University, Long Beach, 1981.

Alfredo Aguayo Mendoza. 'Dialogue with the public: Espejo, Lizardi, and Hidalgo', PhD thesis, University of California, Irvine, 1979.

Richard Kinney Moore. 'Soldiers, politicians, and reaction: the etiology of military rule in Uruguay', PhD thesis, University of Arizona, 1978.

James Roger Norton. 'The life and works of Adolfo Montiel Ballesteros', PhD thesis, University of Missouri, Columbia, 1977.

Francisco E. Panizza. 'The limits of consensus: problems of democracy in a peripheral country', PhD thesis, University of Essex, 1984.

Marie Johnston Peck. 'At the green blade's end: José Pedro Diaz allegorizes Uruguay in crisis', PhD thesis, University of New Mexico, 1974.

Italo L. Ponterotto. 'José Pedro Varela and his contribution to education in Uruguay', PhD thesis, New York University, 1951.

Carlos Alberto Rucks. 'Adoption of improved agricultural practices in Uruguay', PhD thesis, University of Wisconsin, 1969.

Charles Henry Schutter. 'The development of education in Argentina, Chile and Uruguay', PhD thesis, University of Chicago, 1943.

James Rodney Simpson. 'International trade in beef and economic development of selected South American countries', PhD thesis, Texas A&M University, 1974.

Doris Thomason Stephens. 'Delmira Agustini and the quest for transcendence', PhD thesis, University of Tennessee, 1974.

G. T. Stewart. 'The economic development of Uruguay, 1936-61', PhD thesis, University of Alabama, 1967.

Pedro Carlos Máximo Teichert. 'Industrial development policy in Uruguay', PhD thesis, University of Texas, 1955.

Roberto Enrique Vazquez-Platero. 'Decision models for livestock production in Uruguay', PhD thesis, Texas A&M University, 1976.

Martin Weinstein. 'Uruguay: ideology, nationalism and politics in a city-nation-state', PhD thesis, New York University, 1974.

Mary Elizabeth Wilkie. 'The Lebanese in Montevideo, Uruguay – a study of an entrepreneurial ethnic minority', PhD thesis, University of Wisconsin, Madison, 1973.

Peter Edward Winn. 'Uruguay and British economic expansion 1880-1893', PhD thesis, Cambridge University, 1971.

The Country and Its People

1 **Uruguay: a contemporary survey.**
Marvin Alisky. New York: Praeger, 1969. 174p. map. bibliog.
This account of Uruguay adopts a strong North American perspective. Written during the tense period of the late 1960s, the author attributes Uruguay's economic problems to an over-extended welfare state and the strong position of communists in the trade union movement. True or false, the interpretation has little supporting analysis. Unfortunately, factual errors make the descriptive sections on Uruguay's geography, history, etc, not always reliable. The volume contains some photographs.

2 **The republic of Uruguay, South America; its geography, history, rural industries, commerce and general statistics.**
Issued by authority of the Consulate-General of Uruguay. London: Edward Stanford, 1883. 168p. maps.
A valuable and little-known source of information on late-nineteenth-century Uruguay; it is particularly helpful on commercial and financial conditions.

3 **The land and people of Uruguay.**
Lavinia G. Dobler. Philadelphia, Pennsylvania: Lippincott, 1965. 156p.
Apparently intended for school use, this warm but superficial book is the result of a South American tour by a teacher in 1964.

4 **Uruguay.**
[Boulogne], France: Éditions Delroisse, [1979]. 176p.
Like its companion volume *Montevideo: capital of Uruguay* (q.v.), this well-produced volume with over 100 colour plates presents a glossy but unconvincing image of the country. The text, presumably provided by an agency of the dictatorship, praises the neo-liberal economic policies of the time, in English, Spanish, German and French. The intention is plainly the promotion of investment and tourism.

1

5 **Argentina and Uruguay: a tale of two attitudes.**
Russell H. Fitzgibbon. *Pacific Spectator*, vol. 8 (winter 1954), p. 6-20.

Why were – still are – Argentina and Uruguay such different countries? Fitzgibbon, in this lively and provocative (if anecdotal) piece, suggests a variety of reasons for the difference in social psychology of the two peoples. He concludes by emphasizing that Perón's antagonism towards the United States is not shared by Uruguayans.

6 **Uruguay: portrait of a democracy.**
Russell H. Fitzgibbon. London: Allen & Unwin, 1956. 301p. map. bibliog. Reissued New York: Russell & Russell, 1966.

An affectionate and sympathetic study which is well informed and respectful. The author's knowledge of the country was acquired during 1951-53, at the height of Uruguay's post-war boom. Hence his predictions seem wildly optimistic: 'Most of its problems, specific and general, Uruguay has worked out'. In fact they were just beginning to surface, but the book is valuable as a personal view of the country at a period of high national self-esteem. There are some photographs.

7 **A capital for the country-lover.**
Conal Gannon. *Country Life* vol. 153, no. 3945 (1 Feb. 1973). p. 284-5.

A superficial though kindly picture of Montevideo, conveying scarcely a hint of the political disaster about to overtake 'this unspoilt city with its remarkable atmosphere of dignity, liberalism and self-respect'. There are five good photographs.

8 **Inside South America.**
John Gunther. London: Hamish Hamilton, 1967. 610p.

'Uruguay on the rocks' (p. 220-37) develops the author's view that the country had become almost a parody of democracy. 'What does Uruguay need most? 1. More Uruguayans 2. One economist 3. Vitality.' Most of the material is somewhat humorous. The author also reports on an interview with then-President Washington Beltrán.

9 **Paraguay and Uruguay.**
Helene Hanff. New York: Doubleday, 1967. 63p. map.

Illustrated with over thirty photographs and line drawings, this is an extremely undemanding introduction to the country.

10 **Uruguay in pictures.**
Nathan A. Haverstock, John P. Hoover. New York: Sterling Publishing; London; Sydney: Oak Tree Press, 1975. 64p. map. (Visual Geography Series).

With chapters on the land, history, government, people and economy, the view of Uruguay offered is bland but reasonably informative. The 102 illustrations are the book's main asset. A phonetic rendering of Batlle as 'Byé-zhay' is a curiosity.

11 **Nineteenth century South America in photographs.**
H. L. Hoffenberg.   New York: Dover Publications, 1982. 152p.
Twenty of the 205 photographs were taken in Uruguay; some other have Uruguayan interest. There are views of the pier at Pocitos; the (English) Ricketts family on their *estancia*; the famous Hotel Oriental; and a wide variety of others. There are brief notes on five photographers working in the country.

12 **Twentieth century impressions of Uruguay. Its history, people, commerce, industries and resources.**
Reginald Lloyd (Director in Chief), with W. Feldwick, L. T. Delaney, Arnold Wright.   London: Lloyd's Greater Britain Publishing, 1912. 524p. map.
Second only to the *Libro del Centenario del Uruguay* (q.v.) in the quality and quantity of its information (as well as in size and weight), this work gives a remarkable view of Uruguay at an important stage of its development. There are thirty-eight chapters, all serious and substantial pieces of work. Twenty-three have named authors including Carlos Arocena (stock-raising and agriculture); Pablo Blanco Acevedo (old Montevideo); José Irureta Goyena (crime, prisons and police); Julio M. Llamas (external commerce); Raúl Montero Bustamante (literature and art); and Octavio Morató (finance). Other areas covered include geography, population, flora and fauna, education, sport, railways, aborigines, and many others. There are hundreds of photographs, including a very fine full-length formal portrait of President Batlle y Ordóñez which was specially commissioned for this work. The book was produced in Spanish also, and the editors claim to have received no government subsidy. The only map supplied with the book was not actually attached to it, and was unfortunately missing from the copy of the book we examined.

13 **The purple land of Uruguay.**
Luis Marden.   *National Geographic Magazine*, vol. 94, no. 5 (Nov. 1948), p. 623-54. map.
In 1948 there was scarcely any hint of the economic and political misfortunes soon to afflict the country. That is reflected in this relaxed, tourist's view of the country. Marden visited many locations (though not Punta del Este), and writes well, if briefly, on a variety of unrelated topics: among them the salinity of the Plate, the Fortaleza (Fortress) Santa Teresa, amethyst, *gaucho* dress. There are ten monochrome and twenty colour plates, the latter including Pocitos beach before the high-rise building boom, and a painting by Juan Manuel Blanes. Escapist, but recommended.

14 **How to tango: a solo across South America.**
George Mikes, illustrated by Nicolas Bentley.   Harmondsworth, England: Penguin, 1966. 189p. First published as *Tango* by André Deutsch, 1961.
A good-humoured as well as very funny account of Uruguay (p. 81-93) which makes valid points: Uruguay as a displaced European country; national self-deprecation; bureaucracy . . . and so on.

3

The Country and Its People

15 **Let's visit Uruguay.**
Marion Morrison. London: Burke, 1985. 94p. map.
The best and most recent guide for children to Uruguay, the book has chapters on the colonial period, the welfare state, the city that is a nation, the Uruguayans at work, the *gauchos*, along the River Uruguay, and from the Second World War to today. There are 47 excellent photographs, mostly in colour.

16 **Montevideo: capital of Uruguay.**
[Montevideo]: Municipality of Montevideo and Éditions Delroisse, 1980. 148p.
The main feature of this volume is the high quality of its 159 colour plates, which present a cheerful tourist image of the country entirely at odds with the reality of the final years of the military dictatorship. There is brief text prepared by the Publications and Press Service of the Municipality.

17 **The 20 Latin Americas.**
Marcel Neidergang, translated by Rosemary Sheed. Harmondsworth, Middlesex: Penguin, 1971. vol. 1. 415p.
First published in French in 1962, this general introduction to the country, its history and politics (p. 193-206) is somewhat marred by the statement that Uruguay has sixty million cattle and twice as many as sheep. Wishful thinking! Actual numbers are approximately eight million and twenty-five million respectively.

18 **Uruguay.**
Washington, D.C.: Pan American Union, 1962. 48p. map. (American Republics Series no. 20).
A very general and useful though dated description of the country. The sections on education and culture are fuller than might be expected. There are twenty-seven illustrations.

19 **The lands and peoples of Paraguay and Uruguay.**
George Pendle. London: A. and C. Black, 1959. 95p. map. bibliog.
This is a rather slight exploration of the country (p. 53-87), intended for a young readership, and illustrated with ten monochrome plates.

20 **Uruguay: South America's first welfare state.**
George Pendle. London; New York: Royal Institute of International Affairs, 1963. 3rd ed. 128p. maps. bibliog.
This is a sound, factual (though of course dated) introductory survey. The principal chapters examine in detail the welfare state, finance, production, foreign trade, arts and the media, foreign policy and party politics, and culture. The tone is objective, avoiding extremes of praise or criticism. In one of his few judgments, the author suggests that Uruguay's great problem will be to extend Montevideo's level of welfare to the rural districts.

4

21   **Three antipodean republics: I. Uruguay, the welfare state.**
Michael Teague.   *Geographical Magazine*, vol. 31, no. 1 (May 1958),
p. 1-11. maps.
Excellently illustrated with fourteen photographs by the author, this is a friendly and
well-written account. The author plainly enjoyed his stay among Uruguayans. 'If they
could lose some of their idealism and become slightly more practical, they might yet
win for their small country the utopian status so liberally granted to it by foreign
journalists.'

22   **Latin America and the Caribbean: a handbook.**
Edited by Claudio Véliz.   London: Anthony Blond, 1968. 840p. maps.
bibliog.
The main section on Uruguay (p. 126-35) is by George Pendle, consisting of an
introductory essay and basic information, much of it in tabular form. There is also
Uruguayan material in other chapters on, for example, Latin American theatre, and a
painting by Joaquín Torres-García ('Uruguay') is reproduced.

23   **Area handbook for Uruguay.**
Thomas E. Weil (et al.).   Washington: American University, 1971.
440p. map. bibliog. (Foreign Area Studies series 550-97).
'This volume is one of a series . . . designed to be useful to military and other
personnel who need a convenient compilation of basic facts about the social, economic,
political, and military institutions and practices of various countries.' Coverage is in
four sections: social; political; economic; and national security. Of these the first is
perhaps the most valuable. It extends to almost half the book; and whereas much of
the material in the other sections is readily accessible elsewhere, it includes good
surveys of, amongst other topics, education, the arts and religion. Though now needing
to be up-dated, this is close to an encyclopaedia on Uruguay.

24   **El libro del centenario del Uruguay 1825-1925.** (The centenary book of
Uruguay, 1825-1925.)
Montevideo: Capurro, 1925. 1096p. maps.
The least remarkable feature of this volume is that it weighs seven kilos. Published
semi-officially to celebrate the centenary of Independence, it escapes the temptation to
present a glorified account of the nation's progress. Instead it offers a series of
authoritative surveys of just about every aspect of Uruguay in the mid-1920s: natural
resources, history, demography, social welfare and public health, sport and recreation,
education, literature, the arts, architecture, communications, the economy, agriculture
and manufacturing, the legal system, religion; almost everything is included.
Unexpectedly interesting and valuable are accounts of individual manufacturing
enterprises. A particular feature of the book is the copious amount of illustration,
giving the reader a complete and vivid picture of the country: there are 3500
photographs, 25 colour plates, 40 maps and plans, and 150 tables.

Travellers' Accounts

General

25 **South America rediscovered.**
Tom B. Jones.   Minneapolis, Minnesota: University of Minnesota
Press, 1949. 285p. map. bibliog.

The aims of this delightful book are 'first, to reconstruct southern South America as
foreigners saw it in the years from 1810 to 1870; and second, to enumerate and to
discuss briefly the sources that may be employed for such a task'. Plainly the work was
a labour of love. Chapter 4 (p. 53-78) contains most of the Uruguayan interest, drawn
in the main from other works in this section of Travellers' Accounts. One
bibliographer admires another whose annotation on a work entitled *Dust and foam* is
'Just that'.

26 **Accounts of nineteenth-century South America: an annotated check-list of
works by British and United States observers.**
Bernard Naylor.   London: Athlone Press, for the Institute of Latin
American Studies, University of London, 1969. 80p. (Institute of Latin
American Studies, Monograph 2).

Sixty-seven items are listed for the River Plate, divided into sub-periods 1800-30, 1830-
70, and 1870-1900. Not all of these have material on Uruguay; others that do may be
found in the 'General' and 'Brazil' sections. Annotations are brief but indicate
geographical coverage where the work's title does not.

27 **Travel accounts and descriptions of Latin America and the Caribbean, 1800-1920; a select bibliography.**
Thomas L. Welch, Myriam Figueras.   Washington, D.C.: Organization of American States, 1982. 292p. (Documentation and Information Series, no. 6).

The section on Uruguay (p. 248-52) lists thirty-nine titles, mostly in English, which deal wholly or partly with the country. Other relevant works not having Uruguay or River Plate in the title are in the section on South America. There are no annotations.

Before 1900

28 **An account of a voyage up the River de la Plata, and thence over land to Peru. With observations on the inhabitants, as well Indians and Spaniards; the cities, commerce, fertility, and riches of that part of America.**
Mons. Acarete du Biscay.   London: printed for Samuel Buckley, 1698. 79p. map.

The author, a Frenchman, arrived in the River Plate from Cadiz in April 1658. His observations on the territory of Uruguay are very brief (p. 7-9) but of immense interest. He found it 'Inhabited by none but Savages, call'd Charuas . . . those I met were well made, with long Hair and very little Beard; they wear nothing but a great Skin, made of little ones patch'd together, that hangs down to their heels, and a piece of Leather under their Feet, ty'd with straps about their Ankles. For Ornament, they bind a Fillet of some Stuff about their Heads, which comes over the Fore-head, and keeps the hair back behind. The Women have no other Garment but these Skins, which they gird about their Wastes, and cover their heads with a sort of little Hats made of Rushes of divers Colours'. North of the Río Negro 'the Country is well stockt with Bulls and Cows'. The map is naturally crude, and locates Montevideo at the mouth of the river.

29 **Argentine, Patagonian and Chilean sketches, with a few notes on Uruguay.**
Charles Edmond Akers.   London: Harrison, 1893. 190p.

Chapter 16 'Uruguay' (p. 182-90) is an account of Montevideo in the wake of the financial collapse of 1890. 'In nearly every block of houses the Nemesis of wild speculation is apparent', nowhere more so than in the Barrio Reus. 'Montevideo today bears a very poverty-stricken appearance.' There is discussion of the continuing depressed state of the nation's finances.

30 **Travels in Buenos Ayres and the adjacent provinces of the Rio de la Plata. With observations intended for the use of persons who contemplate emigrating to that country; or, embarking capital in its affairs.**
J. A. B. Beaumont. London: James Ridgway, 1828. 270p. map.

The author arrived at Montevideo in May 1826 in charge of 200 agricultural emigrants from Britain heading for Entre Rios, only to find the River Plate blockaded by Brazilian forces. Fifty landed at Montevideo (the rest returning to Plymouth) where many apparently established themselves. The chapters of the book deal with the history of the River Plate provinces, natural conditions, population, principal buildings, problems of emigration, and travel. There is a general description of Montevideo and the Banda Oriental on pages 67-72, and an especially interesting section on the political future of the country on pages 240-43. 'Whichever [Buenos Ayreans or Portuguese] remain master of the Banda Oriental, then, it is likely to be the seat of war for many years to come . . . The only way, apparently, in which it can be rescued from this series of wars . . . is, by rendering it an independent state, under the guarantee of a great maritime power, such as Great Britain.'

31 **A visit to South America; with notes and observations on the moral and physical features of the country, and the incidents of the voyage.**
Edwin Clark. London: Dean, 1878. 355p.

The author, a civil engineer, was resident in the River Plate region during 1876-77. 'Matters of business connected with the North-Western railway of Montevideo lead to a lengthened residence in the northern part of Uruguay, and afforded one of the most interesting episodes in my travels . . . The lonely and lovely spot selected by my wife and myself for a three-month residence' was a remote wooden cottage by the railway bridge over the valley of the Arapey river, 45 miles north of Salto. His account of the obviously happy experience, mostly of the meteorology of the district (having set up his own instruments) and its flora and fauna, is to be found on pages 205-63.

32 **La Plata countries of South America.**
Eliza Jane McCartney Clemens. Philadelphia: Lippincott, 1886. 511p. map.

Part I 'A journey and a glance at Uruguay' (p. 11-91) has chapters on scenes in Montevideo; popular amusements; burial customs; 'business conveniences'; and a general description. With accounts of bull-fighting and sea-bathing this is clearly not a heavyweight analysis; but the author did find that 'next to Rio de Janeiro, Montevideo is the finest city in the world south of the equator'.

33 **South American sketches.**
Robert Crawford. London: Longmans, Green, 1898. 280p.

A volume of reminiscence by an engineer who worked on the construction of the Central Uruguay Northern Extension Railway during the period 1889-92. The material is mostly anecdotal, much of it trivial, with little about the railway or indeed specifically about Uruguay, though there are notes on, for example, flora and fauna, and climate. 'Political revolution and discord' are the obstacles to progress in South America generally.

34 The capitals of Spanish America.
William Eleroy Curtis. New York: Harper, 1888. 715p. map.

The chapter on Montevideo (p. 591-622) gives an interesting and lively account of the politics, personalities and economy of the country as a whole. Written apparently in 1886, the account is extremely optimistic, but offers no great depth of insight. The book was reprinted by Praeger, New York, in 1969.

35 The voyage of the *Beagle*.
Charles Darwin, with an introduction by H. Graham Cannon. London; Toronto: Dent, 1959. Everyman's Library. 487p.

In July 1832 the *Beagle*, with Darwin on board, entered the River Plate and anchored at Montevideo. 'The Plata looks like a noble estuary on the map but is in truth a poor affair. A wide expanse of muddy water has neither grandeur nor beauty'. Between then and November 1833 Darwin journeyed from Maldonado ('a most quiet, forlorn, little town') to Colonia, and north to Mercedes and the Río Negro. He was not much taken with Montevideo, perhaps because 'the gauchos, or countrymen, are very superior to those who reside in the towns'. But there are fine descriptions of *estancias*, of the customs of the land, and of course of its natural history, in chapters 3 (p. 36-59) and 8 (p. 134-50). See also *Charles Darwin's* Beagle *diary*, edited by Richard Darwin Keynes (Cambridge: Cambridge University Press, 1988), 464p., maps, for more immediate, frank and arresting observations. On the Cerro (across the bay from Montevideo), for example, 'The view from the summit is one of the most uninteresting I ever beheld . . . Whoever has seen Cambridgeshire, if in his mind he changes arable into pasture ground & roots out every tree, may say he has seen Monte Video . . . yet there is a charm in the unconfined feeling of walking over the boundless turf plain'. He learned to dislike the élite of Montevideo, and 'The politicks of the place are quite unintelligible'. Keynes's edition replaces that of Norah Barlow (*Charles Darwin's diary of the voyage of H.M.S. 'Beagle'* [Cambridge: at the University Press, 1933. 443p. maps]).

36 Letters from Paraguay: describing the settlements of Monte Video and Buenos Ayres.
John Constanse Davie. London: G. Robinson, 1805. 293p.

The letters from Montevideo are dated January-February 1797 (p. 27-42). Davie had arrived in the River Plate by chance (if he is to be believed). Montevideo was found to lie 'at the foot of a conical mountain of a stupendous height'. The fort and church are described, 'though, God knows, besides the river and the mountain there is but little to excite a traveller's curiosity'. Davie claims to have had an interview with Governor Blas D'Hinojosa, and speculates on how Montevideo 'if once in the possession of the English, be found a very valuable key to the riches of the southern world'. The main obstacle to that was not in his view Spanish arms, but the mudbanks in the River Plate (of which the most notorious near Montevideo was already known as the English bank).

37 Zephyrus: a holiday in Brazil and on the River Plate.
Edward Robert Pearce Edgcumbe. London: Chatto and Windus, 1887. 242p. maps.

Edgcumbe's experiences in Uruguay (p. 92-179) were important and unusual. They began with six days' quarantine on the Isla de Flores. Montevideo, though 'unquestionably a fine city', did not detain him long, and he then sailed up the

9

Uruguay River to Salto. Here he witnessed at first hand the preparations for and aftermath of the rising of 1886 against the government of Santos. He has valuable observations on that, on the significance of Brazilian traffic to the North West of Uruguay Railway, on the importance of the Midland Railway which would connect Salto with the south, on the meat industry, and on the life of the town. The book is illustrated with the author's own neat sketches.

38 Brazil, the River Plate, and the Falkland Islands; with the Cape Horn route to Australia.
William Hadfield. London: Longman, Brown, Green and Longmans, 1854. 384p. map.

The author, as Secretary to the newly-formed but ill-fated South American and General Steam Navigation Company, is much concerned to proclaim the advantages and promote the use of steamships between Liverpool and the Atlantic coast ports, but also gives much useful material on general commercial and political conditions. The chapter on Montevideo (p. 229-58) describes its battered appearance at the end of the Great War, its history, trade, etc, and emphasizes the role of Brazil as exercising the role of benign protector or policeman. There are five illustrations. Later editions of the book omit the background material and update the assessment. In *Brazil and the River Plate in 1868: showing the progress of those countries since his former visit in 1853* (London: Bates, Hendy, 1869. 271p.), the author comments: 'The impressions conveyed in my former narrative as to the development of Monte Video were favourable, but I hardly expected to see the place grown half as large again since that time'. Nonetheless cholera, the assassination of General Flores and impending commercial crisis ('The only thing wanting to Monte Video is business') dampened his enthusiasm (p. 25-30). In *Brazil and the River Plate 1870-76* (Sutton, Surrey: W. R. Church; London: Edward Stanford, 1877. 327p.), conditions were not improved in 1870 (p. 135-38) and worse still in 1876 (p. 253-56), though the dictatorship of Latorre was thought to promise better times.

39 South American sketches.
Thomas Woodbine Hinchliff. London: Longman, Green, Longman, Roberts, and Green, 1863. 414p. map.

Hinchliff spent little time in Montevideo in 1861, except to visit the *quinta* (estate) of M. Buschenthal, now the Prado park (p. 89-92). He then travelled up the Uruguay River to an *estancia* near Paysandú (p. 136-91), where he spent most of his time shooting partridge. Some vignettes of *gaucho* life are recorded in a lordly manner. His experiences earlier in Brazil gave rise to some offensive expressions of racism.

40 Buenos Ayres and Argentine gleanings: with extracts from a diary of *salado* exploration in 1862 and 1863.
Thomas J. Hutchinson. London: Edward Stanford, 1865. 321p. map.

Chapter 1 (p. 1-9) gives his favourable impressions of Montevideo while en route to Buenos Aires. Some of the Argentine material, for example his description of a *saladero*, is also relevant.

41   **Twenty-four years in the Argentine republic; embracing its civil and
     military history, and an account of its political condition, before and
     during the administration of Governor Rosas; his course of policy; the
     causes and character of his interference with the government of Monte
     Video . . .**
     John Anthony King.   New York; Philadelphia: Appleton; London:
     Longman, Brown, Green and Longmans, 1846. 324p.
King, 'an officer in the army of the republic' from 1817 to 1841, narrated this book to
its writer, Thomas R. Whitney. The Uruguayan interest is principally in chapter 1, a
confused but victorious account of a skirmish with 'the seditious Artegas' in 1817
(p. 20-24), and chapter 25 (p. 307-16) concerning the policy towards Uruguay of the
Argentine dictator Rosas and his Uruguayan lieutenant Oribe in 1840-41, in which
there is a reference to 'Señor Garribaldi, an Italian'.

42   **The states of the River Plate: their industries and commerce.**
     Wilfrid Latham.   London: Longmans, Green, 1868. 2nd ed. 381p. map.
Since the two republics are analysed together, Argentina inevitably is more prominent.
Nonetheless, this is a fascinating and vivid account of rural life in the River Plate
region in the 1860s. A sheep-farmer in Buenos Aires province since the early 1840s,
Latham had first-hand knowledge of technical, commercial and political conditions
which he describes precisely and even-handedly. Written shortly before the advent of
meat-freezing technology, his frustration with earlier and inferior methods of
conserving River Plate beef for sale in England is very clear. Liebig's factory at Fray
Bentos is briefly mentioned. Other comments on Uruguay have to be looked for, but
are often illuminating: for example, he notes that the foreign elements in Montevideo
which withstood the siege (1843-51) during the Great War had prospered greatly, 'not
being personally interfered with, nor sensibly impeded in their avocations'. The first
edition of the book, with only 200 pages, appeared in 1866.

43   **A five years' residence in Buenos Ayres, during the years 1820 to 1825:
     containing remarks on the country and inhabitants; and a visit to Colonia
     del Sacramento.**
     By an Englishman [George Thomas Love].   London: G. Herbert, 1825.
     176p.
The author made a short visit to Colonia in December 1821 (p. 159-64) and spent
rather less time in Montevideo. He found Colonia a poor place of 800 inhabitants,
occupied at the time by Brazilian forces. 'Buenos Ayres would seem its more natural
protector'; nonetheless, 'every thing leads me to think its present occupants will long
keep possession'. An appendix (p. 167-76) has instructions for navigation between
Buenos Aires and Montevideo.

44   **Two thousand miles' ride through the Argentine provinces: being an
     account of the natural products of the country, and habits of the people;
     with a historical retrospect of the Rio de la Plata, Monte Video, and
     Corrientes.**
     William MacCann. London: Smith, Elder, 1853. 2 vols. 295p., 323p.
     map.
MacCann arrived in the River Plate in 1842, but although knowledgeable about

Uruguay he admits that he never in fact visited the country. In volume II (p. 186-323) he outlines British policy at the time of the invasion and towards Rosas, and gives recommendations as to future British policy. The English text of the treaty between Uruguay and Brazil (1851) is given. He believed that Montevideo, by reason of harbour, territory and climate, 'is destined to be the ultimate metropolis of this coast'.

45   **The republic of Uruguay, Monte Video, geographical, social, and**
     political. To which is appended, Life in the River Plate. A manual for
     emigrants.
     [John McColl.]   London: Effingham Wilson, 1862. By authority of the
     Monte Videan government. 72p. maps.

'The common error of confounding the Oriental Republic of Uruguay with the Argentine Confederation . . . and the little knowledge possessed in Europe of the economical and political institutions of this fine country, have determined the publication of the geographical and statistical information contained in these pages. They show, in a complete manner, the surprising wealth that Providence has bestowed on this country, and the superior advantages it offers over many others better known to the capitalist and the labourer.' This is an important source, full of detail (some of it optimistic), attractively illustrated with sketches. McColl, to whom the whole work is generally attributed, is named as author of 'Life in the River Plate' (p. 47-59). 'All that is wanted is population and capital.' There are also letters concerning beef preservation and land sales, and a detailed map of the 80,000-acre estate of the Baron de Mauá near Mercedes.

46   **Paraguay, Brazil and the Plate. Letters written in 1852-1853.**
     Charles Blachford Mansfield, with a sketch of the author's life by the
     Rev. Charles Kingsley.   Cambridge: Macmillan, 1856. 504p. map.

In letters which convey immediate emotion rather than considered reaction, the author details a ten-month expedition to Paraguay. En route he visited Montevideo (p. 122-50) as the guest of Samuel Lafone in August 1852, a few months after the siege of the Great War. Notwithstanding that, 'the town looks now more lively and flourishing than Buenos Ayres'. From the bay it was 'a curious-looking place, with a Moorish, oriental air; all the houses flat-topped, terrace-roofed, and with tall church-towers like minarets'. Though he probably saw little of the interior, 'the Banda Oriental is almost one entire beautiful meadow'. A vegetarian, he gives an appalled description of the slaughter-houses.

47   **Travels in the interior of Brazil, particularly in the gold and diamond**
     districts of that country, by authority of the Prince Regent of Portugal:
     including a voyage to the Rio de la Plata, and an historical sketch of the
     revolution of Buenos Ayres.
     John Mawe.   London: Longman, Hurst, Rees, Orme and Brown, 1812.
     366p.

'In the year 1804, I was induced to undertake a voyage of commercial experiment, on a limited scale, to the Rio de la Plata. On my arrival at Monte Video, the ship and cargo were seized; I was thrown into prison, and afterwards sent into the interior, where I was detained until the taking of that place by the British troops under Sir Samuel Auchmuty.' Pages 1-46 give a vivid account of these extraordinary experiences. His harsh treatment he blames on Governor Huidobro: 'I did not perceive any disposition on the generality of the people to injure or oppress me', though Mawe did notice how Montevideo had profited from the English defeat at Buenos Aires and failed English commercial speculations. His banishment was to an *estancia* on the Barriga Negra, north of Minas. There are fine descriptions of rural life, and of Montevideo itself. 'Such is the profusion of flesh-meat, that the vicinity for two miles round, and even the purlieus of the town itself, present filthy spectacles of bones and raw flesh at every step, which feed immense flocks of sea-gulls.'

48   **The English in South America.**
Michael George Mulhall.   Buenos Ayres: 'Standard' Office; London: Ed. Stanford, 1878. 641p.

Although it was not the author's purpose 'to write an apotheosis of my countrymen', there appears 'in every page . . . the unquestionable proofs of the indomitable energy of our race'. Much of this was historical writing. Sections with Uruguayan interest include the capture of Montevideo in 1807 (p. 107-15), including the text of Auchmuty's victorious despatch dated 6 February 1807; and accounts of early English settlers, including Young and Stirling (1823), Fair (1824), Jackson (1825), Lafone, Hughes and many others (p. 336-43).

49   **Handbook of the River Plate republics. Comprising Buenos Ayres and the provinces of the Argentine Republic and the republics of Uruguay and Paraguay.**
Michael George Mulhall, Edward T. Mulhall.   London: Edward Stanford; Buenos Ayres: M. G. and E. T. Mulhall, 1875. 478p. maps.

Although printed in London, the *Handbook* is an authentic and first-hand guide and directory to the River Plate. Other editions were published in 1863, 1869 and 1892. It is a compendium of detailed geographical and commercial information, and is a particularly valuable source for details of large land-holdings and meat-salting plants (*saladeros*), especially those owned by British residents. The chapters dealing with Uruguay occupy pages 310-84. There is a street map of Montevideo. The Mulhalls were not in fact travellers but residents of Buenos Aires.

50   **Travels in Uruguay, South America; together with an account of the present state of sheep-farming and emigration to that country.**
Rev. John H. Murray.   London: Longmans, E. Stanford, 1871. 234p.

The author ('late chaplain in Colonia') arrived in Montevideo in February 1868. His eighteen days there gave him 'no prepossessing idea of the place or people'. This was partly because his stay coincided with a cholera epidemic, but mainly because his brief visit included the 19th of that month ('engraved', in the words of the Uruguayan historian Juan E. Pivel Devoto, 'in the annals of the country as one of its most tragic days', item no. 166, q.v.). The assassination that day of General Flores and of Bernardo Berro, as well as the killing of many of their respective supporters, must have unsettled the new arrival, but he gives an important account of these events (p. 44-50). If that were not enough, he also had to report that 'there is nothing attractive, picturesque, or worth noticing in either Monte Video or Buenos Ayres'. Thereafter he was engaged for nine months travelling in the interior, near Colonia. There are notes on the rural population, natural history and natural phenomena, and a long appendix (p. 155-234) on sheep farming and the merits of emigration to South America as a whole. Murray cannot be counted a gifted observer, but the book is important, and enlivened by numerous sketches.

51 **Description of views in South America, from original drawings made in Brazil, the River Plate, the Parana etc etc.**

Sir William Gore Ouseley. London: Thomas McLean, 1852. 118p.

The description of Montevideo (p. 65-69) is interesting because it was made during the siege by the forces of Oribe and Rosas which Ouseley, as British minister in Buenos Ayres in 1845-46, actively opposed. He records that the siege, among other inconveniences, caused dredging of the harbour to be suspended, but it did not reduce trade and population to their earlier low levels. The besieging forces were located at Cerrito on the edge of the city, and had artillery which, however, 'are not, either by position or strength, sufficient to decide the contest or even seriously to damage the defences'.

52 **La Plata, the Argentine Confederation, and Paraguay.**

Thomas Jefferson Page. London: Trubner, 1859. 632p. map.

'Being a narrative of the exploration of the tributaries of the River La Plata and adjacent countries during the years 1853, '54, '55, and '56, under the orders of the United States government.' Chapter 18 (p. 318-31) describes the navigation of the Uruguay River by Page, a US naval officer aboard the *Water Witch*. Paysandú in 1855 was found to be 'forlorn, dilapidated', whereas Salto was 'rather a bustling place'.

53 **Letters on Paraguay: comprising an account of a four years' residence in that republic, under the government of the dictator Francia.**

John Parish Robertson, William Parish Robertson. London: John Murry, 1838-39. 3 vols. 359p., 342p., 400p.

JPR was fifteen years old when he arrived off Montevideo in 1807 in time to witness Auchmuty's assault on the city. Even better than that eye-witness account (from the ship) is his report on the reception given to the British subsequently ('One of a nation of invaders, I was individually cherished as a friend by those invaded'); the arrival of Whitelocke and defeat at Buenos Aires; and the evacuation of Montevideo (vol. 1, p. 96-134). There is also material by WPR on how Artigas ('in his habits only a better sort of Gaucho . . . He was the Robin Hood of South America') was perceived in Buenos Ayres in 1813-14 (vol. 2, p. 178–99). Best of all, volume 3, which bears the additional title *Francia's reign of terror*, has JPR's vivid and well–known account of Artigas in 1815–16, 'seated on a bullock's skull, at a fire kindled on the mud floor of his hut, eating beef off a spit, and drinking gin out of a cow-horn' (p. 100-10).

54 **Letters on South America; comprising travels on the banks of the Paraná and Rio de la Plata.**

John Parish Robertson, William Parish Robertson. London: John Murray, 1843. 3 vols. 320p., 300p., 345p.

This work continues the account by the two Scottish merchants of their activities in the River Plate region, and of the political history of the period, until their final returns to Britain in 1830 and 1834 respectively. The Irish *gaucho* Pedro Campbell, who deserted from Beresford's army and became a lieutenant of Artigas, appears in volume 1. The men of the Banda Oriental are described as more 'hardy, resolute and daring' than those of Corrientes. On the relationship between the Robertson brothers and Artigas, see John Street, *Artigas and the emancipation of Uruguay*, p. 266-78.

55 **Picturesque illustrations of Buenos Ayres and Monte Video, consisting of twenty-four views; accompanied with descriptions of the scenery, and of the customs, manners, etc. of the inhabitants of those cities and their environs.**
Emeric Essex Vidal. London: R. Ackerman, 1820. 115p.

'The author of this work contented himself with sketching . . . some of the characteristic features presented by the cities of Buenos Ayres and Monte Video', leaving larger issues 'to the professed historian and political economist.' Irrespective of their considerable historical significance, the colour plates are quite beautiful. There are four of specifically Uruguayan scenes. 'Monte Video from the anchorage outside the harbour' (p. 1-4); 'Estantia (farm) on the River San Pedro' (p. 71-84) is said to be located 16 miles north of Colonia, and is accompanied by a description of the estate and of rural life almost as vivid as the picture; 'Balling ostriches' (p. 85-88); and 'Paolistas, soldiers of the east bank of the Plata' (p. 107-10), described as 'Cossacks of America' and depicted at the door of a *pulpería* (store) in Montevideo. The size of the book is approximately 50 × 35 cm. Essex is said by B. Naylor (q.v.) to have been purser on H.M.S. *Hyacinth* at the time.

56 **Narrative of a voyage to the southern Atlantic Ocean, in the years 1828, 29, 30, performed in H.M. Sloop *Chanticleer*.**
William Henry Bayley Webster. London: Richard Bentley, 1834.
2 vols. 399p., 398p. map.

In the course of a scientific expedition, the author (the ship's surgeon) was at Montevideo during August-October 1828, and records his impressions in chapters 3 and 4 (p. 58-93). The period is particularly interesting because of the Brazilian occupation of the time. Webster did not find great interest in Montevideo, though like other observers he was intrigued by the *miradores* (look-outs) on the house-tops by which notice of shipping arrivals could be gained. He gives an enthusiastic account of the manners and dress of the *gaucho*, and reports on a public execution. Also, the cupola of the cathedral 'being roofed with good plates and dishes of Staffordshire blue ware, has an odd appearance. They are intended, no doubt, as a substitute for the Dutch tile; the idea is said to have originated with Artegas, a native chief, and the effect altogether is not amiss'.

After 1900

57 **Men, manners and morals in South America.**
J. O. P. Bland. London: Heinemann; New York: Scribners, 1920.
319p.

The (British) author's experiences in Uruguay are described (p. 172-309) in a patronising, racist, but not always unperceptive manner. The account of *estancia* life is probably the most valuable chapter. Batlle, consistently mis-spelled Battlé, is nonetheless assessed more objectively than was the custom amongst the author's fellow-countrymen, and Uruguay is said to be governed 'with more educated intelligence than any country south of Panamá'. The author was in Uruguay during 1916-19. There are a dozen photographs.

58 **Tales of Uruguay.**
Old Woking, Surrey: The British Uruguayan Society, 1988. 91p.

Contains twenty brief contributions of expatriate reminiscence by British former residents in Uruguay. Diplomatic activity, the railways, the *Graf Spee*, the British School, *estancia* life, and birdwatching all figure.

59 **South America: observations and impressions.**
James Bryce. New York: Macmillan, 1920. new ed. 611p. maps.

Chapter 10 (p. 349-65) deals briefly with Uruguay. It notes that Uruguay has 'all the material conditions required for prosperity and happiness', with the former not retarded by recurrent civil wars. Two peculiarities are noted: 'ideas tending towards state socialism', and the antagonism of the dominant party towards the church. Both are regarded as alien imports from southern Europe.

60 **South America to-day.**
Georges Clemenceau.   London; Leipzig, Germany: T. Fisher Unwin, 1911. 315p.

Chapter 11 (p. 208-25) records the impressions of a brief visit to Montevideo by the former (and subsequently) Prime Minister of France. The most striking feature of Uruguayans is 'a mental activity that is sometimes carried to excess'. They are distinguished from Argentinians by 'impulsive idealism'. The author is optimistic about future progress in Uruguay once revolutions are suppressed.

61 **The states of South America, the land of opportunity: a complete geographical, descriptive, economic and commercial survey.**
Charles Domville-Fife.   London: G. Bell, 1920. 287p. maps.

The two chapters on Uruguay (p. 201-26) contain general and commercial surveys, but have little that is original. There are five plates.

62 **South American memories of thirty years.**
E. F. Every.   London: Society for Promoting Christian Knowledge, 1933. 210p.

The 'Reminiscences of Uruguay' (p. 64-74) are a sad relation of how progressive, secular, state policies have eroded Christian practice generally, and in particular were threatening the English Church of Holy Trinity in Montevideo which stood in the way of the projected Rambla Sur construction. Happily it survived (rebuilt a short distance away, in 1935), but the British community in the interior did not. The author, who had evidently returned to Britain after a long ministry in the Anglican Church in South America, records that the British had taken advantage of rising land values to sell up and leave, since Uruguay 'is not suitable as a permanent home for our race'. The book is a curiosity of gloomy evangelical racism.

63 **Eight republics in search of a future: evolution and revolution in South America.**
Rosita Forbes, with a preface by Viscount D'Abernon.   London: Cassell, 1933. 340p.

The two chapters on Uruguay (p. 77-93) offer colourful description and exaggerated generalization about society, life and politics, but no analysis. The main interest of the

16

book lies in the author's observations on the perceived effects of the Ottawa Agreements on Uruguay's access to the British beef market, and her obsessive belief that Uruguay was the Russia of South America. 'South American revolutions of a Communist nature are generally planned in Uruguay'!

64 **Working north from Patagonia: being the narrative of a journey, earned on the way, through southern and eastern South America.**
Harry A. Franck. London: T. Fisher Unwin, 1921. 650p. map.

It is not made clear when this journey was undertaken – publication was delayed by the First World War. The chapter on Uruguay (p. 111-37) is above average in quality of observation and writing, and is illustrated by a few photographs.

65 **South American journey.**
Waldo Frank. London: Victor Gollancz, 1944; New York: Duell, Sloan and Pearce, 1943. 215p.

Chapter 3 'Uruguayan Interlude' (p. 91-101) is brief but interesting: about Montevideo as a provincial city; the nature of the *gaucho*; and the roots of Uruguayan independence. There are allusions to interviews with President Alfredo Baldomir, and the poet Juana de Ibarbourou.

66 **The Argentine through English eyes; and a summer in Uruguay.**
J. A. Hammerton. London: Hodder and Stoughton, [n.d.] 367p.

The author's impressions of Uruguay, probably published in 1914, are in chapters 20 and 21 (p. 298–344). They are in general those of an intelligent tourist, and on the whole favourable. The quality of education and the democratic spirit of the people are praised. The social life of Montevideo is preferred to that of Buenos Aires. There is an attempt to distinguish between the Colorado and Blanco political parties, and President José Batlle y Ordóñez is criticized for his constitutional reform proposals. There are seventeen plates.

67 **The great south land: the River Plate and southern Brazil of to-day.**
W. H. Koebel. London: Thornton Butterworth, 1919. 314p.

Though there are references to Uruguay throughout the book, chapter 14 (p. 249-68) is devoted to an account of the country. Eight years on from his monograph (see following item), the author remains well disposed to Uruguay and so little ashamed of his circumlocutions in that book that he repeats the worst. Economic progress is still disappointing, a legacy of past political unrest. Batlle y Ordóñez is credited with 'some daring but intelligent social experiments' and blamed only for 'a certain amount of tacit encouragement to strikes among the employés of the foreign-owned industrial companies'. But the future looked rosy for this 'land of fine soil, charming climate, and friendly inhabitants'.

68 **Uruguay.**
W. H. Koebel. London: T. Fisher Unwin, 1911. 350p. maps.

A friendly but verbose and dull study of the country ('he would be no real friend of Uruguay who strove to show that the march of the country has not been rudely arrested on innumerable occasions'). History and travel within the country receive most attention: commerce and finance are rather neglected. There is a chapter on the Indian tribes, and fifty-five photographs.

17

69 **Through five republics (of South America): a critical description of Argentina, Brazil, Chile, Uruguay and Venezuela in 1905.**
Percy F. Martin. London: Heinemann, 1905. 487p. maps.

The six chapters (p. 361-417) devoted to Uruguay provide one of the most interesting accounts of the country in travel books of this kind. Following two general chapters on political and living conditions, there is extended treatment of the British-owned railways, other public utilities, and the beef industry. Martin's visit followed the civil war of 1904 and he was perhaps prejudiced against Batlle for that reason ('violations of the Constitution are of daily occurrence . . . the word "liberty" is a farce'). But he found it difficult to speak well of any Uruguayan, and impossible to criticize any Englishman in Uruguay. If one can ignore the author's bile and prejudice, there is much useful factual and technical material, and sixteen photographs mostly of railways and the cattle industry, as well as sharp comment.

70 **Diplomatic terminus: an experience in Uruguay.**
Jefferson Patterson. Cambridge, Massachusetts: Riverside Press, 1962. 113p. maps.

In 1956 the author arrived in Montevideo as ambassador of the United States to Uruguay, a post which he held until his retirement from diplomatic life in 1958. This elegantly produced and privately printed memoir, with twenty-four photographs, does little more than record impressions of the country with some condescension, very little malice, and no profundity at all. There are references to 'the infiltration of communist agents' and 'politically contrived "agrarian reform" ', but there are no deliberately controversial observations, and for the most part the book is an anodyne self-indulgence. Batlle is mis-spelled throughout.

71 **Argentina and Uruguay.**
Gordon Ross. London: Methuen, 1917.

This is a lively and attractive account of the two nations, based on a period of residence in 1911, but useful more as a source of opinion and insight than of information. The principal chapters deal with government, the cities, the First World War, finance and commerce, railways, agriculture, literature and art. Perhaps in spite of its dedication to Sir Robert Kennedy, British Minister in Montevideo until 1911 and implacable critic of Batlle y Ordóñez, Ross is not harsh in his judgments. There are thirteen photographs.

Samuel Walters, Lieutenant, R.N.: his memoirs.
See item no. 147.

Tourism and Travel Guides

72 **The South American Handbook.**
Edited by John Brooks. Bath, England: Trade & Travel Publications.
annual. maps.

Even seasoned travellers to Latin America find room for the *South American Handbook*. Its hallmarks are an immense amount of highly detailed factual information, and an informal personal style. There is an implicit message that those who expect to enjoy the best of Latin America should be prepared to forsake five-star hotels. Those who have visited are encouraged to pass on the benefits of their experience to the editor, and their contributions are duly acknowledged. Only pages 799-824 of the 1389 pages of the 65th edition (1988) are devoted to Uruguay, but the *Handbook* is indispensable nonetheless. Concise, accurate and up-to-date information on geography, history, population and government is followed by a detailed account of Montevideo with the names and addresses of over fifty hotels with price ranges and brief assessments. Restaurants, night-clubs, tea-shops, travel agents, shopping, theatres, museums, sports, churches, travel, and an abundance of other information is also included. The towns of the interior, their facilities and attractions, are treated similarly. The *Handbook* specializes in telling the visitor what (s)he needs to know but is unlikely to find out elsewhere: thus 'Never ring the bell on a bus to get off; ask the conductor and he will ring it'. None of the other travel guides are in the same class as this publication.

73 **South America on a shoestring.**
G. Crowther. London: Lonely Planet Publications, 1986. 3rd ed. 734p.
maps.

This guide provides brief but useful and accurate information on Uruguay on pages 698-711.

74 **Hints to exporters: Uruguay 1986/87.**
London: Department of Trade and Industry, British Overseas Trade
Board. 52p. map. bibliog.

A valuable publication for visitors on business, its main sections are: general
information (area, population, health, customs, hours of business, etc); travel; hotels
(six in Montevideo with phone numbers and prices as at July 1985); postal, telegraph,
telex and telephone facilities; economic factors; import and exchange control
regulations; methods of doing business; and government and commercial organizations.

75 **Guía de Montevideo.** (Guide to Montevideo.)
Montevideo: Mapas y Guías 'Eureka', 1988. 176p. maps.

This is the standard, generally available, and frequently revised guide for those living
in Montevideo. There are street maps for the whole of the Department, in fifty-four
sections, showing street numbers at each block, and bus routes. There is an index to
street names, etc. Bus routes are also listed numerically, with first and last bus times
and frequency of service. There are some useful telephone numbers. No tourist
information as such is given, but any visitor who prefers to use public transport rather
than be enclosed in a taxi will find this an indispensable aid to getting round
Montevideo.

76 **Fodor's South America.**
Edited by Robert C. Fisher, Leslie Brown. London: Hodder and
Stoughton. annual.

The chapter 'Uruguay: the tight little city-state' (p. 573-608 in the 1979 edition) is
contributed by Henry Lee. He achieves the apparently impossible task in the
background section of discussing the contemporary politics of Uruguay without
mentioning that Uruguay was ruled by a military régime. President Bordaberry, it is
said, had 'popular support for the elimination of the slums', but there is no suggestion
that after three repressive years he was himself abruptly removed from office. Other
information is more acceptable, though Garibaldi did not of course fight 'against
Spanish royalists during the independence struggle'. Eight Montevideo hotels are
mentioned, but no prices are given.

77 **Frommer's South America on $25 a day.**
Arnold and Harriet Greenberg. biennial. map.

The relevant section of this guide is to Montevideo only, not Uruguay. The emphasis is
on detailed information about hotels, with plenty of sensible advice and information.
Other sections cover restaurants, Montevideo by day and night, shopping, and
transportation. All the expensive hotels are in fact included, and the stress is on value
for money, rather than economy.

78 **The Jewish travel guide.**
Edited by Sidney Lightman. London: The Jewish Chronicle. annual.

The entry for Uruguay in the 1987 edition (p. 279) estimates a Jewish population of
30,000, and gives addresses and telephone numbers of the Comité Central Israelita and
the four separate Montevideo Kehillot, other synagogues, and details of the
Jewish/Yiddish media.

79   **Descubre Uruguay.** (Discover Uruguay.)
     Montevideo: Ministerio de Turismo, 1987.

Rather than a book, this is a wallet of useful materials for tourists, especially for those planning to travel within the country (there is rather little about Montevideo). The information includes sheets of general introduction and practical material; a road and airport map with distances and flight times; detailed notes on suggested tours within the interior, to the thermal springs, to the various resorts along the coast, and to the hills of Maldonado; and an excellent physical map (scale 1:1,000,000) provided by the Servicio Geográfico Militar (SGM), complete with extensive information on each Department. The sheets are in Spanish and (embarrassingly bad) English. The whole is available without charge from the Ministerio de Turismo, Cerrito 282, Montevideo.

80   **Michael's guide to South America: vol.1 Argentina, Chile, Paraguay, Uruguay.**
     Michael Schichor.   Tel Aviv: INBAL Travel Information, 1985. 183p. maps.

The introduction is relatively extensive, with some emphasis on the information requirements of backpackers. Material on Uruguay is confined to pages 167-81, perhaps because 'From a tourist standpoint Uruguay is of limited interest'. Information is thus brief, and a number of words are mis-spelled. Five Montevideo hotels are recommended, but without prices. Carrasco is said to be 10 minutes by bus from downtown Montevideo (of which there is a street map). Punta del Este is the only 'interior' town treated. The 1988 edition for the whole of South America in one volume discusses Uruguay on pages 663-80.

81   **Myra Waldo's travel guide to South America.**
     Myra Waldo. New York: Collier, 1983. rev. ed. 391p. maps.

In addition to introductory material on South America for intending travellers (from the United States), there is a chapter on Uruguay (p.328-52) in which lethargy, licence and communism are blamed for the country's problems. However, 'the country is now enjoying a period of calm and tranquillity'; 'this very democratic country hardly seems concerned at all about the democratic process and the right to vote in a free election'. One almost expects a travel guide to be patronising, but this one is offensively so. Only three hotels in Montevideo are found worthy of mention (no prices).

Latin America and Caribbean review.
See item no. 658.

Geography

General

82 **Latin America: a regional geography.**
Gilbert J. Butland. London: Longmans, 1960. 373p. maps. bibliog.
Uruguay is treated (p. 282-90) in two parts, the Plata-Uruguay agricultural lowland (extending as a coastal-littoral margin from Maldonado to Salto) and the pastoral plateau interior. There are two plates.

83 **Uruguay.**
Raymond E. Crist, Edward P. Leahy. In: *South America.* Edited by Alice Taylor. New York: Praeger; Newton Abbot, Devon: David & Charles, 1973, p. 217-27. maps. bibliog. (Published in cooperation with the American Geographical Society).
A geographical, historical and economic survey, necessarily superficial in some judgments but certainly not vacuous. It concludes optimistically, expressing ill-founded 'confidence that the nation will reorganize and institute the measures needed to reduce social and economic inequalities and restore political stability'.

84 **The River Plate countries.**
J. Colin Crossley. In: *Latin America: geographical perspectives.* Edited by Harold Blakemore, Clifford T. Smith. London; New York: Methuen, 1983, p. 383-455. 2nd ed. maps. bibliog.
'River Plate' here means primarily Argentina, and treatment of Uruguay is rather thin. However the strongly regional perspective is itself valuable, especially in discussion of the livestock industry.

85   **The agricultural land use regions of Uruguay.**
Ernst Clark Griffin.   *Revista Geográfica* vol. 76 (1972), p. 121-51.
bibliog.

Griffin begins by commenting on the paucity of geographical analyses of Uruguay, a void which his paper seeks to fill 'by presenting a descriptive analysis of Uruguay's agricultural land use regions'. They are seven: orchard–vineyard; intensive crop production; cereals; dairy; cereals–livestock; extensive sheep grazing; and cattle grazing. For each there is analysis of location, farm size, production patterns, and production problems. The text is supported by twelve maps. This is a useful work which may be compared with the similar analysis (which does not however distinguish between the sheep and cattle grazing regions) in CLEH-CINAM, *Situación económica y social del Uruguay rural* (q.v.).

86   **Testing the Von Thünen theory in Uruguay.**
Ernst Clark Griffin.   *Geographical Review*, vol. 63, no. 4 (Jan. 1973), p. 500-16. maps.

Griffin argues that Uruguay is a suitable location in which to test the Von Thünen theory of intensity of land use, and finds that the theory fits well with the four bands of diminishing land use intensity round Montevideo. The main deviation from the model's prediction occurs to the east of Montevideo, where there is direct passage from the most intensive zone (horticulture) to the least intensive (livestock). This is explained primarily in terms of soil fertility, but limited use of modern technical inputs, traditional settlement patterns and foreign market competition are also perceived to be relevant. There are nine excellent maps supporting the argument.

87   **Uruguay: el país urbano.** (Uruguay: the urban country.)
Jaime Klaczko, Juan Rial Roade.   Montevideo: Ediciones de la Banda Oriental, 1981. 144p. maps. bibliog.

'This work analyses the structure of the urban system in Uruguay, as the ordering principle of an initially empty space, in consequence of the various efforts deployed in the organization of the territory resulting from economic, social, political, and ideological stimuli, located in the context of its historical evolution'. The rise of a network of towns but the continuing dominance of Montevideo is analysed with the aid of ten maps and twenty-six tables.

88   **South America.**
Arthur S. Morris.   London: Hodder & Stoughton, 1981. 2nd ed. 276p. maps. bibliog.

The conclusions of this attractive introduction to the (mainly economic) geography of Uruguay (p. 129-37) are unexpectedly positive, though ambitious and even unproven. They are that economic opportunity still beckons, provided that there is intensification of agricultural land use following reform; that government action is taken to stimulate growth outside Montevideo; and that there is favourable treatment from the Latin American Free Trade Association (which expired in 1980!) to promote greater integration with the River Plate–São Paulo axis. The bibliography unfortunately runs together two separate works by Brannon and Fitzgerald.

89 **The climate of Argentina, Paraguay and Uruguay.**
Fritz Prohaska. In: *Climates of Central and South America*. Edited by
Werner Schwerdtfeger. Amsterdam; Oxford; New York: Elsevier
Scientific Publishing, 1976, p. 13-112. bibliog. (World Survey of
Climatology, vol. 12).

This is an authoritative and detailed account of the climate of the region, supported by
fifty-four tables and thirteen figures. Only a minority of these relate exclusively to
Uruguay, but they include climatic tables for Artigas (annual averages for the period
1944-60); Paso de los Toros (1937-60); Treinta y Tres (1939-60); Punta del Este (1940-
60); and Montevideo (1901-50).

90 **Selective annotated bibliography on the climates of Paraguay, Uruguay
and Argentina.**
Mary L. Rice. *Meteorological Abstracts and Bibliography*, vol. 3, no. 3
(March 1952), p. 243-90.

Numerous annotated references are listed, mostly to works in Spanish and English,
under these principal headings: meteorological services and observation; data; analysis
and forecasting; temperature; wind; fog, clouds and hydrometeors; hydrology;
climatology; and miscellaneous phenomena and applications.

91 **The grasslands of Latin America.**
G. M. Roseveare. Aberystwyth, Wales: Imperial Bureau of Pastures
and Field Crops, 1948. 291p. maps. bibliog. (Bulletin 36).

Although Miss Roseveare is credited as author, her task was to assemble a report
based on information collected by the Bureau since about 1930. In the case of
Uruguay, most of the information originated with Dr. Alberto Boerger (who checked
the work in manuscript) and his team at the research station La Estanzuela
(Department of Colonia). The main section on Uruguay (p. 34-50) has detailed
information on grass types in various localities of sixteen departments, based on a
survey in 1937-38. A theme of the report is gradual botanical deterioration and soil
degradation. The failure of lucerne cultivation is attributed to 'compact soils with
impermeable subsoil'. There are also brief sections on research and conservation, and
six plates.

92 **Urban places in Uruguay and the concept of a hierarchy.**
David E. Snyder. *Northwestern University Studies in Geography*,
vol. 6 (1962), p. 29-46. maps.

Snyder maps the location of eighty-nine urban centres, finds the Christaller model of
urban hierarchies too formal, but successfully imposes a pattern of equidistant
polygons based on departmental capitals. Passenger carrier routes are then mapped
and analysed. He concludes that 'It is probably improper to suggest that a hierarchy of
central places exists in other than arbitrary form. However, it can be concluded that,
within the limits of the various assumptions, both explicit and implicit, the empirical
pattern of passenger linkages among Uruguayan urban places does approach a form
and a composition which in many respects is consistent with the concept of an urban
place hierarchy'. Professional geographers will find most enlightenment.

93 **Urbanization in twentieth century Latin America: a working bibliography.**
Compiled by Denton R. Vaughan.   University of Texas at Austin,
Institute of Latin American Studies, Population Research Center, 1970.
122p.
Twenty-three items are listed for Uruguay on pages 88-90. Most are Spanish-language
references, and there are no annotations.

Geology

94 **Bibliography and index of geology.**
American Geological Institute. Monthly and annual accumulated vols.
A complete unannotated listing of geological monographs and articles.

95 **Carta geológica del Uruguay.** (Geological map of Uruguay.)
Jorge Bossi (et al.).   Montevideo: Dirección de Suelos y Fertilizantes,
1979.
A geological map of the country, scale 1:1,000,000.

96 **Geología uruguaya.** (The geology of Uruguay.)
Juan A. Caorsi, Juan C. Goñi.   Montevideo: Imprenta Nacional, 1958.
73p. maps. bibliog.
A standard general geology of the country, with forty-one excellent plates.

97 **Geology and geomorphology of the coastal plain of Rio Grande do Sul,
Brazil and northern Uruguay.**
Patrick J. V. Delaney.   Baton Rouge, Louisiana: Louisiana State
University Press, 1966. 58p. maps. bibliog. (Louisiana State University,
Coastal Studies Series, 15).
Because of the vast area covered, 'this project must be considered a semi-detailed
reconnaissance study'. The main sections are natural setting; geological framework and
history; stratigraphy; and palaeoclimates. It continues and revises a previous work by
Delaney, no. 7 in the same series, 'Outline of the geologic history of the coastal plain
. . .' (1963). There are fourteen plates and an annotated bibliography.

98 **The groundwater resources of Uruguay.**
Y. Gilboa.   *Hydrological Sciences Bulletin*, vol. 22, no. 1 (March 1977),
p. 115-26. maps. bibliog.
The author reconstructs the generalized hydrogeological model of the country, and
evaluates groundwater resources for the country based on recharge values obtained
from studies relating to São Paulo (Brazil). 'The estimates presented are of a most

preliminary nature, only hinting at the relative importance of the main aquifers and the possibilities of utilizing the groundwater potential.' Less than five per cent of the potential is exploited.

99 **Bibliografía sobre geología y paleontología del Uruguay.** (Bibliography of the geology and palaeontology of Uruguay.)
Boletín, Instituto Geológico del Uruguay, no. 38 (1981), p. 95-162.
Lists 825 references.

100 **Morphological, physical and chemical properties of major soils from Calagna in northwestern Uruguay.**
M. A. Lugo-López, Juan P. Carnelli, G. Acevedo. *Soil Science Society of America Journal*, vol. 49, no. 1 (Jan.-Feb. 1985), p. 108-13.
A somewhat technical and small-scale but nonetheless significant study of about 5000 hectares near a modern sugar-cane mill at Bella Unión. Potassium and phosphorus levels were found to be 'strikingly low', but with suitable fertilizer use and efficient irrigation techniques (because of erratic rainfall) the soils of Calagna are well suited to production of a range of field and horticultural crops.

101 **A geo-paleontological synthesis of the Gondwana formations of Uruguay.**
Alvaro Mones, Alfredo Figueiras. In: *Gondwana five: selected papers and abstracts of papers presented at the fifth international Gondwana symposium.* Edited by M. M. Cresswell. Rotterdam: Balkema, 1981, p. 47-52. bibliog.
'The Gondwana formations of Uruguay occupy two basins. The most extensive one occupies the northern departments of the country and is subdivided into two parts: one in the NE, filled mainly with Eogondwanic rocks (Carboniferous–Permian), and one in the NW, filled mainly with Neogondwanic rocks (Jurassic–Cretaceous). The other basin lies in SE Uruguay and contains Jurassic–Cretaceous rocks without equivalents in Argentina and Brazil. Brief lithological descriptions and fossil lists for each formation are given.' Most of this paper is technical and in note form, but there is a table which correlates the Gondwanic formations of Uruguay and her two neighbours. (Gondwana-land was the super-continent of the southern hemisphere which united the present continents 200 million years ago.)

102 **Bibliography of economic geology of South America.**
Joseph T. Singewald, Jr. Geological Society of America, 1943.
159p. (Geological Society of America, Special Papers, 50).
Lists twenty-eight titles for Uruguay (p. 150-51), many in English, and many published before 1920. There are no annotations.

103 **Noteworthy features of Uruguayan soils.**
Frederick R. Troeh. *Soil Science Society of America Proceedings*, vol. 33, no. 1 (Jan.-Feb. 1969). p. 125-28. map. bibliog.
The author worked in Uruguay for a year, contributing technical guidance to a reconnaissance soil survey, associated with the US Agency of International Development. Following a useful introduction on topography, climate, vegetation and soil

parent materials, soil characteristics are discussed. The principal soils are found to occur commonly in a catena sequence, and different types are analysed. Troeh concludes: 'There are few if any countries in the world where the mollic epipedon is more nearly universal than in Uruguay. This asset gives Uruguay a high potential crop production that has yet to be realised'. Internal drainage problems and phosphorus deficiency on unfertilized soils are the main problems.

104 **The Rivera gold belt of Uruguay.**
N. W. Wilson. *Mining Magazine*, vol. 59 (1938), p. 201-10. maps. bibliog.

During 1937-38 the author spent four months examining the San Gregorio gold mine, and shorter periods at other workings. San Gregorio had closed in 1916, and that effectively ended gold mining's forty-year history. Wilson's fascinating study examines the location, topography, climate, history, communications, labour supply and geology of the industry and its area. He concludes that in spite of renewed interest in gold mining, 'optimism about revenue-producing possibilities does not seem to be warranted, for there are no known mines in the Rivera gold belt that could yield reasonable returns on big capital investments.' That left only the possibility of small-workers (i.e. independent and without capital) who would need government assistance if they were to work below water-level.

Maps and gazetteers

105 **Indice toponímico de los lugares poblados.** (Index of place-names of population centres.)
Montevideo: Dirección General de Estadística y Censos, 1972. 528p.

Based on the enumeration of places made for the 1963 census of population and housing, the index lists in alphabetical order 5019 place-names. The majority of these have no population, and their location is given solely in administrative terms (judicial section and department). Geographical reference (to rivers, roads, railways) is additionally given for those which are populated. They are categorized as to the type of settlement, and there is information on the number of males, females and dwellings in the location. Appendix tables list the settled places in each department.

106 **Carta del Uruguay al millonésimo.** (Map of Uruguay scale 1:1,000,000.)
Montevideo: Servicio Geográfico Militar, 1971.

This useful map shows the frontier with Brazil, cities and towns, departmental boundaries, principal highways (with their numbers), railways, rivers and marshes. Contours are indicated at 100-metre altitude intervals. Land over 300 metres (of which there is very little) is not clearly shown, though a limited number of spot heights are indicated. Similar information is given for adjacent regions of Argentina and Brazil. The map is based on 1:50,000 mapping by the SGM.

107   **Uruguay: official standard names approved by the United States Board on Geographic Names.**
United States, Office of Geography, Department of the Interior, Washington, D.C.: 1956. 126p. (Gazetteer no. 21).
About 8,600 names of places and features in Uruguay are listed, together with latitude and longitude coordinates (to the nearest minute), identification of the place/feature within forty-one categories (area, bay, bank, beach, cape, etc), and reference to seven maps or charts on which it may be located. Variant names are listed, and are cross-referenced to approved standard names.

Descubre Uruguay. (Discover Uruguay.)
See item no. 79.

Uruguay: the problem of etymology of place names of Guaraní origin.
See item no. 224.

Flora and Fauna

108 On the birds of Uruguay.
Oliver Vernon Aplin, with an introduction and notes by Philip Lutley
Sclater. *The Ibis* ser. 6, vol. 6, no. 22 (April 1894), p. 149-215. map.
In his introduction, Sclater (editor of *The Ibis*) records the origins of this work in his
collaboration with W. H. Hudson on a book on Argentine birds in which he discovered
a comparative dearth of information on those of Uruguay. At his instigation Aplin
spent seven months in Uruguay in 1892-93, and returned with specimens of 93 species.
They and a further 46 are described here, with mention of 24 others seen only as
museum specimens. The field-notes are interesting though generally confined to
behavioural characteristics, and the local Uruguayan name is not given in most cases.
There is a colour plate of eight eggs.

109 Insectos y aracnidos. (Insects and spiders.)
Carlos S. Carbonell. Montevideo: Editorial 'Nuestra Tierra', 1969.
72p. bibliog. (Nuestra Tierra 15).
A well-illustrated guide to Uruguay's scorpions, ants, bees, flies, cockroaches, spiders,
locusts, etc. The general rule seems to be that the worse they look (in the ninety
photographs) the less harmful they are.

**110 Pflanzengesellschaften der Küstendünen von Argentinien, Uruguay und
Südbrasilien.** (Plant communities of the coastal dunes of Argentina,
Uruguay and southern Brazil.)
U. Erskuche. *Vegetatio*, vol. 28, no. 3-4 (Sept. 1973), p. 201-50. map.
bibliog.
There is an English summary of this work on pages 245-49. Six principal plant
communities, most of which occur in Uruguay, are identified, and there are six
photographs.

111 **Las aves del Uruguay.** (The birds of Uruguay.)
Michael E. J. Gore, Alfredo R. M. Gepp. Montevideo: Mosca
Hnos, 1978. 283p. map. bibliog.

This is the definitive work on Uruguayan ornithology. Details of identification, habitat,
status, global distribution, and brief notes on observations by the authors, are given for
376 species. There are 109 photographs (by the authors), including twenty-six in
colour, and useful sections on Uruguayan geography and climate, habitats and bird
populations, migration, the conservation issue, and ornithological history. The text is
in Spanish, but the book is the product of an Anglo–Uruguayan collaboration and all
species are identified by their English, Uruguayan and specific names. In addition there
are notes for English readers and a Spanish–English glossary.

112 **Birds of the Uruguayan swamplands.**
Michael E. J. Gore. In: *The Third Birdwatchers' Book*. Compiled and
edited by John Gooders. Newton Abbot, Devon: David and Charles,
1976, p. 114-24.

A general account of some of the principal species of the habitat, mainly ducks, waders
and birds of prey. Problems of controlling those which are agricultural pests are
discussed, as well as more general conservation issues and the practice of trapping to
supply cagebirds. There is one illustration.

113 **The potatoes of Argentina, Brazil, Paraguay, and Uruguay: a
biosystematic study.**
J. G. Hawkes, J. P. Hjerting. London: Oxford University Press,
1969. 675p. maps. bibliog.

A work of immense, indeed astonishing, scholarship, this study of the tuber-bearing
wild potato (*Solanum*) species relates only in part to Uruguay. In fact the first species
in the group was collected from Montevideo by the French explorer Commerson in
1767, and *S. commersonii* is by far the most abundant in the country. The general
chapters in the first part are: historical survey; wild potato collections; distribution and
ecology of the wild species; taxonomy and evolutionary relationships; breeding value;
taxonomic methods used; and classification of the genus *Solanum*. There follows a
detailed taxonomy developed by the authors of 19 species in 6 series, and a further
three cultivated species. There are 150 full-page photographic plates, 13 maps, and
numerous line drawings and tables. The bibliography contains some 700 items. A truly
majestic volume.

114 **Birds of La Plata.**
William Henry Hudson, with a note by R. B. Cunninghame Graham.
London; Toronto: J. M. Dent; New York: E. P. Dutton, 1923. 405p.
(Collected works of W. H. Hudson, vol. 6)

Hudson records in his introduction (October 1920) that this work derives from his two-
volume *Argentine Ornithology* (1888-89). Although it covers the La Plata district of
Argentina, the overlap with Uruguayan birds is extensive. There are descriptions of
190 species, but the delight of this book is the care and detail in the observation and
anecdote, and the quality of the writing. Oddly, Hudson finds a close resemblance
between the Dominican or kelp gull (*Larus dominicanus*) and the Great (not Lesser)
Black-backed gull of the northern hemisphere.

115 **The naturalist in La Plata.**
William Henry Hudson. London; Toronto: J. M. Dent; New York:
E. P. Dutton, 1923. 392p. 1st ed. published in 1892 (Collected works of
W. H. Hudson, vol. 20).
To be read as much for pleasure as for zoological enlightenment, Hudson describes in
an unsystematic manner a variety of mammals, insects and birds to be found in the La
Plata region of Argentina (and in Uruguay though he does not say so).

116 **Anfíbios y reptiles.** (Amphibians and reptiles.)
Miguel A. Klappenbach, B. R. Orejas-Miranda. Montevideo:
Editorial 'Nuestra Tierra', 1969. 68p. bibliog. (Nuestra Tierra 11).
As with the other volumes in the series, though intended for popular consumption this
is an authoritative account of the species to be found in Uruguay. Illustrated with line
drawings and photographs.

117 **Flora arborea y arborescente del Uruguay.** (Trees and shrubs of
Uruguay.)
Atilio Lombardo. Montevideo: Consejo Departamental de
Montevideo, Dirección de Paseos Públicos, 1964. 2nd ed. 151p.
First published in 1946, this most useful guide is illustrated with line drawings of the
leaves, fruit and flowers of most of the 224 species (belonging to fifty-two families)
listed. The main section has descriptive notes on each and an account of its distribution
within the country. Specific and common names are given. There is a list of botanical
terms used, with their meanings, and an identification key. The bibliography which
apparently featured in the first edition has disappeared in the second, but the work is
fully indexed. A more accessible work for the general reader by the same author is
Arboles y arbustos (Trees and shrubs), Montevideo: Editorial 'Nuestra Tierra', 1969,
72p., bibliog. (Nuestra Tierra 27).

118 **A guide to the birds of South America.**
Rodolphe Meyer de Schauensee. Edinburgh: Oliver and Boyd, 1970.
470p.
There are short descriptions of 2924 species with some differentiation of sub-species,
and brief notes on distribution. Fifty plates, many in colour, are an aid to
identification. See also the same author's *The species of birds of South America and
their distribution* (Narberth, Pennsylvania: Livingston, 1966, 577p.).

119 **Hierbas del Uruguay.** (Grasses of Uruguay.)
Osvaldo del Puerto. Montevideo: Editorial 'Nuestra Tierra', 1969.
68p. bibliog. (Nuestra Tierra 19).
The plants are described according to their habitat (marshland, grassland, sand dunes,
etc). There are some good drawings but the photographs are of indifferent quality.

31

Flora and Fauna

120 **The Uruguayan fur-seal islands.**
Hugh M. Smith. *Zoologica*, vol. 9, no. 6 (Sept. 1927), p. 271-94.
map.

In December 1922 the author visited what constituted the largest fur-seal herd in the South Atlantic, on three groups of islands: the Lobos Islands near Punta del Este; the Torres and Castillos Islands off Cabo Polonio; and, further north still, the Coronilla Islands. The species, *Arctocephalus australis*, coexists easily with the 'sea-lion', *Otaria jubata*, whose skin is less valuable. Smith's main concern was less the preparation of a scientific paper than to give warning that 'the present Uruguayan seal herd is a mere remnant fast approaching commercial extinction under existing conditions'. There are interesting notes on other mammals, birds and fish which he observed, as well as on evidence that the Charrúas had made use of the seals. There are six plates.

121 **Peces del Uruguay.** (The fish of Uruguay.)
Raúl Vaz-Ferreira. Montevideo: Editorial 'Nuestra Tierra', 1969.
72p. bibliog. (Nuestra Tierra 23).

An authoritative study of fresh and saltwater fish, illustrated by line drawings and a small number of photographs.

122 **Observations on the birds of Argentina, Paraguay, Uruguay, and Chile.**
Alexander Wetmore. Washington: Government Printing Office, 1926.
448p. map. (Smithsonian Institution, United States National Museum, Bulletin 133).

During a ten-month expedition to South America, the author was in Uruguay in January-February 1921, visiting Montevideo, La Paloma, Castillos, (Minas de) Corrales and Río Negro. The main purpose was to assess the status of birds that migrate to the northern hemisphere, but there was also 'abundant opportunity to make representative collections of native birds'. This work thus consists of 'an annotated list of the species of birds collected, with observations on a few of which no specimens were taken'. Lucky few. If one can cope with the fact that any bird which interested the author was immediately shot, the account which he gives of their field characteristics is valuable. Against that, the species are identified only according to their scientific nomenclature; English or Spanish names are not given.

The voyage of the *Beagle*.
See item no. 35.

The grasslands of Latin America.
See item no. 91.

The criollo: Spanish cattle in the Americas.
See item no. 431.

Prehistory and Archaeology

123 **Uruguay: monumentos históricos y arqueológicos.** (Uruguay: historical and archaeological monuments.)
Alfredo Castellanos. México, D.F.: Instituto Panamericano de Geografía e Historia, 1974. 175p. bibliog. (I.P.G.H. publication no. 337, Monumentos Históricos y Arqueológicos de América, vol. 16).

The first four chapters give historical background to and discuss the buildings or artefacts of the pre-Hispanic, Hispanic (1700-1814), Luso-Brazilian (1817-28) and nineteenth-century periods. State policy on protection of national monuments is then discussed. There are forty-seven plates.

124 **El Uruguay indígena.** (Indigenous Uruguay.)
Renzo Pi Hugarte. Montevideo: Editorial 'Nuestra Tierra', 1968. 68p. maps. bibliog. (Nuestra Tierra 1).

A brief all-embracing study of the indigenous cultures of Uruguay, especially that of the Charrúa Indians. The book is well illustrated.

125 **Uruguayan archaeology.**
B. Sierra y Sierra. *Inter-America*, vol. 6, no. 2 (Dec. 1922), p. 128-31.

This brief and rather uninformative note reports on fragments of pottery collected by the author at locations in Uruguay. The Spanish original of this article, published in *Revista Histórica* (Montevideo, Jan.-March 1922), is accompanied by illustrations.

126 **10.000 años de prehistoria uruguaya.** (Ten thousand years of the
prehistory of Uruguay.)
Daniel Vidart.   Montevideo: Fundación Editorial 'Unión del
Magisterio', 1973. 83p. maps. bibliog.
Rather little is known of Uruguayan prehistory, but this is a useful summary. There are
a number of photographs, mostly of artefacts, not very well reproduced.

An account of a voyage up the River de la Plata . . .
See item no. 28.

Uruguay.
See item no. 68.

La arquitectura en el Uruguay. Vol. I. Epoca colonial. (Architecture in
Uruguay. Vol. I. Colonial era.)
See item no. 483.

History

General

127 **Anales históricos del Uruguay.** (Historical annals of Uruguay.)
   Eduardo Acevedo.   Montevideo: Barreiro y Ramos, 1933-36. 6 vols.
This extraordinary work is essentially a mine of information on Uruguayan history
rather than (as the author himself believed it to be) a work which sacrificed detail in
order to assist the student-reader to form his own judgments. There is a mass of factual
and quantitative material, often taken from official publications, which is frequently
indispensable although requiring (in Uruguayan publications as elsewhere) to be
regarded cautiously. The standard format of the volumes is an examination of each
government in terms of political, economic and administrative developments, but these
are interpreted widely and almost everything of any note is recorded. It is rare for any
source for the information to be given. The sequence of volumes is strictly
chronological, and the terminal dates for each are 1838 (1), 1860 (2), 1876 (3), 1894
(4), 1915 (5), and 1931 (6).

128 **Civilization and barbarism: cattle frontiers in Latin America.**
   Silvio R. Duncan Baretta, John Markoff.   *Comparative Studies in
   Society and History*, vol. 20 (1978), p.587-620.
Although this article is not specific to Uruguay, it contains interesting ideas concerning
the changing nature of violence on the cattle frontier as rationalization of production
(particularly the introduction of barbed wire) and the improved equipment of state
forces occurred. There are references to Aparicio Saravia.

129 **Small wars you may have missed.**
   Andrew Graham-Yooll.   London: Junction Books, 1983.
   192p. bibliog.
This delightful book recounts Britain's involvement in small wars in South America,
using extended quotations from *The Times* and the *Manchester Guardian*, and the

writings of British observers. The chapters of greatest Uruguayan interest concern 'Buenos Aires, Brazil and the Banda Oriental, 1826' (p. 37-50), and 'Anglo-French blockade in the River Plate, 1845-1850' (p. 79-94). Published the year following the Falklands conflict, the author expresses the hope 'that readers will look on these pages as an entertainment and will note how ironical and repetitious history and its language tend to be'.

130 **Latin America: a guide to the historical literature.**
   Charles C. Griffin (editor), J. Benedict Warren (assistant editor).
   Austin, Texas; London: University of Texas Press, 1971. 700p.
   (Conference on Latin American History, publication no. 4).
This valuable annotated bibliography is organized in seven sections, covering reference, general, backgound, colonial, Independence, post-Independence, and international relations. The largest section dealing with Uruguay is the post-Independence period (p. 579-95), which is edited with a short introduction by Milton I. Vanger and contains 200 items in Spanish and English.

131 **Cronología comparada de la historia del Uruguay (1830-1945).**
   (Comparative chronology of Uruguayan history, 1830-1945.)
   M. Blanca París de Oddone, Roque Faraone, Juan Antonio Oddone.
   Montevideo: Universidad de la República, 1968. 189p. maps. bibliog.
For anyone requiring a swift and remarkably detailed guide to historical events and 'facts', this chronology is almost indispensable. There are entries for each year under three headings: politics and administration; technology, economy and society; and culture. Each heading also has parallel but briefer notes on developments elsewhere in the world. Legislation and elections predictably bulk large, but regular sub-headings also include population; production; foreign trade; communications; energy; education; music; and art and literature. There are indexes to geographical place-names; personal names; and institutions (subdivided into nine categories).

132 **Historiography and historical studies in Uruguay.**
   Juan Rial, Jaime Klaczko.   *Latin American Research Review*, vol. 17, no. 3 (1982), p. 229-50.
Eleven works dealing with Uruguayan history of the twentieth century (mostly published in Montevideo during 1979-81) are assessed in this review article, which, however, also addresses more general issues concerning the nature and difficulties of historical scholarship in the country.

133 **Surprisingly profitable ventures in Uruguay.**
   J. Fred Rippy.   In: *British investments in Latin America, 1822-1949: a case study in the operations of private enterprise in retarded regions.*
   Hamden, Connecticut: Archon, 1966. Original edition published 1959 by University of Minnesota Press, Minneapolis, Minnesota, p. 142-49. map.
This chapter in Rippy's book first appeared as an article in *Journal of Business* for 1952. He reviews the rate of return on the various British investments in Uruguay, and concludes that in spite of the tensions which existed between British capitalists and the host country, 'it is likely that their investment in Uruguay yielded as high returns over

the years as their capital in almost any other Latin-American country'. Oddly, he seems unaware that Liebig's Extract of Meat Co. sold their Fray Bentos plant to Vestey's and left Uruguay in 1924.

134 **Research tools for Latin American historians.**
David P. Werlich. New York; London: Garland, 1980. 269p.
(Garland reference library of social science, vol. 60).
In addition to guides, indexes and bibliographies relating to Latin America as a whole, there are twenty-four annotated bibliographical entries for Uruguay (p. 240-43), mostly in Spanish.

135 **South American dictators during the first century of independence.**
Edited by A. Curtis Wilgus. New York: Russell & Russell, 1937. 502p.
Lewis Winkler Bealer contributed two studies to this collection, though it is hard to see how the first qualifies under the volume's title. They are: 'Artigas, father of federalism in La Plata' (p. 35-57); and 'Fructuoso Rivera, colorado caudillo of Uruguay' (p. 114-24).

Discovery and colonial period

136 **Economic growth and regional differentiations: the River Plate region at the end of the eighteenth century.**
Juan Carlos Garavaglia, translated by Diane Meléndez. *Hispanic American Historical Review*, vol. 65, no. 1 (Feb. 1985), p. 51-89.
'We feel that the image of an immense pampa traversed by a handful of horse-riding gauchos, busy with their lassoes and strumming their guitars – a dearly-loved simplification of a whole genre of representations of the past of our Litoral – is false.' This conclusion derives from an attempt to examine the nature of economic growth and how it was distributed in the region in the period which was influenced by the Bourbon reforms. There is thus an estimate of the relative productive strengths of Buenos Aires and Montevideo; but even more interesting is the suggestion (based partly on evidence of tithes) that there was a shift from cereal production to cattle in the Colonia–Soriano region at the end of the century, whereas for Montevideo, Maldonado (and Buenos Aires) grain production was dominant throughout this period.

137 **The conquest of the River Plate.**
Robert Boutine Cunninghame Graham. London: Heinemann, 1924. 313p. map. bibliog.
The author emphasizes in his preface that this popular and colourful account of the conquest aims less to give a scholarly account of what happened than 'to present some of the conquerors of the River Plate as human beings, and try to show that, taking into consideration the times in which they lived, they did not differ greatly from ourselves'. He makes the point that almost no eye-witness accounts are available. The book opens with Solís sailing into the River Plate in 1515, and dying at the hands of the Charrúas. Thereafter specific references to Uruguay are infrequent.

138 **Bruno Mauricio de Zabala: the founder of Montevideo.**
Raúl Montero Bustamante. *Inter-America*, vol. 2, no. 5 (June 1919),
p. 272-79.
A biographical sketch, with no great pretensions to historical scholarship, of the man
who founded Montevideo in 1724.

139 **The European discovery of America: the southern voyages AD 1492-
1616.**
Samuel Eliot Morison. New York: Oxford University Press, 1974.
758p. map. bibliog.
The discovery of the River Plate by Juan de Solís (1516) is described on pages 297-303;
the voyage of Magellan in 1520 on pages 362-63; the voyage of Sebastian Cabot in 1527
on page 548; and the conquest of the River Plate 1534-80 on pages 562-82. Clearly the
River Plate explorations rate comparatively modest attention. The author's style is racy
and forthright. R. B. Cunninghame Graham's *The conquest of the River Plate* (q.v.) he
describes as 'slapdash and uncritical'.

140 **The Solís, Cabot, and Mendoza expeditions to the Río de la Plata.**
In: *New Iberian world: a documentary history of the discovery and
settlement of Latin America to the early 17th century.* Edited, with
commentaries, by John H. Parry and Robert G. Keith, with the
assistance of Michael Jimenez. New York: Times Books and Hector
Rose; Toronto: Fitzhenry and Whiteside, 1984. Vol. 5: *Coastlines,
Rivers, and Forests*, p. 246-76. maps. bibliog.
Following a short introduction by the editors, chapter 61 of this elegantly produced
five-volume work recounts the story of the early expeditions to the River Plate by
means of extracts from contemporary or early accounts. The authors of those accounts
(translated into English) are Antonio de Herrera (on the voyage of Juan de Solís); Luis
Ramírez (1530, on Cabot); Cabot himself (1530); Francisco Villalta (1556); and others.
Most of the material refers to Buenos Aires or Paraguay, but Herrera gives an account
of the killing of Solís by the Charrúas. A number of early maps of the region are
reproduced, including those attributed to Gaspar Viegas (1537); Cabot (1544); Alonso
de Santa Cruz (after 1545); and others.

141 **Dom Pedro of Braganza and Colônia do Sacramento, 1680-1705.**
Mario Rodríguez. *Hispanic American Historical Review*, vol. 38,
no. 2 (May 1958), p. 179-208.
The city of Colonia was founded in 1680 by Portugal, opposite Buenos Aires and
essentially to challenge its control of the River Plate. The author, whose work is
closely based on primary sources, examines this motivation and evaluates the history of
the settlement to the end of Dom Pedro's reign. He concludes that in a narrow sense
the Colonia enterprise was a failure economically, but that it had the long-term benefit
of stimulating agricultural activity in southern Brazil.

142 **Estructura económico-social de la colonia.** (Economic and social structure of the colony.)
Lucía Sala de Touron, Nelson de la Torre, Julio C. Rodríguez.
Montevideo: Editorial Pueblos Unidos, 1967. 200p.

The authors aim to analyse the specific nature of the socio-economic structure of colonial Uruguay, in which late colonization, the lack of a submissible Indian population or precious metals, and the failure to secure effective state power over the whole territory, were key elements.

143 **Evolución económica de la Banda Oriental.** (The economic evolution of the Banda Oriental del Uruguay.)
Lucía Sala de Touron, Julio C. Rodríguez, Nelson de la Torre.
Montevideo: Ediciones Pueblos Unidos, 1968. 2nd ed. 302p. maps.

Based essentially on sources in Buenos Aires and in the Archivo General de la Nación and the Museo Histórico Nacional, the authors analyse the process of primitive capital accumulation through trade, the growth of the meat-salting plants, and the appropriation of land and cattle, throughout the colonial period up to 1815. Class formation and the nature of class conflict up to 1815 are also assessed.

144 **Trade and proletarianization in late colonial Banda Oriental: evidence from the Estancia de Las Vacas 1791-1805.**
Ricardo Salvatore, Jonathan C. Brown. *Hispanic American Historical Review*, vol. 67, no. 3 (Aug. 1987), p. 431-59. bibliog.

Using the records for 1791-1805 of this estate, which was located on the Uruguay River, the authors examine the way in which fluctuations in the dominant commercial activity, the export of hides, combined with the life-style and work habits of the *gauchos* to ensure their resistance to the process of proletarianization. Because changing demand for labour dictated that comparatively little labour was permanent, *gauchos* could retain their distinctive preferences in regard to the duration of employment and work discipline. These were rooted not only in the wandering life and lack of attachment to place or job, but also in limited consumption needs, and the fact that 'the gaucho identified his subsistence with appropriation and not with wage labor. Illegality provided him with an alternative to work . . .'. The analysis in this valuable article, which is supported by quantitative material from the estate records, primarily concerns the labour process on the estate and the relationship of that to fluctuating world demand; the nature of *gaucho* habits is mainly derived from published sources.

English invasions 1806-7

145 **Military memoirs of four brothers (natives of Staffordshire) engaged in the service of their country, as well in the New World and Africa, as on the continent of Europe.**
By the survivor, Captain Thomas Ferneyhough. London: John Masters, 1838. 3rd ed. 324p.
The journals of Lieutenant Robert Ferneyhough while serving in the Home Popham invasion force in the River Plate in 1806-7 are to be found on pages 82-130. The main Uruguayan interest is a short account of Montevideo, which Robert passed through with the defeated forces of Whitelocke in 1807.

146 *The Southern Star*, **Montevideo 1807.**
Instituto Histórico y Geográfico del Uruguay, with a prologue by Ariosto González. Montevideo: Barreiro y Ramos, 1942.
During the period of the British occupation of Montevideo, a newspaper in English and Spanish, *The Southern Star*, was published in the city between 23 May and 4 July 1807. This is a facsimile edition.

147 **Samuel Walters, Lieutenant, R.N.: his memoirs.**
Edited with an introduction and notes by C. Northcote Parkinson.
Liverpool: Liverpool University Press, 1949. 154p.
'It was suggested by Sir Home Popham and the General [Beresford] that we, with a small force, might succeed in making a landing in the River Plate.' The author was on board one of the vessels which accompanied Popham on his extraordinary invasion in 1806, and his experiences and impressions during 1806-7 are recorded on pages 41-63. There are especially vivid accounts of the capture by British forces of Maldonado (October 1806) and Montevideo (January–February 1807), accompanied by sketch-maps of the two towns. At Montevideo Walters estimated British losses at 200 dead and 'great numbers' on the Spanish side. Nonetheless, 'The fact was, in two day's time the inhabitants open'd their shops. The melancholy appearance wore off by degrees, they soon became cheerful . . .'.

148 **An authentic narrative of the proceedings of the expedition under the command of Brigadier-Gen. Craufurd, until its arrival at Monte Video; with an account of the operations against Buenos Ayres under the command of Lieu.-Gen. Whitelocke.**
By an officer of the expedition. London: printed for the author, 1808. 216p. maps.
Craufurd's small force sailed from Britain a month after Auchmuty, and arrived at Montevideo (which Auchmuty had captured in February) in June 1807. The author, who may be Captain James Thomson, gives a second-hand account of the capture, with a very detailed map, and a description of the city (p. 95-114), and a participant's view of the embarkation at Montevideo of Whitelocke's forces for their ill-fated attempt to retake Buenos Aires. The narrative concludes with details of the evacuation af all British forces from Montevideo in August 1807. Even at that time it was possible to

guess at the significance of the invasions: 'it is problematical whether Buenos Ayres, and perhaps all South America, will not be more irrecoverably lost to the Spanish nation, by the issue of the English invasion, than if it had fallen under our subjugation at this moment'.

149 **A narrative of the operations of a small British force, under the command of Brigadier-General Sir Samuel Auchmuty, employed in the reduction of Monte Video, on the River Plate, A.D. 1807.**
By a field officer on the staff [J. G. P. Tucker].   London: John Joseph Stockdale, 1807. 60p. map.

The narrative opens with the landing in 'Carittas bay' (apparently where the Montevideo golf course is now located, near Punta Carretas) on 16 January 1807, and is limited to the military exercise of capturing the city. There is no mention of the reception given by the population to the invaders. The difficulty of the feat is not minimized: 'The rock of Gibraltar, it is asserted by those who have seen it, is not more strongly fortified than the peninsula of Montevideo'. Auchmuty's despatch of 6 February is reproduced, and there is an account of the House of Commons debate when the news was received. The map shows the disposition of forces as far east as Buceo.

José Gervasio Artigas (1764-1850) and Independence (1810-28)

150 **Contribution to a bibliography on Artigas and the beginnings of Uruguay, 1810-1820.**
Lewis Winkler Bealer.   *Hispanic American Historical Review*, vol. 11, no. 1 (Feb. 1931), p. 108-34.

Comprises a list of 236 printed items on the career of Artigas, almost all to be found in the general library of the University of California, the Bancroft Library, or Stanford University Library. There are brief annotations. Some items are in English though all are, of course, somewhat dated.

151 **The navy and South America 1807-1823: correspondence of the commanders-in-chief on the South American station.**
Edited by Gerald S. Graham, Robert Arthur Humphreys.   Printed for the Navy Records Society, 1962. 394p. map. (Publications of the Navy Records Society, 104).

This collection of documents is of considerable interest, since during most of this period the Spanish American colonies were in open revolt but their independence had not yet been recognized. The Royal Navy commanders therefore acted as 'amphibious plenipotentiaries', communicating between the Foreign Office and the revolutionary authorities, as well as transmitting political reports and naval intelligence to London. The status of Montevideo, the Portuguese occupation and the fortunes of Artigas are amongst the Uruguayan issues which were the subject of reports.

152 **The Spanish American revolutions 1808-1826.**
John Lynch.   London: Weidenfeld & Nicolson, 1973. 433p. maps.
bibliog.

Lynch gives a marvellously clear and concise account (p. 88-104) of the independence
process in Uruguay, in the course of which he points out that 'Artigas was a victim of
his own ideals, destroyed by the very provincialism he had helped to create'. This is a
very valuable reference.

153 **Artigas, the founder of Uruguayan nationality.**
Percy Alvin Martin.   *Hispanic American Historical Review*, vol. 19,
no. 1 (Feb. 1939), p. 2-15.

Avoiding the 'dithyrambic enthusiasm for their hero' of many Uruguayan historians,
Martin observes that 'though Artigas was instrumental in securing the freedom of his
native land from both Spain and Portugal, his greatest achievement, the foundation of
an independent state was – ironically enough – one on which he set little store and
which for a time he even opposed'. This is an excellent and straightforward
introduction to the role of Artigas in the achievement of nationhood. Unfortunately
there are no bibliographical references.

154 **Artigas and the emancipation of Uruguay.**
John Street.   Cambridge: Cambridge University Press, 1959. 406p.
maps. bibliog.

'This book is a study of the origins of Uruguayan nationality, in the development of
which the career of Artigas was one of the most important forces . . . The book is not
a biography of Artigas, and its unity is to be found in the greater theme of the birth of
a new nation.' The standard work of scholarship in English on the process which
culminated in Independence, the book examines the tensions between Buenos Aires
and Montevideo, the impact of the English invasions of the River Plate in 1806-7, the
nature of Artigas' command over his followers, his federalism, the Portuguese invasion
of 1816, and British mediation resulting in the creation of an independent nation with
its own constitution in 1830. Street presents the hero, Artigas, in a favourable light,
but is not uncritical of his military record. There are brief accounts of his family
origins, and his exile in Paraguay during 1820-50.

155 **Lord Strangford and Río de la Plata, 1808-1815.**
John Street.   *Hispanic American Historical Review*, vol. 33, no. 4
(Nov. 1953), p. 477-510.

Because Strangford, British Minister in Rio de Janeiro from 1808 to 1815, was head of
Britain's only diplomatic mission in South America, and because of Portuguese designs
on the Banda Oriental (now Uruguay), Strangford's diplomacy was an important factor
in the complex process which led eventually to Uruguayan independence. This (fairly
dense) account of British policy deals with the problem of the Río de la Plata region as
a whole, in which the situation of the Banda Oriental was nonetheless a major
element.

156 **La revolución agraria artiguista, 1815-1816.** (The agrarian revolution of
Artigas, 1815-1816.)
Nelson de la Torre, Julio C. Rodríguez, Lucía Sala de Touron, with an
introduction by Eugenio Petit Muñoz.   Montevideo: Ediciones
Pueblos Unidos, 1969.˙438p.
This is an immensely detailed and scholarly work, based on archival sources in
Montevideo and Buenos Aires. The agrarian revolution is examined as a process in
Part I, and in geographical terms in Part II.

19th century

157 **Uruguay en el siglo XIX: acceso a la modernidad.** (Uruguay in the
nineteenth century: entry to modernity.)
Roberto Ares Pons.   Montevideo: Ediciones del Río de la Plata, 1964.
109p.
Originally delivered as six lectures, these studies are exercises in ideas and
interpretation. They deal with the country's Hispanic roots; the Banda Oriental; the
rising of 1811; the ideas of Artigas; the transition stage in traditional Uruguay; and the
modernization of Uruguay. There are few 'facts', and no sources or bibliography are
given.

158 **Apogeo y crisis del Uruguay pastoril y caudillesco, 1839-1875.** (Zenith
and crisis of the Uruguay of pasture-land and landowner-chieftains,
1839-1875.)
José Pedro Barrán.   Montevideo: Ediciones de la Banda Oriental,
1977. 3rd ed. 139p. bibliog.
This is a straightforward history of an under-studied period, in which the traditional
Uruguay of primitive livestock production and decentralized authority began to be
undermined by early representatives of capitalism in commerce, among landowners,
and in the form of foreign capital. The political parties failed to establish the conditions
necessary for the development of the new forces – principally internal peace and
security – opening the way to military rule after 1875.

159 **Uruguayan rural history.**
José Pedro Barrán, Benjamín Nahum.   *Hispanic American Historical
Review*, vol. 64, no. 4 (Nov. 1984), p. 655-73.
This short article presents an overview of the conclusions to the authors' monumental
seven-volume *Historia rural del Uruguay moderno* (Rural history of modern Uruguay)
(Montevideo: Ediciones de la Banda Oriental, 1967-78). Barrán and Nahum, who may
be said to work in the *Annales* tradition, are the best known of the modern generation
of Uruguayan historians, and this article is valuable for making available to a wider
audience something of their work. Themes discussed include the conservative impact
of world demand on rural society, the comparatively autonomous character of
Uruguay's dependent development, the persistence of *latifundismo*, the conflict

between the interests of the commercial and livestock sectors, and an especially interesting comparison with the development of New Zealand. Unfortunately, the translation into English is not good. The serious reader will in any case want to consult the original work, which made extensive use of (and quotes copiously from) contemporary publications, especially of the *Asociación Rural*. The seven volumes are: *Historia rural del Uruguay moderno 1851-1885* (Part I 659p., Part II 367p., 1967); *Historia rural del Uruguay moderno 1886-1894* (685p., 1971); *Recuperación y dependencia 1895-1904* (Recovery and dependency 1895-1904, 519p., 1973); *Historia social de las revoluciones de 1897 y 1904* (Social history of the revolutions of 1897 and 1904, 212p., 1972); *La prosperidad frágil 1905-1914* (Fragile prosperity 1905-1914, 187p., 1977); *La civilización ganadera bajo Batlle 1905-1914* (Livestock-raising civilization under Batlle 1905-1914, 487p., 1977); and *Agricultura, crédito y transporte bajo Batlle 1905-1914* (Agriculture, credit and transport under Batlle 1905-1914, 217p., 1978).

160 **Uruguay under Juan Idiarte Borda: an American diplomat's observations.**
Victor C. Dahl. *Hispanic American Historical Review*, vol. 46, no. 1 (Feb. 1966), p. 66-77.

'A former California gold miner . . . merchant, rancher, dispenser of vigilante justice, and politician', who in addition was deep in debt, might seem an odd choice to be US minister in Uruguay. Granville Stuart had hopes of wealth from involvement in the cattle business, but in fact his period of office in Uruguay (May 1894 to January 1898) coincided with disturbed conditions which reached a climax with the first revolt of Aparicio Saravia in late 1896 and the assassination of President Idiarte Borda in August 1897. This valuable account of the period balances the generally adverse view of the president with the defence of him published by his daughters in 1939.

161 **Who invested in Argentina and Uruguay?**
Charles Jones. *Business Archives*, number 48, vol. 4, no. 4 (Nov. 1982), p. 1-23.

The author attempts to answer his own question, as far as British investors are concerned, by analysing the share registers nearest in date to 1895 of seventy-one Anglo–River Plate companies. A principal conclusion is that about a sixth of British investment in such companies (there is no separate treatment of Uruguay) was controlled by only sixty-eight individuals or companies. They are listed individually, with the value of their portfolios, in seven tables and four appendices. The article is an important contribution to an understanding of British interest in the River Plate at the end of the nineteenth century.

162 **A century of banking in Latin America: to commemorate the centenary in 1962 of the Bank of London and South America Limited.**
David Joslin. London: Oxford University Press, 1963. 307p. map.

The London and River Plate Bank (L&RP) opened a branch in Montevideo in January 1863, a few days after starting business in Buenos Aires. This, 'the oldest and most successful British bank in South America', was also one of the first commercial banks to trade in Uruguay. By 1890 it had been joined by four other British banks, but none had the stability and repute of the London and River Plate, which in 1923 merged with the London and Brazilian Bank to form the Bank of London and South America (BOLSA). This major study of banking enterprise, substantially based on surviving records of the L&RP, contains material on its history in Uruguay where George Drabble, chairman of the L&RP for thirty years, was also chairman of the Central Uruguay Railway.

163   **The River Plate republics from independence to the Paraguayan war.**
John Lynch. In: *The Cambridge history of Latin America, Vol. 3: From independence to c.1870.* Edited by Leslie Bethell. Cambridge: Cambridge University Press, 1985, p. 615-76, 896-901. map. bibliog.

The early decades in Uruguay's nationhood have been almost ignored by historians writing in English. Happily this magisterial survey fills the gap, and succeeds brilliantly in bringing some sense to a chaotic period. The fortunes of independent Uruguay throughout this period were closely bound up with tendencies and events elsewhere in the River Plate region, but a section (p. 659-66) within this chapter looks directly at the country. 'Uruguay after independence possessed a pastoral economy, an export trade, an international port and a liberal constitution. These assets were first squandered and then plundered'. This period saw the emergence of the Blanco and Colorado parties, and of the rivalry which developed into the Guerra Grande (Great War), the involvement of the Argentine dictator Rosas, and the siege of Montevideo from 1843 to 1851. The nature of this conflict, the devastating effect on the economy, and the process by which Uruguay was drawn into a triple alliance with Argentina and Brazil against Paraguay, are all discussed. There is a separate bibliographical essay. The chapter is reprinted as 'The River Plate republics' in Leslie Bethell (ed.) *Spanish America after independence, c.1820 – c.1870* (Cambridge: Cambridge University Press, 1987), p. 314-75, 406-11.

164   **Orleanist diplomacy and the French colony in Uruguay.**
Iwan Morgan. *International History Review*, vol. 5, no. 2 (May 1983), p. 201-28.

The Anglo-French blockade of the River Plate in 1845-46, during the Guerra Grande (Great War), is the climactic event of the period examined in this study, but the focus is given by France's interests in the region. The article in fact 'seeks to analyze the development of Orleanist interest in Uruguay, the intervention of the immigrant colony in the Platine war, and the collapse of French interests in South America during the 1840s'. By 1842, indeed, the French colony in or near Montevideo numbered over 17,000, and French policy in the Plate was dominated by the need to protect its growth. Although Garibaldi's Italian batallion is better known, it numbered only some 700 compared with the peak of 3500 in the French legion defending Montevideo against Oribe. This is a somewhat dense article which nonetheless makes sense of a complex period, especially the lack of common interest underlying Anglo-French actions.

165   **The formation of modern Uruguay, c.1870-1930.**
Juan Antonio Oddone. In: *The Cambridge history of Latin America, Vol. V: c.1870-1930.* Edited by Leslie Bethell. Cambridge: Cambridge University Press, 1986, p. 453-74. bibliog.

The sixty years covered by this authoritative survey were crucial to the process of modernization. After outlining the nature of traditional Uruguay, a land of cattle and *caudillos*, Oddone goes on to observe the progressive strengthening of central government and the consolidation of a modern state structure, while the livestock industry was reorganized to suit the requirements of the world market. During 1904-18, between the defeat of the last military *caudillo* of the Blancos and the collegiate constitution, the reformism of José Batlle y Ordóñez was dominant, creating what has been loosely called a 'welfare state'. These years were also the expansive phase of the meat-packing industry. After 1918 the limits to reformism became apparent, as government came to depend on agreements between the parties, and divisions within the ranks of the Colorados deepened. Throughout this stimulating essay, ideas and trends are emphasized, rather than facts and dates. It is complemented by an annotated bibliography.

166   **Historia de la República Oriental del Uruguay 1830–1930.** (The history of Uruguay 1830–1930.)
Juan E. Pivel Devoto, Alcira Ranieri de Pivel Devoto.   Montevideo: Editorial Medina, 1966. 3rd ed. 495p.

With less than thirty pages devoted to the period after 1897, this standard general history of Uruguay (first published in 1945) is best regarded as a history of the nineteenth century. The senior author (JEPD) may be regarded as the 'father' of the modern historiography of Uruguay. The work is broadly political and chronological in character, but chapters 5 and 10 offer more general perspectives on the country at mid- and end-century, with material on its economic, social and cultural development.

167   **El patriciado uruguayo.** (The patrician class of Uruguay.)
Carlos Real de Azúa.   Montevideo: Ediciones de la Banda Oriental, 1981. 2nd ed. 133p.

Real de Azúa was one of Uruguay's outstanding intellects of the twentieth century, and this book, first published in 1961, was one of his most important works. The *patriciado* was the ruling class in Uruguay in the first half of the nineteenth century, whose influence began to decline at the end of the Great War (1839-52) and was extinguished with Batlle at the beginning of this century. It was composed of landowners, merchants, bureaucrats, soldiers, scholars and churchmen. Inevitably therefore there were deep internal tensions, but there was nonetheless a unity of interests, ideals and way of life. The author analyses the economic base – urban as much as rural – and political career of this group of 100 or so eminent men. Although Real de Azúa is not easy to read, this is a key work for an understanding of the period. A review by Tulio Halperín Donghi, first published in 1965, is reprinted as a prologue to the second edition.

168   **Observations on blacks and bondage in Uruguay, 1800-1836.**
John Hoyt Williams.   *Americas*, vol. 43, no. 4 (April 1987), p. 411-27.

Lamentably little is known about Uruguay's early demographic history. Williams reports on investigations among early census documents held in the Archivo General de la Nación in Montevideo, in an attempt to answer basic questions about the size and character of the black population. His findings are tentative because of problems in the material, but they are very significant. The proportion of blacks in Montevideo's population was very considerable at this time (33 per cent in 1800) and in spite of European immigration the proportion remained high. Clearly there was a stream of black immigration, the nature of which is made plain by the fact that a very high (82 per cent in 1800) and increasing proportion of blacks over the period were declared to be slaves (and were characteristically younger than the free blacks). All of this 'hints strongly at an ongoing and substantial illegal slave trade which continually refreshed the numbers of and added youth to the Uruguayan black community'.

169 **British informal empire in Uruguay in the nineteenth century.**
Peter Edward Winn. *Past and Present*, no. 73 (Nov. 1976), p. 100-26.
This wide-ranging, strongly argued essay employs the concepts of informal imperialism and collaborating élites to analyse and evaluate Britain's role in Uruguay between the pre-Independence period and 1914. After a false start, followed by an interval in mid-century of Brazilian ascendancy, British trade and investment secured positions of pre-eminence after 1864 which were scarcely challenged until the decade preceding the First World War. The adverse implications of this relationship for Uruguay – as well as its benefits – are briefly argued, focusing in particular on railways, banking and meat-processing. Winn's interpretation of Anglo–Uruguayan relations in their expansive phase (the 'special relationship' did not end until after the Second World War) is challenging and provocative.

20th century

170 **An interview with Doctor Brum, the President of Uruguay.**
A correspondent (anonymous). *Inter-America*, vol. 3, no. 1 (Oct. 1919), p. 3-8.
The interview was first published in *Myriam* (Buenos Aires), but unfortunately there are no clues as to the date on which it took place. Baltasar Brum was elected as first president under the constitution of 1919 which divided executive authority between the president and a presidential *colegiado* ('college'). During 1919 Brum formed his own faction of the Colorado party and was later accused (on negligible evidence) of plotting a coup that year, but there is little hint here of such excitements below the surface. The interview is interesting but rather bland, and the translation into English is dreadful. There follows (p. 9-10) a brief note on the 1919 constitution.

171 **Batlle, los estancieros y el imperio británico.** (Batlle, the landowners, and British imperialism.)
José Pedro Barrán, Benjamín Nahum. Montevideo: Ediciones de la Banda Oriental, 1979-87. 8 vols.
The 2000 pages of this remarkable historiographical achievement analyse in close detail the relationships between José Batlle y Ordóñez, the landowning class, and the representatives of British capital and the British government in Uruguay, during the period 1903-16. The central theme is the reformism of Batlle, and the conflicts with nationally and internationally dominant groups. The wide range of sources, from which there is abundant quotation, include parliamentary debates, British and Uruguayan newspapers, business archives, and Foreign Office files held at the Public Record Office in London. Volume 1 (*El Uruguay del novecientos*, The Uruguay of 1900) examines the social, cultural and political background at the turn of the century. Volume 2 (*Un diálogo difícil 1903-1910*, A difficult dialogue 1903-1910) analyses the reformist plan and the reaction of the conservative classes during Batlle's first administration and up to his candidacy for a second term. Volume 3 (*El nacimiento de batllismo*, The birth of *batllismo*) traces the origins and consolidation of *batllismo* as a modern political movement, volume 4 (*Las primeras reformas 1911-1913*, The first reforms 1911-1913) covers the great reforms of the first two years of Batlle's second

administration: economic, social, rural, fiscal, 'moral' and political reforms. The opposition to them is the subject of volume 5 (*La reacción imperial-conservador 1911-1913*, The imperial–conservative reaction 1911-1913). Volume 6 (*Crisis y radicalización 1913-1916*, Crisis and radicalization 1913-1916) argues that the more fundamental reforms of this period were impelled by the pre-war and war-time economic crisis and *batllismo's* declining popularity, factors which brought about the movement's defeat in 1916. Volume 7 (*Lucha política y enfrentamiento social 1913-1916*, Political struggle and social confrontation 1913-1916) focuses on the correspondence between the political parties and defined social interests; and volume 8 (*La derrota del batllismo 1916*, The defeat of *batllismo* 1916) analyses the reverse suffered by Batlle in the 1916 election for delegates to the assembly to consider his proposed collegiate constitution. No one seriously interested in the foundations on which modern Uruguay is built can afford to ignore this book; moreover, it is written in a style which is clear, lively and direct. The result is a vivid picture.

172 **Breve historia de la dictadura (1973-1985).** (A short history of the dictatorship, 1973-1985.)
Gerardo Caetano, José Rilla. Montevideo: Centro Latinoamericano de Economía Humana (CLAEH) – Ediciones de la Banda Oriental, 1987. 151p.

Most of this brief but perceptive account of the military régime is modestly sub-titled 'The facts'. Apart from the excellent choice of documents emanating from the régime which are reproduced here, the tone of this work is judiciously analytical rather than 'factual'.

173 **The economic and social situation of Uruguay.**
César Charlone. *International Labour Review*, vol. 33, no. 5 (May 1936), p. 607-18.

Charlone, who wrote this bland and curiously lifeless account of the state of the economy and social welfare legislation, was at that time Minister of Finance (an office he was again to hold at the end of the 1960s). His description of the 1934 constitution, as enshrining 'the most novel and advanced principles of democratic public law', is ironic since it originated in Gabriel Terra's *coup d'état* in 1933 and was itself supplanted in 1942. Interestingly, Terra, rather than Batlle y Ordóñez or any of the loyal *batllistas*, is credited with inaugurating the study of social problems. The most significant material concerns the speed of economic recovery and the policy controls employed to achieve it.

174 **El Uruguay neo-batllista, 1946-1958.** (*Neo-batllista* Uruguay, 1946-1958.)
Germán D'Elía. Montevideo: Ediciones de la Banda Oriental, 1983. 113p. (Temas del siglo XX, 8).

In spite of its clear importance in the formation of modern Uruguay, historians have sadly neglected the period in which, freed of the constraints of Terra's régime and of the Second World War, the country sought to return to the principles of the first *batllista* period. In spite of industrialization and a new collegiate constitution, however, the outcome of state interventionism and income redistribution was very different from the earlier experience. The six chapters of this useful book examine the consequences of the interwar depression; accelerated economic development during 1946-55; the *neo-batllista* ideology; the political process 1946-54; the economic crisis of the mid-1950s; and political developments during 1954-58 which culminated in the electoral victory of the Blanco party. It is a pity that the author's final words, that this was a period which revealed Uruguay's structural dependence on the Centre countries, thus conditioning its evolution and limiting its possibilities of self-sustained development, are rather unenlightening.

175 **El Uruguay en que vivimos, 1900-1968.** (The Uruguay in which we live, 1900-1968.)
Roque Faraone. Montevideo: Editorial Arca, 1968. 2nd ed. 141p.

This is a splendid little book providing succinct factual information and brief but intelligent interpretation on almost all aspects of Uruguay's twentieth-century history. The material is organized in chapters based on five sub-periods. The author himself modestly sees the book's main weakness as the paucity of fact and interpretation for the final thirty years (a reflection of the dominant historiographical tradition which has emphasized nineteenth-century studies).

176 **Three perspectives on the crisis in Uruguay.**
Martin Henry John Finch. *Journal of Latin American Studies*, vol. 3, no. 2 (Nov. 1971), p. 173-90.

This article suggests that the fundamental causes of the crisis of the 1950s and 1960s are to be found 'in the manner in which modernizing forces were reconciled to traditional structures in the early decades of this century'. The perspectives are economic, political and historical.

177 **Baldomir y la restauración democrática (1938-1946).** (Baldomir and the restoration of democracy, 1938-1946.)
Ana Frega, Mónica Maronna, Yvette Trochon. Montevideo: Ediciones de la Banda Oriental, 1987. 151p. (Temas del siglo XX, 39).

Baldomir was elected to succeed Gabriel Terra as president in 1938, but in 1942 he dissolved the constitution of 1934 (the *golpe bueno*, 'good coup'). He thus brought to an end the illiberal and undemocratic régime imposed by Terra, paving the way for the return of the *batllista* wing of the Colorado party and the *neo-batllista* phase of Uruguay's history. This transitional period, deeply affected by economic change at home and by the implications of the Second World War, has been relatively neglected by historians, but the gap is well filled by this short book.

178 **Utopia in Uruguay: chapters in the economic history of Uruguay.**
Simon G. Hanson. New York: Oxford University Press, 1938. 262p.

This is one of the most important references in the historiography of Uruguay, and a pioneering study in English. Hanson is interested primarily in the achievements of Batlle y Ordóñez in enlarging the public sector of the economy and in promoting social legislation. His analysis is detailed, factual and balanced. After examining the state insurance bank, electricity utility, state railways, port authority and state banks, and the organization of the public sector, Hanson concludes that 'government enterprises have been run at a profit, service in some cases has improved and in most cases has not deteriorated, costs to the consumer frequently have been lowered'. His verdict on social welfare is sympathetic but less generous. On the impact of *batllismo* on foreign investment, 'there is little justification for the belief that a policy of unfriendliness to foreign capital checked the inflow of funds with consequent large national loss'. The book is an indispensable reference, especially for the period before 1930. See also, by the same author, 'State ownership in Uruguay', *Southwestern Social Science Quarterly* vol. 16 (1935), p. 14-32.

179 **Uruguay 1929-1938: depresión ganadera y desarrollo fabril.** (Uruguay 1929-1938: depression in the livestock industry and the development of manufacturing.)
Raúl Jacob. Montevideo: Fundación de Cultura Universitaria, [1981]. 433p.

Jacob collected an enormous amount of previously unpublished information and quotation in writing this book, and the result is a very detailed and factual survey of the post-depression decade. Particularly valuable is the material on foreign investments in Uruguay, and on the interests and connections of leading industrialists, merchants and lawyers. The result is a massive and indispensable reference on the economic history of Uruguay which nonetheless contrives to be disappointing in that (as the author admits) there is little in the way of penetrating generalization; and, moreover, his unhelpful paragraph structure makes the task of building an argument very problematic. Readers may find this book valuable and frustrating in equal and abundant measure.

180 **El Uruguay de Terra, 1931-1938: una crónica del terrismo.** (The Uruguay of Terra, 1931-1938: a chronicle of *terrismo*.)
Raúl Jacob. Montevideo: Ediciones de la Banda Oriental, 1983. 141p. (Temas del siglo XX, 11).

Uruguayans have traditionally felt some embarrassment about Gabriel Terra's coup in 1933 which overthrew the constitution of 1919 and installed Terra in the presidency until 1938. That may explain the neglect of the 1930s by Uruguayan historians. However, Jacob's book succeeds admirably in explaining the background to the coup (Part I), and in outlining in the chapters of Part II the political and economic history of the period, and developments in social, educational and foreign policy. It is certainly the best available work on the period.

181 **Uruguay's new path: a study in politics during the first *colegiado*, 1919-33.**
Göran G. Lindahl. Stockholm: Library and Institute of Ibero-American Studies, 1962. 369p. map. bibliog.

This is the classic account of the operation of the 1919 constitution which introduced the collegiate executive to Uruguay and was overthrown by the *coup d'état* of 1933. Indeed the wealth of detail in the analysis is unlikely ever to be replicated, so this will surely remain the standard work on the period. That said, although there are helpful biographical notes and tables on the composition of governments, this is not an easy book for readers without a background knowledge of the period. The most accessible chapters are 5 'The significance of the first *colegiado* Constitution' (which contains a helpful section on the idea of co-participation in Uruguay) and 6 'The political parties'. The author's general view of the constitution is positive, judging it to have been 'an expression of social realities'.

182 The career of José Batlle y Ordóñez.
Percy Alvin Martin. *Hispanic American Historical Review*, vol. 10,
no. 4 (Nov. 1930), p. 413-28.
Assessing the achievement of Batlle (who died in 1929), Martin argues that 'the
foremost institutions of this progressive nation are indeed but the lengthened shadow
of this remarkable man'. After observing the collegiate executive (which shared
executive powers with the president) in action over several months, the author plainly
felt that the innovation 'more than justified itself'.

183 **El impulso y su freno: tres décadas de batllismo y las raíces de la crisis
uruguaya.** (The thrust and its brake: three decades of *batllismo* and the
roots of the Uruguayan crisis.)
Carlos Real de Azúa. Montevideo: Ediciones de la Banda Oriental,
1964. 107p.
'Why did the progressive thrust which one party – Batllismo – impressed on Uruguay
in the early decades of this century come to a halt?' Real de Azúa's answer to his own
question, in the conclusion to his analysis, is that *batllismo* created an image of the
country which it found acceptable and had no reason to change; when the image was
broken by outside events, *batllismo* was no longer in a position to repair it or invent
another; having lost its impetus, the attempt to renovate *batllismo* threatened its
structures and the movement therefore opted for survival. In between question and
answer is a wealth of subtle argument and penetrating observation which is still
required reading for anyone seeking to understand Uruguay's crisis of the third quarter
(or second half) of the twentieth century. The analysis is neither easy, nor comfortable:
'we have come to be a society which is economically stagnant, politically sick, and
ethically without tone . . . overall we appear to be incompetent for the times we live in
and its implicit challenges'.

184 **The Uruguayan *coup d'état* of 1933.**
Philip B. Taylor. *Hispanic American Historical Review*, vol. 32, no. 3
(Aug. 1952), p. 301-20.
The coup staged by Gabriel Terra was the first interruption of constitutional
government in Uruguay this century. This is a valuable account which points out that
even by 1952 'few Uruguayans find it possible to defend the Terra regime', but that it
had little lasting effect. Taylor's analysis is conducted almost entirely at the political
level. There is no mention of the role of the landowning class, threatened by restricted
access to the British beef market, or of foreign interests who welcomed the coup.

185 **The innovator: José Batlle y Ordóñez.**
Folco Testena. *Inter-America*, vol. 1, no. 6 (Aug. 1918), p. 384-88.
This remarkable article, first published in Buenos Aires, reports on an interviewer's
impressions of Batlle. The great man is praised, but this is the opposite of an empty
eulogy: instead there are vivid word-pictures and perceptive insights into the
ambiguities of Don Pepe. Thus 'in spite of his comprehension of the socialist ideal,
José Batlle y Ordóñez is bourgeois by condition, by mentality, by education, by spirit:
he is bourgeois par excellence'; and 'he has all the greatest defects that a man of
politics can have . . . and these defects trouble even his friends'; and 'this man
automatically weighs his speech, word by word, wishing to know if his voice expresses
faithfully his thought; he has something like a scruple lest he may involuntarily deceive

us, hiding from us an idea or presenting it incomplete, altered'. Batlle is quoted on the Blancos: 'it is the party that does not read'. And which non-Uruguayan could disagree with Testena's opening sentiment: 'I do not know the real value of Artigas'?

186   **José Batlle y Ordoñez of Uruguay: the creator of his times, 1902-1907.**
Milton I. Vanger.   Cambridge, Massachusetts: Harvard University
Press, 1963. 320p. maps. bibliog.

Vanger's political biography of Batlle (who, says the author, did not accent the second syllable of 'Ordóñez' when signing his own name) is a work of fundamental importance to an assessment of this remarkable figure. The author was the first historian to be given access to Batlle's private papers. On the basis of those and other sources he argues that the explanation of Batlle's rise to power and consolidation in it 'lay in his use of the Colorado political organization and tradition, not in his response to class needs and demands', and that his opposition to the propertied classes was based not on a rival class coalition but on a united Colorado party. It is fair to add that few historians have so far followed Vanger in this interpretation, but none can ignore it. The volume runs from the eve of the first administration in 1902 to his departure for Europe in 1907, and deals extensively with Saravia's revolt of 1904. The narrative is vivid, and is illustrated with fifteen photographs.

187   **The model country: José Batlle y Ordoñez of Uruguay, 1907-1915.**
Milton I. Vanger.   Hanover, New Hampshire; London: University
Press of New England for Brandeis University Press, 1980. 436p. map.

This second volume of Vanger's political biography follows Batlle to Europe in 1907 (where he wrote of making Uruguay 'a small model country'), and through his second presidency of 1911-15. It was during this administration that most of his reformist measures in the fields of economic and social policy, including the proposal for constitutional reform to introduce the collegiate executive, were brought forward, so this volume is of even greater general interest than its predecessor. The author maintains his interpretation of Batlle of the earlier volume, and this time confronts his adversaries in the social sciences directly in three inserts labelled 'Appraisals': they 'misinterpret Batlle's intentions, narrow the scope of his policies, and underestimate his radicalism'. Whether one agrees or not, the author contributes enormously to the understanding of Batlle (as family man as well as public figure) and his times. There are more remarkable photographs.

188   **El reto financiero: deuda externa y desarrollo en el Uruguay (1903-1933).** (The financial challenge: foreign debt and development in Uruguay, 1903-1933.)
Carlos Zubillaga.   Montevideo: Editorial Arca – Centro
Latinoamericano de Economía Humana (CLAEH), 1982. 296p.
bibliog.

This is a major study of the role and nature of external financing of Uruguayan development, from the first administration of Batlle y Ordóñez to the coup of 1933 which brought Gabriel Terra to power. The uses made of the foreign loans, and their results, are discussed. There is a statistical appendix.

El libro del centenario del Uruguay 1825-1925. (The centenary book of Uruguay, 1825-1925.)
See item no. 24.

Surprisingly profitable ventures in Uruguay.
See item no. 133.

The Negro in the Viceroyalty of the Rio de la Plata.
See item no. 203.

Latin America and the war.
See item no. 348.

The United States and the Southern Cone: Argentina, Chile, and Uruguay.
See item no. 353.

Latin America and the Second World War.
See item no. 360.

A political economy of Uruguay since 1870.
See item no. 375.

Historical dictionary of Uruguay.
See item no. 657.

Population

General

189 **Población y desarrollo de un pequeño país: Uruguay 1830-1930.**
(Population and development of a small country: Uruguay 1830-1930.)
Juan Rial Roade. Montevideo: Acali Editorial, 1983. 187p. maps.
bibliog.

Rial examines the evolution of demographic variables and their interrelationship with Uruguay's pattern of economic development, focusing on the way the labour market functioned and its impact on fertility rates. In parts the analysis is admitted to be conjectural, but there is an abundance of quantitative material deployed in support.

190 **Sources for studies of historical demography in Uruguay (1728-1860).**
Juan Rial Roade. *Latin American Research Review*, vol. 15, no. 2
(1980), p. 180-200. maps. bibliog.

'Demographic studies in Uruguay are in their infancy; work in historical demography has been meager and, in almost all cases, the work has concerned the statistical period, when government data have been published. This article will describe sources for the proto-historical period, seeking to call attention to them, in order to prompt further research.' These sources, mostly survey data, are held at the Archivo General de la Nación in Montevideo.

191 **Evolution of fertility in Argentina and Uruguay.**
Ana M. Rothman. In: *International Population Conference / Congrès
International de Population, London, 1969*. Liège: International Union
for the Scientific Study of Population, 1971. vol. 1, p. 712-32. bibliog.

Compared with the rest of Latin America, and even with Argentina, the crude birth rate in Uruguay throughout this century has been low. This important work offers estimates of population and the major demographic variables as five-year averages

54

from 1895-99 to 1960-64, and age-specific fertility rates for 1948, 1953, 1957 and 1963. The work is presented as an interim statement on a continuing research programme, and there is little analysis of the determinants of fertility levels. The data are contained in seven tables and five figures.

Immigration and emigration

192 **Uruguay: país de emigración.** (Uruguay: a country of emigration.)
César Aguiar. Montevideo: Ediciones de la Banda Oriental, 1982.
130p. bibliog. (Temas del siglo XX, 3).

'Here is a book which explains how many went, who went, where they went, analyzes the significance of this loss of human capital for the nation, and warns about a possible repetition.' Its subject is the huge population loss by emigration between the census years 1963 and 1975, estimated at 200,000 persons, but the book does more than document this process so admirably. In particular it points out that the traditional idea of the importance of immigration in populating the nation in the twentieth century is a myth. In fact the country has throughout this century sent away immigrants and forced out native-born Uruguayans.

193 **The Lebanese war and Lebanese immigrant cultures: a comparative study of Lebanese in Australia and Uruguay.**
Michael Humphrey. *Ethnic and Racial Studies*, vol. 9, no. 4 (Oct. 1986), p. 445-60. bibliog.

Humphrey has written an exceptionally interesting account of the impact of the war in Lebanon over the last decade on the community of 30,000 Maronite Lebanese in Uruguay. They are 'a small, largely third-generation population who are culturally inconspicuous, whose memory of Lebanon is remote and whose knowledge of Arabic is very limited'. Despite this high level of assimilation, the community has retained its cultural identity as West-facing Maronites; hence 'the strong feeling of crisis and loss over Lebanon mirrors their own experience of political repression and economic decline in Uruguay'.

194 **Immigration and settlement in Brazil, Argentina and Uruguay: II.**
Fernand Maurette, Enrique Siewers. *International Labour Review*, vol. 35, no. 3 (March 1937), p. 352-83.

The section dealing with Uruguay (p. 373-80) contains interesting material on state assistance for settlers, restrictions on immigration introduced in 1932, and on possibilities for settlement. The state of arable agriculture, and especially the low likelihood of Uruguay emerging as a crop exporter on an important scale, are analysed. The report concludes that in the short term Uruguay is not capable of receiving a large number of immigrant settlers.

Population. Immigration and emigration

195 **La formación del Uruguay moderno: la inmigración y el desarrollo económico-social.** (The formation of modern Uruguay: immigration and socio-economic development.)
Juan Antonio Oddone. Buenos Aires: Editorial Universitaria de Buenos Aires, 1966. 106p. bibliog.

This well-known introduction to the role of immigrants contains much interesting material, including extracts from nineteenth-century reports of representatives in Montevideo of countries of emigration. However, the analysis needs to be treated cautiously, as Oddone's estimates of the size of net immigration in the early twentieth century are a huge exaggeration of the probable figure.

196 **Consequences of Uruguayan emigration: research note.**
José Luis Petruccelli. *International Migration Review*, vol. 13, no. 3 (Fall 1979), p. 519-26.

A succinct account of the process and implications of population loss by emigration in the 1960s and 1970s. The author predicts that continuing economic stagnation will reinforce the outflow, and intensify Uruguay's dependency on its larger and more dynamic neighbours.

197 **El legado de los inmigrantes.** (The legacy of the immigrants.)
Renzo Pi Hugarte, Daniel Vidart. Montevideo: Editorial 'Nuestra Tierra', 1969. 2 vols. 60p., 60p. maps. bibliog. (Nuestra Tierra 29, 39).

The first volume of this excellent and well-illustrated study examines slavery in Uruguay, and the frontier populations adjacent to Brazil and Argentina. The second deals with European immigration, especially from France, Spain and Italy. The legacy is assessed primarily in its social and cultural aspects.

198 **Socioeconomic structure and population displacements: the Uruguayan case.**
Danilo Veiga. *NorthSouth* vol. 6, no. 12 (1981), p. 1-25. maps. bibliog.

Veiga presents a wide-ranging study of internal and international population movements affecting Uruguay. He identifies basic push-and-pull factors, and notes the transition from an internal migration model in which Montevideo was an attraction, to the pattern of the 1960s and 1970s in which the city became a source of emigrants to other countries.

199 **La inmigración europea en el Uruguay: los italianos.** (European immigration in Uruguay: the Italians.)
Silvia Rodríguez Villamil, Graciela Sapriza. Montevideo: Ediciones de la Banda Oriental, 1982. 144p. bibliog.

The first part of this valuable work deals with European immigration in general between 1830 and 1930. Part II studies aspects of Italian migration in particular, including the Italian colony in Salto. In their conclusion the authors address the debate on the quantitative importance and demographic significance of immigration in the early twentieth century. Their conclusion is intermediate: although the scale of immigration was much reduced compared with earlier decades, it continued to make an important contribution to total population growth.

200 **La emigración uruguaya, 1963-1975.** (Emigration from Uruguay, 1973-1985.)
Israel Wonsewer, Ana María Teja. Montevideo: Centro de Investigaciones Económicas (CINVE) – Ediciones de la Banda Oriental, 1985. 174p. bibliog. (Estudios CINVE, 5).
During the 1960s and 1970s the scale of emigration from Uruguay assumed alarming proportions. This book, subtitled 'its economic determinants' and prepared with the assistance of Martín Rama and Nelly Niedworok, is a detailed analysis of the process supported by fifty tables. Following introductory chapters on the long-run economic stagnation and social perspectives of the 1950s and 1960s, there are studies of the emigration itself, characteristics of the migrants, the labour market, and factors of attraction and expulsion.

Minorities

201 **Jews in Latin America.**
Jacob Beller. New York: Jonathan David, 1969. 303p.
Chapter 17 'Jews in Uruguay: the democratic model' (p. 218-30) traces the formal foundation of the Jewish community (estimated in the late 1960s at 40,000) up to 1907. Official Uruguayan support for the establishment of the state of Israel is recalled, and the extent of anti-Semitism is assessed. Luis Batlle Berres is remarkably renamed Luis Batlle Herrera!

202 **Negro anthology.**
Compiled by Nancy Cunard. London: Nancy Cunard at Wishart & Co., 1934. 855p.
This extraordinary volume is a radical and angry anthology 'of the struggles and achievements, the persecutions and revolts against them, of the Negro peoples'. The section on Uruguay (p. 518-22) has articles on 'The negro race in Uruguay' by Elemo Cabral and 'Rituals and "Candombes"' by Marcellino Bottaro. There is also a translated poem 'Song of the washboard' by Ildefonso Pereda Valdés (p. 433).

203 **The Negro in the Viceroyalty of the Rio de la Plata.**
Irene Diggs. *Journal of Negro History*, vol. 3 (1951), p. 281-301.
Although the article deals with the Viceroyalty as a whole, there is material specifically on the black population of Montevideo which dates from the early eighteenth century. By 1743 Montevideo was trading in slaves, and blacks constituted up to one-third of the total population in the final decades of the century and the period up to Independence. There is some account of the role of blacks in colonial economy and society, and of the transition from the predominantly domestic service of slaves to the military service of ex-slaves in the abolitionist decree of 1842.

204 **Britons at Maldonado.**
Lloyd Hirst. Montevideo: Ediciones Gemini, 1975. 148p. map.
Books like this one, written in English but published in Montevideo, are rare. The author, long resident in the River Plate region and with periods of service in the Royal Navy, died just before its publication. It is an anecdotal account of Britons and British shipping in and off Maldonado, in the nineteenth century and earlier. No sources are cited or bibliography given.

205 **Race and ethnic relations in Latin America and the Caribbean: an historical dictionary and bibliography.**
Robert M. Levine. Metuchen, New Jersey; London: Scarecrow Press, 1980. 252p.
Contains fourteen unannotated bibliographical references to Uruguay.

206 **The *gaucho*: cattle hunter, cavalryman, ideal of romance.**
Madaline Wallis Nichols. New York: Gordian Press, 1942. Reprinted 1968. 152p. bibliog.
'This book tells how the highly disreputable gauchos emerged from the background of a pastoral society and how those gauchos came to win honor.' It does so by examining how they lived and hunted cattle; their role in contraband, as frontiersmen, and in war; and the romanticization of the *gauchos* in literature and art. The author makes extensive use of nineteenth-century travellers' accounts. A feature of the book is the enormous bibliography (not annotated) containing 1431 items published before 1942.

207 **El negro en el Uruguay: pasado y presente.** (The black population in Uruguay: past and present.)
Ildefonso Pereda Valdés. Montevideo: Revista del Instituto Histórico y Geográfico del Uruguay, 1965. 300p. maps. bibliog.
This work by Pereda Valdés is very significant, and not merely because the literature on the black population of Uruguay is so small. It surveys a substantial quantity of source material, with many interesting documents reproduced in a long appendix. The first and most extensive part deals with black slavery in Uruguay: origins, extent, legal status, customs and religious practice. Part 2 treats, rather briefly, aspects of the abolitionist movement in Uruguay leading to final abolition in 1846. Part 3 examines Afro-Uruguayan folklore, especially dance (including *calenda*, *bámbula* and *candombe*); drum-bands; carnival; and the African contribution to River Plate speech. The final section assesses the situation of the estimated 40,000 blacks. They are found to occupy a very low socio-economic position, victims of racial prejudice and discriminatory employment policies. The black community has nonetheless supported a lively cultural, especially literary, tradition. There are interesting photographs of dance, a transcription of *bámbula* music, and facsimiles of documents.

208 **The passing of the Afro-Uruguayans from caste society into class society.**
Carlos M. Rama. In: *Race and class in Latin America.* Edited by Magnus Mörner. New York; London: Columbia University Press, 1970, p. 28-50.
This is a major contribution to the study and interpretation of the Afro-Uruguayan population. Rama argues that 'the crisis of the caste system in Uruguay began around

the turn of the nineteenth century and entered its critical phase during the era of revolution between 1810 and 1830 . . . Thus the caste system, which had never become firmly entrenched in Uruguay, was replaced by an incipient, indeed premature, capitalist society of open classes'. The analysis sustaining this argument is restricted to the nineteenth century, and the contemporary situation of blacks is not discussed. However, the most contentious observation is certainly that 'race prejudice has been replaced generally by class prejudice'. There are population estimates (whites, slaves, freedmen and Indians) for Montevideo for various years between 1726 and 1843. The text is translated and abbreviated by Arnold Clayton from the Spanish original.

209   **The African experience in Spanish America: 1502 to the present day.**
       Leslie B. Rout, Jr.   Cambridge: Cambridge University Press, 1976.
       404p. bibliog.

The brief review (p. 197-205) of the history and present position of the black population in Uruguay concludes: 'the great prejudice in Uruguay seems to be that the white population is loathe to admit that racial prejudice exists. This means that, because of their relatively small number, Afro-Uruguayans may scream, but few will listen to the message that they are trying to get across'.

Observations on blacks and bondage in Uruguay, 1800-1836.
See item no. 168.

The Waldenses in the New World.
See item no. 233.

Demographic yearbook.
See item no. 470.

Language and Dialects

210 **English influence on the common speech of the River Plate.**
Américo Barabino. *Hispania*, vol. 33, no. 2 (May 1950), p. 163-65.
This is an informal article examining a number of words and phrases in common usage on both sides of the River Plate which have English origins but which have changed their spelling, or their meaning, or both. The author suggests that English and American companies, and Hollywood, have been the principal sources, though he also notes that sport has originated the greatest number of new words.

211 **The French influence on the Spanish of the River Plate.**
Paul-Vincent Cassano. *Orbis*, vol. 21, no. 1 (June 1972), p. 174-82.
This article seeks 'to plot the phonological interference of a language contact situation wherein the language of importation [i.e. French] has always been considered a language of great prestige and culture'. The main features of this process are indicated, in terms which will be of interest primarily to students of linguistics. In the text the author speaks frequently of Argentina, but his analysis evidently applies also to Uruguay.

212 **The Spanish language in Uruguay.**
Mary Weld Coates. *Hispania*, vol. 41, no. 2 (May 1958), p. 206-8.
These brief notes by a high-school teacher from the United States visiting Uruguay do no more than provide basic guidance for those needing to adjust their Spanish to Uruguayan usage. But she gives encouragement: Uruguayans 'speak distinctly and forcefully and their Spanish is therefore in the main clear and easy to understand'.

213 **The Spanish of Argentina and Uruguay: an annotated bibliography for 1940-1978.**
Jack Emory Davis. Berlin; New York; Amsterdam: Mouton, 1982.
360p.
This bibliography is indispensable for anyone seriously interested in the language of

the River Plate countries. Items relating specifically to Uruguay have generally to be searched for amongst the 1227 entries, most of which inevitably refer to Argentina. They are organized thematically, and the annotations are helpful in both summary and comment.

214 **Address forms in Montevideo Spanish.**
Adolfo Elizaincín. In: *Proceedings of the Twelfth International Congress of Linguists*, Innsbruck, 1978, p. 264-67.
This paper is a sociolinguistic study of role relations between speaker and listener, focusing especially on the pronouns *tú* and *vos*, as well as use of titles, surnames, nicknames, etc. The author argues that their use is governed 'by scales of solidarity and power'.

215 **The emergence of bilingual dialects on the Brazilian–Uruguayan border.**
Adolfo Elizaincín. *Linguistics*, no. 177 (1976), p. 123-34.
A device in the mid-nineteenth century for resisting Brazilian penetration into northern Uruguay was the establishment of border settlements, one of which, Rivera, provides the evidence for this report. The strength of Brazilian influence has resulted in patterns of bilingualism; of Portuguese and Spanish amongst the more educated, and a new somewhat paradoxical pattern in which *fronterizo*-speaking monolinguals are becoming *fronterizo*/standard Spanish bilinguals as a result of the spread of primary schooling in towns like Rivera. *Fronterizo* is perceived as a language of the lower classes, a deformed Spanish which is likely neither to develop nor to disappear.

216 **Diccionario del lenguaje campesino rioplatense.** (Dictionary of rural speech in the River Plate region.)
Juan Carlos Guarnieri. Montevideo: Editorial Florensa y Lafon, 1968. 144p.
This dictionary gives the meanings of and comments on about 3000 words and sayings, collected from two sources: the literature of the *gaucho*, and the compiler's own knowledge of rural life. Although the extension of this material to the River Plate as a whole is no doubt justified, there is a strong emphasis on Uruguayan usage throughout. The definitions given are expressed in simple terms, making this dictionary particularly useful to strangers as well as to Uruguayans. The compiler based this volume on his earlier *Nuevo vocabulario campesino rioplatense* (Montevideo, 1957); from it he took the brief but interesting introduction, in which he notes that *gaucho* speech (as opposed to a language) originated in the vulgar Spanish brought with them by mostly illiterate emigrants, which retained its special character in the isolation of rural life. The very limited occurrence of Portuguese and Indian words (except in the frontier region, or as names for flora and fauna, respectively) is emphasized.

217 **El habla del boliche: diccionario del lenguaje popular rioplatense.** (Bar speech: a dictionary of popular speech in the River Plate region.)
Juan Carlos Guarnieri. Montevideo: Editorial Florensa y Lafon, 1967. 212p.
The meanings and typical usage of about 4000 words and sayings are indicated in this dictionary. Where appropriate they are categorized as belonging to *lunfardo* (the slang of Buenos Aires in particular), *vesrre* (another slang tradition in which typically syllables are transposed), or rural speech. There is some etymological information. The

Introduction emphasizes the limited contribution of European languages other than Italian in River Plate Spanish. J. E. Davis (see item no. 213) comments: 'an unusually fine regional lexicon'. A *boliche* in its fuller sense is a meeting place for the men of the *barrios* of Montevideo and Buenos Aires.

218   *Fronterizo*: a case of phonological restructuring.
       Fritz (Frederik Gerald) Hensey. In: *Three essays on linguistic diversity in the Spanish-speaking world.* Edited by Jacob Ornstein. The Hague; Paris: Mouton, 1975, p. 47-59.

This rather technical paper examines the Portuguese which is spoken in areas of northern Uruguay, generally by older Uruguayans living in isolated communities. The language is effectively a set of dialects termed *fronterizo* which is changing (and disappearing) as bilingualism spreads in this border region.

219   Livramento/Rivera: the linguistic side of international relations.
       Fritz (Frederik Gerald) Hensey. *Journal of Inter-American Studies*, vol. 8, no. 4 (1966), p. 520-34.

This article reports on a survey of schoolteachers in communities on both sides of the Brazilian–Uruguayan border on their evaluation of bilingualism and language loyalty. It concludes that while relations across the border are 'exceptionally harmonious', problems deriving from language contact are much greater in Rivera (Uruguay) since there is far less penetration of Spanish in Brazil. Two explanations of the dominance of Portuguese are posed: past settlement by Brazilians in northern Uruguay; and the contemporary economic strength of Brazil compared with Uruguay.

220   The sociolinguistics of the Brazilian–Uruguayan border.
       Frederik Gerald Hensey. The Hague; Paris: Mouton, 1972. 115p. bibliog.

Uruguay's border with Brazil runs for 600 miles. Since the Brazilian occupation in the early nineteenth century, the frontier region has been open to Brazilian penetration in various forms. Hensey's study is primarily linguistic and somewhat technical, but has material of more general interest. Focusing on the urban community of Livramento (Brazil)/Rivera (Uruguay), where circulation, employment and residence across the border are virtually unrestricted, and the more rural area of Jaguarão (Brazil)/Rio Branco (Uruguay), the analysis deals in particular with the Portuguese spoken by Uruguayan bilinguals, mainly in terms of phonology and lexicon. Some interviews are transcribed. *Fronterizo* Spanish is not extensively dealt with, but because of extensive interference between the two languages the author concludes: 'As urban and rural workers and their families achieve upward mobility, substandard Spanish and the (related) consequences of bilingualism will increasingly become problems for the people of Rivera and other parts of northern Uruguay'.

221   The influence of locally spoken Italian dialects on River Plate Spanish.
       Herman James, Julio Ricci. *Forum Italicum*, vol. 1, no. 1 (1967), p. 48-59.

To what extent have Italian dialects influenced the phonology of River Plate Spanish (RPS)? The answer here is somewhat inconclusive. Many of its particular features are found in other parts of lowland Spanish America far removed from Italian influence.

'Only the distribution of the morpheme of plurality and the consequent extension of the vowel system seem to be exclusively RPS features', and Italian influence is possible.

222 **El lenguaje de los gestos en el Uruguay.** (The language of gestures in Uruguay.)
Giovanni Meo-Zilio. Montevideo: Imprenta Libertad, 1961. 154p.

Personal communication in Uruguay is enriched by a variety of non-verbal forms of expression. '*Ojo!*', with the finger on the lower eye-lid, is a well-known example. This book manages to be both immensely scholarly and fascinating to the general reader. It gives a general introduction to the study of gestures, with detailed and illustrated descriptions of a large number commonly used by Uruguayans. Very few are thought to be exclusive to the River Plate region, the majority being imported from Italy. The book is also published as a contribution to *Boletín de Filología* (Santiago de Chile), vol. 13 (1961), p. 75-163.

223 **El elemento italiano en el habla de Buenos Aires y Montevideo.** (The Italian element in the speech of Buenos Aires and Montevideo.)
Giovanni Meo Zilio, Ettore Rossi. Florence: Valmartina, 1970. 183p. bibliog.

Because of the scale of Italian emigration to the River Plate, the contribution of Italian to River Plate Spanish has been very great. Most of the predecessors to this book made only limited reference to Uruguay, but as the authors point out, Uruguay is an important and distinctive sector of this linguistic community. The first author spent many years in Uruguay, with the result that this book gives unusual prominence to the speech of Montevideo, while pages 24-32 of the Introduction analyse the routes and vehicles by which Italian words and phrases have been adopted or adapted in Uruguay. The substance of the book gives the meanings and derivations for about 500 of these, grouped according to national or regional source in Italy, and there are notes also on the pronunciation and spelling of Italian surnames.

224 **Uruguay: the problem of etymology of place names of Guaraní origin.**
José Pedro Rona. *Names*, vol. 8 (1960), p. 1-5.

Although no Guaraní Indians inhabited Uruguay, about 80 per cent of place-names dating from the earliest period of conquest and colonization are of Guaraní origin, probably because of the role of Guaraní-speaking interpreters between the Spaniards and the indigenous Indians. Because Guaraní dialects are agglutinant, Spanish speakers cannot interpret the meaning of these names. By enlisting the aid of Guaraní speakers, the author is able to argue that the meaning of 'Uruguay' must be 'tail of the *urú* bird'. However, 'it is hard to explain how this name has been given to a river'.

Religion

225 **Racionalismo y liberalismo en el Uruguay.** (Rationalism and liberalism in Uruguay.)
Arturo Ardao. Montevideo: Universidad de la República, 1962. 398p.

A major study of the advance of liberalism in religious thought in Uruguay in the nineteenth century, culminating in the secularization of national institutions in the first years of this century. The first hundred pages in fact deal with rationalism in general. The analysis of rationalism in Uruguay which follows is in four sections: origins; Masonic catholicism (1865-80); deist rationalism (1865-80); and anticlerical liberalism (1880-1925).

226 **The River Plate republics: a survey of the religious, economic and social conditions in Argentina, Paraguay and Uruguay.**
Webster E. Browning. London; New York: World Dominion Press, 1928. 139p. maps.

The survey is primarily of religious conditions, and includes an account of the coming of the evangelical missions, as well as of the slow growth of Protestant Christianity in the region.

227 **Aspectos religiosos de la sociedad uruguaya.** (Religious aspects of Uruguayan society.)
Montevideo: Centro de Estudios Cristianos, 1965. 143p.

The principal contribution to this volume is an analysis of a survey of religious attitudes undertaken by a public opinion polling agency, presented here in forty-three tables. There are also essays on the process of secularization in Uruguay by Julio de Santa Ana; religion in contemporary Uruguayan prose writing by Híber Conteris; and superstitions in Uruguay by Romeo Fiore.

228 **The evangelical church in the River Plate republics: a study of the economic and social basis of the evangelical church in Argentina and Uruguay.**
J. Merle Davis. New York; London: International Missionary Council, 1943. 119p.

Although Uruguay is not treated separately from Argentina, this is a detailed and factual report on the position of the evangelical church. Of greatest interest are accounts of the Central Methodist Church of Montevideo; the Waldensians in Colonia Valdense and thirteen other colonies; the social problems of the suburb of Malvín and the ministry of the Methodist church; and the work of Friendship House in the Cerro district.

229 **The political impact on religious development in Uruguay.**
Russell H. Fitzgibbon. *Church History*, vol. 22, no. 1 (March 1953), p. 21-32.

Apart from Mexico, 'Uruguay's is the first large-scale American experiment in the rejection of the norms and mores of a dominant Church as projected especially into the political realm but felt also in economic, social, and intellectual spheres'. Three factors are offered in explanation: late colonization; an influx of non-Catholic foreigners in the revolutionary period; and mass immigration in the late nineteenth century from Catholic countries but from socio-economic strata whose attachment to the church was limited.

230 **La iglesia en el Uruguay: libro conmemorativo en el primer centenario de la erección del obispado de Montevideo. Primero en el Uruguay, 1878-1978.** (The church in Uruguay: a volume commemorating the first centenary of the bishopric of Montevideo. The first in Uruguay, 1878-1978.)
Montevideo: Instituto Teológico del Uruguay, 1978. 356p. bibliog.

A collection of fifteen essays on the church in Uruguay was assembled to commemorate the centenary. Three are by Juan Villegas SJ, who in addition put together the extensive bibliography. There is also a chronology, an index of names, and notes on the authors. The majority of the essays are historical, and 'church' means strictly 'Roman Catholic church'.

231 **Separation in Uruguay.**
J. Lloyd Mecham. In: *Church and state in Latin America: a history of politico-ecclesiastical relations*. Chapel Hill, North Carolina: University of North Carolina Press, 1966. rev. ed., p. 252-60. bibliog.

Mecham's book was written with the specific intent 'to shed a little light on the meaning of Latin-American anti-clericalism'. The chapter on Uruguay might therefore have been expected to bulk rather larger, given that 'the Uruguayans are not a religious people. In fact there is probably more general religious indifference than in any other country in Latin America'. But in spite of Batlle y Ordóñez' vehement anti-clericalism early in the century, indifference seems to have been the keynote of church–state relations. When President Rivera suppressed the Franciscan convents in 1838, the move was designed to promote population growth rather than attack religious observance. And when the church was disestablished in the 1919 constitution, 'considering the feeble ties which had joined Church and State, . . . the act of separation cannot be regarded as a radical step. Nor, indeed, did the reform encounter serious opposition in any quarter'. And since then 'there has been a remarkable absence of any issue to becloud Church–State relations'. The author includes the standard clichés of Uruguayan anti-clericalism – Tourist Week instead of Holy Week, *dios* instead of *Dios* (God) in Batlle's newspaper *El Día* – but this is overall a dispassionate, judicious and highly authoritative (if brief) review of the place of the church in Uruguay.

232 **Protestantism in Latin America: a bibliographical guide.**
Edited by John H. Sinclair. South Pasadena, California: William Carey Library, 1976. 414p.

Part 1 is the 1967 edition (2044 items) with over 1000 further entries in Part 2 which update the work. References are annotated, and are mostly to works in English or Spanish. The Uruguay sections list twenty-two items, but references for Argentina should also be checked. There is an author index.

233 **The Waldenses in the New World.**
George B. Watts. Durham, North Carolina: Duke University Press, 1941. 309p. bibliog.

The Waldensians in Uruguay, who established the Colonia Valdense in 1858, are the largest such community in South America. Chapter 6 (p. 45-56) examines their successful history and expansion (from 1876) to form new colonies in Uruguay. Government assistance in the early years of this century is recorded. Earlier years were not free from stress, however, and the second leader of Colonia Valdense, Jean P. Salomon, left in 1874 to lead the first group of members of the sect to the United States, declaring that Montevideo was one of the three curses of the Waldensians.

234 **Nationalism and religion in Argentina and Uruguay.**
Arthur P. Whitaker. In: *Religion, revolution, and reform: new forces for change in Latin America*. Edited by William V. D'Antonio, Fredrick B. Pike. London: Burns and Oates; New York: Praeger, 1964, p. 73-90.

Whitaker reviews the unfolding of church–state relations in Uruguay, noting in particular the provision for freedom of worship in the 1830 constitution; the growth of secular education from the 1870s; and separation in 1919. In comparison with Argentina there is a long tradition of secular state policy, and he takes issue with the view that Uruguay is a Catholic country but the people are not religious, suggesting that the reverse is true. He also contrasts a tendency to extreme political views in the Argentine Catholic church with the moderate and unified views of Uruguayan Catholics, especially as expressed through the Unión Cívica party.

South American memories of thirty years.
See item no. 62.

The Jewish travel guide.
See item no. 78.

Social Conditions and Social Structure

235 **Los 'marginados' uruguayos: teoría y realidad.** (The marginalized
population of Uruguay: theory and reality.)
Danilo Astori, José Luis Castagnola, Jorge Ferrando, Mirtha Marinoni,
Horacio Martorelli.   Montevideo: Ediciones de la Banda Oriental,
1984. 97p. (Temas del siglo XX, 16).

The four papers in this collection deal with the problem of marginality in Uruguay
from the perspective of the economist (Astori); sociologist (Martorelli); and
psychologist (Marinoni and Ferrando). Castagnola questions the usefulness of the
concept.

236 **Migración interna en el Uruguay.** (Internal migration in Uruguay.)
Néstor Campiglia.   Montevideo: Universidad de la República, 1968.
193p. maps.

In 1959, a sample of 2415 families living in Montevideo were the subject of a detailed
survey concerning the geographical origin of the head of family, and his/her parents
and grandparents, their occupations, and their age when they migrated to Montevideo.
The results are presented in ninety-three tables which take up more than half of this
important book. The analysis of the tables is in three chapters: migration in earlier
generations; migration in the present generation; and national migration to Montevideo. The work is thus not confined exclusively to internal migration, since there is
information also on country of origin.

237 **La mujer en el Uruguay: ayer y hoy.** (Woman in Uruguay: yesterday
and today.)
Nea Filgueira, Juan Carlos Fortuna, Nelly Niedworok, Susana Prates,
Silvia Rodriguez Villamil, Graciela Sapriza.   Montevideo: Ediciones
de la Banda Oriental, 1984. 142p. (Temas del siglo XX, 15).

Produced by the Grupo de Estudios sobre la Condición de la Mujer en el Uruguay
(GRECMU, Study Group on the Condition of Woman in Uruguay), this volume

provides a socio-economic and cultural perspective on the position of women in Uruguayan society past and present. The chapters examine the increasing participation of women in the Montevideo labour force in the later 1970s (Prates); women, family and labour in rural Uruguay (Niedworok); from biological differences to social inequalities: an ideology for the construction of the feminine 'ideal' (Filgueira); domestic ideology and the subordination of woman (Fortuna); female labour in Montevideo 1880-1914 (Rodríguez Villamil); and images of women at the beginning of the century (Sapriza).

238 **Moral reform and feminism: a case study.**

Cynthia Jeffress Little. *Journal of Interamerican Studies and World Affairs*, vol. 17, no. 4 (Nov. 1975), p. 386-97. bibliog.

The subject of this pioneering study is Paulina Luisi (1875-1950), 'an Uruguayan doctor whose lifelong dedication to moral reform and feminism earned her an international reputation as a fighter for one sexual moral standard and women's rights'. Moral reform for Luisi particularly concerned aspects of social hygiene (venereal disease, the white slave trade, and opposition to the control of prostitution), and her activities in this field expressed her feminism in urging women to take more control over their lives ('more conscientious wives, better mothers, and involved citizens'). Luisi, a member of a remarkably talented family, was the first woman to take a bachelor's degree (1899) and to become a physician and surgeon. In 1932 she was Uruguay's delegate to the League of Nations Disarmament Conference. Perhaps only in Uruguay amongst Latin American nations was such a career possible for a woman at this time. Little's brief biography is based on secondary sources, especially Luisi's own works. Although the article is not primarily concerned with the issue, she concludes that moral reform failed to eradicate social ills because 'it never seriously confronted the link between poverty, prostitution, and a capitalist economy'.

239 **The ecology of malnutrition in eastern South America.**

Jacques Meyer May, Donna L. McLellan. New York: Hafner Press; London: Collier Macmillan, 1974. 558p. maps. bibliog. (Studies in Medical Geography, vol. 13).

The chapter on Uruguay of this multi-volume work, sponsored by the United States Army, occupies pages 359-419. It contains an analysis of food resources and their adequacy, diets, and nutritional disease patterns, supported by much tabular information. The conclusions are that without question 'Uruguay can provide its population with an abundant and nutritious diet', and that 'very little nutritional pathology exists in Uruguay'. The pockets of under-nutrition which do exist 'do not exceed in size and public health importance what is found in many highly developed countries'.

240 **Las clases sociales en el Uruguay: estructura, morfología.** (Social classes in Uruguay: structure, morphology.)

Carlos M. Rama. Montevideo: Ediciones Nuestro Tiempo, 1960. 304p. maps.

An early attempt to estimate empirically the size and structure of social classes in Uruguay, this book was written at a time when some of the most basic social statistics were still unavailable in the country. The work is nonetheless extremely valuable. Chapters deal with society, economy and power; social stratification; upper class; middle classes; and lower classes.

241 **El desarrollo social del Uruguay en la postguerra.** (The social
development of Uruguay since the war.)
Aldo E. Solari. Montevideo: Editorial Alfa, 1967. 225p.

In spite of its age, this book remains of fundamental importance to any reader seeking
to understand the nature of contemporary Uruguayan society. It originated, like so
much Uruguayan social science of the 1960s, in the planning effort of the early years of
the decade led by Enrique Iglesias. Statistical information is deliberately kept to a
minimum; the strength of this book consists in its immensely stimulating ideas and
perception. In that sense the chapters resemble essays. They deal with recent economic
development; the demographic process; urbanization; structure of the economically
active population; social classes; international migration; ideologies and social change;
the political system; and some hypotheses on the society's value system. The
conclusion is remarkable for being a pioneer within Latin America of 'dependency'
analysis, but it by no means suffers from the determinism which afflicted later
interpretations in this vein.

242 **Sociología rural nacional.** (Rural sociology of Uruguay.)
Aldo E. Solari. Montevideo: Facultad de Derecho y Ciencias Sociales
de la Universidad de la República, 1958. 2nd ed. 576p. bibliog.

A huge and somewhat indigestible work, the book is divided into five parts: sociology
and rural society; the rural population (size and distribution, composition, fertility and
mortality, health and physical characteristics, social psychology); the land (soil and
climate, land ownership, land tenure, land-use systems); social differentiation (groups,
classes, the family, education and social control); and social dynamics (social change,
mobility, rural migration). Amongst other conclusions, the author argues that the rural
upper class is less closed than in Argentina, and that it shows less family continuity and
greater vertical mobility.

243 **The family in Uruguay.**
Aldo E. Solari, Rolando Franco. In: *The family in Latin America.*
Edited by Man Singh Das, Clinton J. Jesser. Sahibabad, India: Vikas,
1980, p. 46-83. bibliog.

Although rather little information was available on many aspects, it was probably not
difficult for the authors to conclude that Uruguay 'is the Latin American country where
the Western type of family organization is most widespread'. They argue that the
'typical' family unit is nuclear, in which legal matrimony predominates over all forms
of free union. The divorce rate is relatively high for Latin America (though lower than
in many advanced countries), and is rising. The number of children is small. Although
'uniformity is perhaps the central feature of Uruguayan society', variations within these
norms allowed the authors to isolate five family sub-types for analysis: urban middle
class; working class; rural lower class in cattle-raising areas; rural lower class in crop-
farming areas; and upper class. The analysis is supported by fourteen tables.

244 **La vivienda.** (Housing.)
Juan Pablo Terra. Montevideo: Editorial 'Nuestra Tierra', 1969. 60p.
bibliog. (Nuestra Tierra 38).

During 1963-66 the author was head of the housing and physical planning sections of
the Comisión de Inversiones y Desarrollo Económico (CIDE), the authority which

prepared the first National Plan. In this short book he presents a serious, documented, and excellently illustrated account of the growth of construction, the housing situation in the mid-1960s, and the Plan's proposals.

245 **La infancia en el Uruguay (1973-1984): efectos sociales de la recesión y las políticas de ajuste.** (Childhood in Uruguay, 1973-1984: social effects of the recession and adjustment policies.)
Juan Pablo Terra, Mabel Hopenhaym.   Montevideo: Centro Latinoamericano de Economía Humana (CLAEH) – Unicef – Ediciones de la Banda Oriental, 1986. 205p. bibliog.

Behind its somewhat bland title is a document of major importance on the social consequences of the military dictatorship of this period. The four main chapters examine the principal phases of economic policy; the evolution of public expenditure on social security, health, education, and children; changes in general social conditions (demography, employment, incomes, nutrition, and housing); and specific effects on children. Although the period was characterized by a regressive redistribution of income and a general deterioration in most social indicators, the report objectively records a decline in infant mortality. A feature of the analysis are the 103 tables.

246 **Industrialization, values, and occupational evaluation in Uruguay.**
James R. Wood, Eugene A. Weinstein.   *American Journal of Sociology*, vol. 72, no. 1 (July 1966), p. 47-57.

Questionnaire data from a sample of 463 Uruguayan school students aged about fifteen years were used to throw light on the relationship between industrialization and modifications to traditional occupational prestige hierarchies. The students were drawn from seven urban centres varying in the extent of their industrialization. Uruguay is believed to have a Spanish cultural orientation, that is, 'an intense disdain for manual labour' and an 'orientation toward leisure, intellectual pursuits, enlargement of one's self' as opposed to an orientation toward work and achievement. It was found that industrialization (as here defined) does indeed affect the occupational prestige structure. However, this was not because general cultural values had changed. 'Our data seem clearly to contradict our own approach (if we can assume the validity of our measure of Spanish cultural orientation).' If the authors' prejudices are challenged, those of some readers may be confirmed.

Política económica y distribución del ingreso en el Uruguay, 1970-1976.
(Economic policy and income distribution in Uruguay, 1970-1976.)
See item no. 386.

National accounts statistics: compendium of income distribution statistics.
See item no. 473.

Reshaping the urban core: the politics of housing in authoritarian Uruguay.
See item no. 480.

Welfare State

247　Old-age pensions in Uruguay.
E. G. Collado, Simon G. Hanson. *Hispanic American Historical Review*, vol. 16, no. 2 (May 1936), p. 173-89.

'No serious evaluation of the Uruguayan experiment has yet been made . . . In this article the writers examine the history of old-age pensions in Uruguay; the experience in this field illustrates in many ways the nature of the Uruguayan attack on modern economic and social problems.' Introduced in 1919, the system of old-age pensions had to be reorganized in 1925, and was again in deficit and with arrears of payment to beneficiaries at the time of Terra's coup in 1933. This balanced and judicious account concludes that the non-contributory nature of the scheme was not responsible for its difficulties: a contributory basis would indeed have magnified its administrative weaknesses. The essential problems were a low age qualification, and assigned revenues whose yield fluctuated widely. The analysis is supported by four tables.

248　Labor legislation of Uruguay.
Washington, D.C.: Government Printing Office, July 1929. 70p. (U.S. Department of Labor, Bureau of Labor Statistics, Bulletin no. 494).

This is a compilation and translation of all the laws affecting labour which were in force in 1929. There is no commentary, but each is summarized. The principal enactments reproduced here are: workmen's compensation, accident prevention, minimum wages for rural workers, the eight-hour working day, compulsory weekly rest, prohibition of night work, and old-age and retirement pensions.

249　Labor legislation in Uruguay.
Percy A. Martin, Earl M. Smith. *Monthly Labor Review*, vol. 25 (Oct. 1927), p. 726-33.

Not merely the legislation, but also its implementation and effects are briefly reviewed in this article. The fields covered are accident prevention; workmen's compensation; the eight-hour day; weekly day of rest; and minimum wages for rural labour. There are notes also on the Oficina Nacional de Trabajo (National Bureau of Labour); woman and child labour (inadequate protection for which is seen as the major shortcoming of the system); and old-age pensions. It was probably this article which coined the cliché of Uruguay as 'social laboratory'. The conclusions are very positive: 'Not merely has a fairly complete and coherent system of laws been written on the statute books, but the laws are enforced with honesty and intelligence.' That conclusion extends, very surprisingly but on the basis of a claimed knowledge of practice on 'a number of large Uruguayan estancias', to the payment of the minimum wage to rural workers. There is much evidence for the contrary view.

250 **Social security in Latin America: pressure groups, stratification and inequality.**
Carmelo Mesa-Lago. Pittsburgh, Pennsylvania: University of Pittsburgh Press, 1978. 351p.

Chapter 3 (p. 70-112), 'The case of Uruguay', was prepared by Arturo C. Porzecanski. The historical evolution of the system, and its functioning during the late 1960s (the most recent period for which adequate data are available), are discussed in great detail. The study concludes that although the proportion of the population covered by social security (65 per cent in the 1960s) is one of the highest in Latin America, the system 'abounds in flagrant inequities'. A major source of this bias are pressure groups which reflect the power, influence and prestige of particular occupational groups and frustrate collective welfare objectives. The diagnosis, which is supported by quantitative information summarized in fifteen tables, is not outdated.

251 **Social legislation in Uruguay.**
Alberto Sanguinetti Freire. *International Labour Review*, vol. 59, no. 3 (March 1949), p. 271-96.

Written by the Deputy Director of the National Labour Institute, this is a factual survey, with very little analysis, of the labour laws then in force. The material is dealt with under these headings: conditions of work; industrial safety and hygiene; protection of women and child workers; home work; agricultural employment; wages; compensation for dismissal; social insurance; unemployment and the employment exchanges; conciliation and arbitration; and ratification of international labour conventions. The list represents a remarkable legislative achievement.

252 **The development of social insurance in Argentina, Brazil, Chile, and Uruguay.**
A. Tixier. *International Labour Review*, vol. 32, no. 5 (Nov. 1935), p. 610-36; no. 6 (Dec. 1935), p. 751-79.

Tixier, an official of the International Labour Office, visited Montevideo in November 1934 and examined the organization and working of the State Insurance Bank and the pension funds. Longer visits were paid to the other countries. His report is not by country, but by category of insurance: industrial accidents and workmen's compensation; sickness; and compulsory invalidity, old-age, and survivors' pensions. Most of the analysis consists of a rather bland examination of the various schemes, and the Uruguayan pensions attract comment less often than those of the other countries. However, on the compatibility of paid employment and receipt of a pension, the author notes Uruguayan legislation in 1934 to stop the practice (which became so common in the 1950s and later), and observes that few European countries had similar regulations because 'in Europe pensions are as a rule lower than in Argentina, Brazil or Uruguay, and are not sufficient to provide the pensioner with a reasonable minimum of subsistence'.

Utopia in Uruguay: chapters in the economic history of Uruguay.
See item no. 178.

La infancia en el Uruguay (1973-1984): efectos sociales de la recesión y las políticas de ajuste. (Childhood in Uruguay, 1973-1984: social effects of the recession and adjustment policies.)
See item no. 245.

Notes on the pathology of Uruguay's welfare state.
See item no. 366.

A political economy of Uruguay since 1870.
See item no. 375.

Politics

General

253 **Latin American politics: a historical bibliography.**
Santa Barbara, California; Denver, Colorado; London: ABC-Clio
Information Services, 1984. 290p.

Tucked away in the preface is the key to making sense at least of the Uruguayan
section of this bibliography – that it is restricted to periodical literature during 1973-82.
Over 3000 items are listed, without restriction as to language, though Spanish and
English predominate. The extended annotations prepared by a panel of 250
abstractors are a special feature of the volume. Following a section on Latin American
politics in general, the main part of the book is devoted to country studies. Uruguay
occupies pages 208-9, and thirty items are listed. The reader is certain to find
references here that would otherwise have been missed, which is the purpose of a
bibliography, but the title is seriously misleading. The work is indexed by subject and
author.

254 **Inside the company: CIA diary.**
Philip Agee. Harmondsworth, England: Penguin, 1975. 640p.

Agee's account of his twelve years as a Central Intelligence Agency (CIA) secret
operations officer caused a sensation when published. During 1964-66 he was stationed
in Uruguay, and his recollections (p. 325-494) of CIA operations there are
extraordinarily detailed, fascinating, and horrifying. The book is perhaps more
illuminating about dirty tricks and covert operations than it is about Uruguay itself, but
some leading political figures of the period are named as agents or collaborators. So
much incidental or non-controversial material that only the individual reader could
verify proves to be accurate, that there seems little reason to doubt the veracity of the
rest.

255 **Political forces in Latin America: dimensions of the quest for stability.**
Edited by Ben G. Burnett, Kenneth F. Johnson. Belmont, California: Wadsworth, 1968. 587p. bibliog.

The chapter on Uruguay (p. 429-46) is by Donald W. Bray, and the major sections deal with political history and political structures and roles. It constitutes a useful survey, in spite of the rapidity of change occurring at that time. The 1966 election result is little more than noticed, except to hazard the view that the return to the one-person presidency in the 1967 constitution was a formalistic change, unlikely to affect drastically the political system.

256 **Political participation in urban Uruguay: mixing public and private ends.**
Robert E. Biles. In: *Political participation in Latin America*, vol. 1: *citizen and state*. Edited by John A. Booth, Mitchell A. Seligson. New York; London: Holmes & Meier, 1978, p. 85-97.

'The purpose of this paper is to determine the types or modes of [democratic] participation, the amount of participation, and the factors producing it' in the period before the military coup. Much of the paper is concerned to explain the methodology of the analysis. Using data drawn from 850 interviews in a survey of the adult population of Montevideo in 1970, the author found that particularism and patronage had a central role in shaping participation. However, although patronage contributed to social stability initially, as economic decline continued the system became self-defeating. Moreover the political system ceased to function adequately as 'serving short-term clientelist interests substituted for long range rational decision making'.

257 **Latin America, its problems and its promise: a multidisciplinary introduction.**
Edited by Jan Knippers Black. Boulder, Colorado; London: Westview, 1984. 549p. maps. bibliog.

The section on Uruguay (p. 451-60) is by Diego Abente, a gentle introduction to its political history focusing on the decade of the military régime.

258 **The southern cone: realities of the authoritarian state in South America.**
César Caviedes. Totowa, New Jersey: Rowman and Allenheld, 1984. 212p. maps. bibliog.

A somewhat unfocused study of the authoritarian régimes of the southern cone, in which Uruguay is treated *passim*, though there is a section on 'The reduced elites of Uruguay', p. 75-80.

259 **The politics of regional integration: a study of Uruguay's decision to join LAFTA.**
Elizabeth Ann Finch. Liverpool: Centre for Latin American Studies, University of Liverpool, 1973. 70p. bibliog. (Monograph Series, no.4).

This monograph, an abbreviated version of an MA thesis, examines Uruguay's participation in the negotiations to set up the Latin American Free Trade Association, and the executive and legislative processes during 1959-61 which resulted in membership. Based partly on interviews with twenty-three politicians, bureaucrats and private sector representatives, the study concludes that the decision was taken 'with very imperfect knowledge, before careful study of the project and the rather perfunctory consultation with the private sector. No alternatives were put forward, let alone considered, within the Executive'.

260 **Measurement of Latin American political change.**
Russell H. Fitzgibbon, Kenneth F. Johnson. *American Political Science Review*, vol. 55, no. 3 (Sept. 1961), p. 515-26.

In 1945, 1950, 1955 and 1960 Fitzgibbon asked North American specialists in Latin American affairs to assess the extent of democracy in twenty Latin American republics, by awarding points for democratic performance under fifteen headings. In spite of the ambiguity and limitations of such an exercise, it is worth noting that Uruguay was by a substantial margin regarded as the most democratic nation in Latin America in all four years.

261 **Uruguay: a model for freedom and reform in Latin America?**
Russell H. Fitzgibbon. In: *Freedom and reform in Latin America.* Edited by Fredrick B. Pike. Notre Dame, Indiana: University of Notre Dame Press, 1959, p. 231-55.

Fitzgibbon calls into question the optimistic conclusions reached in his own *Uruguay: portrait of a democracy* (q.v.) a few years earlier, in the light of economic and political difficulties in the second half of the 1950s. On the whole his faith is unshaken, but he does have three prescriptions: a centralization of responsibility in government; a programme of austerity; and a selflessness to elevate the general good of the nation above individual, party or class.

262 **Uruguay y la democracia.** (Uruguay and democracy.)
Edited by Charles Gillespie, Louis Goodman, Juan Rial, Peter Winn. Montevideo: Ediciones de la Banda Oriental, 1984-85. 3 vols.

In September 1984 the Latin American Program of the Woodrow Wilson International Center for Scholars staged a conference on Uruguay at which the twenty-two papers in this collection were delivered. They concern the economy, the armed forces, the political parties, the Left and the working class, education, and problems of the transition to democracy. Together they constitute an essential reference on the period of the transition.

263 **Uruguay: political utopia.**
John J. Johnson. In: *Political change in Latin America: the emergence of the middle sectors.* Stanford, California: Stanford University Press, 1958, p. 45-65. bibliog.

Johnson's thesis on the political importance of Latin America's emerging middle classes is not called into question merely by Uruguay's experience. But the ironies are certainly greater here, not only in the false optimism of 'There is little to suggest that the officer corps will develop or will be permitted to develop political ambitions in the years immediately ahead', but also in the perhaps equally false view that Uruguay's middle sectors have a 'greater readiness to modify traditions and cast aside the established economic and political practices'. The author admits that he relied heavily on Russell H. Fitzgibbon, *Uruguay: portrait of a democracy* (q.v.).

264 **Uruguay: government by institutions.**
Göran G Lindahl. In: *Political systems of Latin America*. Edited by
Martin C. Needler. Princeton, New Jersey: Van Nostrand, 1964,
p. 447-61. bibliog.
Although the constitution and much else has changed since this essay was prepared, it
is still one of the best and best-written historical introductions to the political system.
There is some optimism, but 'the political and the economic trends look dark'.

265 **A Uruguayan appraisal.**
Chris Lines. *Contemporary Review*, vol. 229, no. 1329 (1976), p. 189-
93.
A brief journalistic account, unscholarly but perceptive, of the country's plight three
years after the military coup. Unfortunately it is replete with factual errors and mis-
spelled (or wrong) names.

266 **Legislative politics in Uruguay: a preliminary statement.**
Ronald H. McDonald. In: *Latin American legislatures: their role and
influence*. Edited by Weston H. Agor. New York: Praeger, 1971,
p. 113-35.
'No Latin American legislature has a longer record of sustained activity and relevance
than has Uruguay's.' But as McDonald also goes on to observe (on the eve of the coup
which abolished the legislature for twelve years), the parties were profoundly
factionalized, leadership was personalistic, and politics was strained by economic
stagnation. The study ends with the hope that the Tupamaro movement might
precipitate 'the restructuring of legislative functions to include promotion of economic
development and social mobility as well as maintenance of institutional stability': not
many points for prediction, but this is a valuable and still relevant account of
Uruguayan politics with much useful information.

267 **La democracia en Uruguay.** (Democracy in Uruguay.)
Germán W. Rama. Buenos Aires: Grupo Editor Latinoamericano,
1987. 238p. bibliog.
In a subtle essay of great significance, Rama sets out to establish what is specific in
Uruguayan democracy and the evolution of Uruguayan society. He does so in the
context of certain key factors: the dynamic relationship between state and society; the
major role played by the notion of the future of society and the political project
intended to achieve it; the importance of integration in the initial project, leading to a
'hyperintegrated' society; and the importance of social citizenship rather than class
identity within the political system. These elements are worked out in an interpretation
of Uruguay's political development in the twentieth century.

268 **Uruguay's lost paradise.**
Samuel Shapiro. *Current History*, vol. 62, no. 366 (1972), p. 98-103.
Shapiro gives a general account which contrasts Uruguay's current difficulties with its
earlier achievements. He sees the future as lying between reform from within the
existing structure, or radical-revolutionary change instituted by the Tupamaros or the
Frente Amplio. A military régime was apparently not in prospect. The article is

reprinted, somewhat shortened, in *South America: problems and prospects*, edited by Irwin Isenberg (New York: H. W. Wilson, 1975; The Reference Shelf vol. 47, no. 2), p. 104-12.

269 **Government and politics of Uruguay.**
Philip B. Taylor, Jr. New Orleans, Louisiana: Tulane University, 1960. 285p. bibliog. (Studies in Political Science, vol. VII).

An important, immensely detailed study of Uruguay's mounting political and economic problems of the late 1950s. Though scholarly (the footnotes alone occupying 100 pages), the book addresses key issues bluntly; for example, constitutional reform, overhaul of public administration and social welfare, and the voting system. These issues are still important, and in addition the book captures the sense of unease and frustration of the period. Two historical chapters introduce the analysis.

270 **Interests and institutional dysfunction in Uruguay.**
Philip B. Taylor, Jr. *American Political Science Review*, vol. 57, no. 1 (March 1963), p. 62-74.

A wide-ranging critique of functional aspects of the political system, emphasizing the strength of interest groups operating through the political parties and the incapacity of the collegiate executive. Taylor suggests that in some important respects the political system 'achieved its most important goals three decades ago, and today functions only from the momentum of that achievement', and concludes by raising the issue of the extent to which political values and practices (e.g. 'corruption') can be assessed outside the national context.

271 **Uruguay: the costs of inept political corporatism.**
Philip B. Taylor, Jr. In: *Latin American politics and development*. Edited by Howard J. Wiarda, Harvey F. Kline. Boston, Massachusetts: Houghton Mifflin, 1979, p. 262-80. map. bibliog.

This very valuable survey of Uruguay's political development concludes at a moment when, as the author frankly admits, 'the future of the country is literally as unpredictable as tomorrow's news dispatches'. His investigation of Uruguayan history places the political system at the centre of the story: 'After the 1930s the political class became increasingly self-indulgent. Perhaps it had not designed the Byzantine constitutional and electoral system with its own aggrandizement in mind, but this was its effect. The decision process became so convoluted and bureaucratic as to be unresponsive even to client group demands'.

272 **Educational backgrounds of Latin American legislators: a three-country analysis.**
Joel G. Verner. *Comparative Politics*, vol. 6, no. 4 (July 1974), p. 617-34.

Verner analyses the higher educational backgrounds of the 116 Uruguayan legislators (31 senators and 85 of the 99 representatives) elected for 1967-72, alongside their Brazilian and Guatemalan equivalents. Of the 116, 84 had some university credits and 56 had completed their degrees. The educational attainment of senators was somewhat greater than that of representatives. Of those with at least some credits, 77 per cent of senators and 61 per cent of representatives had studied law, followed by medicine (8 per cent and 12 per cent respectively).

273 **Uruguay: democracy at the crossroads.**
Martin Weinstein. Boulder, Colorado: Westview Press, 1988. 160p.
map. bibliog. (Nations of Contemporary Latin America).
Weinstein's concise introduction to the history and contemporary situation of Uruguay
is generally successful and certainly the best book of its kind since R. H. Fitzgibbon's
Uruguay: portrait of a democracy (q.v.). The opening chapters lay the background
under the headings of the land and the people; historical background; the 'Switzerland
of South America'; crisis and decline; and the military dictatorship. The second part
deals with the transition to democracy and subsequent problems, and foreign policy,
and is somewhat pessimistic. The author is particularly critical of the amnesty granted
at the end of 1986 to the military for human rights offences. Unfortunately there are
some factual errors: Batlle did not introduce an urban minimum wage; Uruguay broke
relations with the Soviet Union in 1936, not 'established' them; Viera appears three
times as Rivera; and some dates are questionable. But these do not mar an excellent
introduction to Uruguayan politics.

274 **Uruguay: the politics of failure.**
Martin Weinstein. Westport, Connecticut: Greenwood Press, 1975.
190p. bibliog.
A significant study of the background to Uruguay's political crisis resulting in the
military coup in 1973. Chapters on *batllismo* and counter-ideologies, co-participation,
and social class, are particularly useful. The book's central theme is that *batllismo*, as a
nationalist ideology, failed to shape the values and institutions necessary for its
survival, and ultimately gave way to the personalism and clientelism of a corporatist
political structure. Political theory is very much to the fore, and the argument is
contentious. The economic stagnation of the period does not figure in the analysis. Part
of the book was published as 'Corporatist ideology in Latin America: implications of
the Uruguayan case', in: *Terms of conflict: ideology in Latin American politics*, edited
by Morris J. Blackman, Ronald G. Hellman (Philadelphia, Pennsylvania: Institute for
the Study of Human Issues, 1977), p. 63-96.

Parties and elections

275 **Political parties of the Americas: Canada, Latin America and the West
Indies.**
Edited by Robert J. Alexander. Westport, Connecticut: Greenwood
Press, 1982. 2 vols. 864p. bibliog. (The Greenwood Historical
Encyclopedia of the World's Political Parties).
The section on Uruguay (p. 671-89 in vol. 2, subtitled *Guadeloupe – Virgin Islands of
the United States*) is contributed by Ronald H. McDonald. There is an extended
historical introduction to September 1981, followed by notes on the following: Catholic
party; Christian Civic Movement (MCC); Christian Democrat Party (PDC); Civic
Union (UC); Colorado party; Communist Party (PC); Movement of the Revolutionary
Left (MIR); National (Blanco) party; Popular Action Movement; Socialist Party (PS);
Trotskyists; Uruguayan Anarchist Federation (FAU); and Uruguayan Revolutionary
Movement (MRU). The author was unfortunate in having to prepare material towards

the close of a long period in which political parties were suppressed, since the significance of many of these groups is confined to the 1960s, and the resumption of democracy in 1984 initiated some changes in the party system.

276 **Elections and democratization in Latin America, 1980-85.**
Paul W. Drake, Eduardo Silva. San Diego, California: Center for Iberian and Latin American Studies, Center for US–Mexican Studies, Institute of the Americas, 1986. 335p. bibliog.

Three chapters discuss aspects of Uruguay's return to democracy in the 1980s: 'Prelude to elections: the military's legitimacy crisis and the 1980 constitutional plebiscite in Uruguay' by Howard Handelman (p. 201-14); 'Activists and floating voters: the unheeded lessons of Uruguay's 1982 primaries' by Charles G. Gillespie (p. 215-44); and 'The Uruguayan elections of 1984: a triumph of the center' by Juan Rial (p. 245-71). The second two papers present a quantitative analysis of voting patterns in 1982 and 1984, and the three together constitute a reference of major importance on the democratization process.

277 **Democratisation in Uruguay.**
Henry Finch. *Third World Quarterly*, vol. 7, no. 3 (July 1985), p. 594-609.

The author analyses the election campaign of 1984, and the results in comparison with those of 1971, and argues that elements of conservatism and continuity are still strong in the political system. The article is somewhat pessimistic about the stability of the restored democracy, partly because the military returned to barracks in 1985 in good order, but mainly because of the severity of the economic crisis.

278 **Adoption of a collegiate executive in Uruguay.**
Russell H. Fitzgibbon. *Journal of Politics*, vol. 4, no. 4 (Nov. 1952), p. 616-42.

Enthusiastic as ever for all things Uruguayan, Fitzgibbon suggests of the collegiate executive embodied in the 1952 constitution that 'it is not impossible that this Uruguayan innovation is the most interesting political experiment attempted in the New World since the eighteenth-century revolution of the British colonies in North America'. But there is little hyperbole in the rest of the article, which examines the history in Uruguay of the collegiate idea, the Swiss model, the process by which the new constitution was adopted, and gives a detailed description of it.

279 **Historia del Partido Comunista del Uruguay [hasta el año 1951].**
(History of the Communist Party of Uruguay [up to 1951].)
Published by Eugenio Gómez. Montevideo: Editorial Elite, 1961. 281p.

Gómez insists that this work was written primarily by Francisco Pintos, on the instruction of the Party Executive Committee, and not by him. In addition to what it has to say about the development of the Left, it also contains an interesting foreword by Gómez with comments on the 'coup' within the Party in 1955 by ten 'Trotskyist-opportunists' (including Rodney Arismendi, Enrique Rodríguez and Pintos himself) who accepted Khruschev's revision of the Stalin era. As a result of this schism it was intended to suppress the volume, in which Gómez figures abundantly, but Gómez managed to retain a copy of the manuscript.

280 **Uruguay, 1980-1981: an unexpected opening.**
Luis Eduardo González. *Latin American Research Review*, vol. 18,
no. 3 (1983), p. 63-76.

In November 1980 the military régime in Uruguay staged a plebiscite seeking
endorsement of their constitutional proposals which would, if approved, have
institutionalized military rule. Against all expectations 57 per cent of voters said 'no'.
As the author observes, the poll marked the turning point in the régime's history. This
perceptive article is devoted to an analysis of both civilian and (especially) military
behaviour on the issue. González notes that opposition to the military was drawn from
the political centre and right, as well as the left wing. The notion of the 'good
conscience' of the military is employed to explain its collegial rather than personal
decision-making structure, its apparent belief that military rule was exceptional and
transitory, and the impossibility of identifying it with any particular economic interest
in the country. 'Good conscience' thus dictated, remarkably, that 'after a long and
essentially fraudulent process, the military government unhesitatingly admitted
political defeat'.

281 **Uruguay: election factbook; November 27, 1966.**
Washington, D.C.: Institute for the Comparative Study of Political
Systems, 1966. 53p. maps.

'Factbook' understates the quality of this compact but exceptionally informative and
complete study of the 1966 elections. Main sections are: overview; political history;
elective offices to be filled; electoral timetable; items of electoral significance; who
votes; political parties; political personalities; political groups; election issues; analysis
of elections since 1950; election laws; proportional representation; and structure of
government as defined by the Constitution. There are ten invaluable tables on the
electorate and election results since 1950.

282 **Latin American political movements.**
Ciarán O. Maoláin. Harlow, Essex: Longman; New York: Facts on
File, 1985. 287p.

'The aim of this work is to present in a compact and readily accessible form, basic
factual information on political parties and alliances, guerrilla movements, pressure
groups and other legal and illegal organizations currently active in the ever-changing
political scene . . .' The section on Uruguay occupies pages 242-53, and appears to be
up-dated to March 1985. Following a brief introduction (history, constitutional
background, 1984 election result), thirty-eight political movements are briefly noted.
The large majority are political parties. The most complete entries (e.g. Blanco and
Colorado parties, and the Tupamaros) give address/telephone, leadership, orientation.
history, policies and publications. Others receive barely a line, or are rather
inconclusive, reflecting perhaps a lack of information as much as unimportance. There
is an index of names.

283 **Electoral politics and Uruguayan political decay.**
Ronald H. McDonald. *Inter-American Economic Affairs*, vol. 26,
no. 1 (Summer 1972), p. 25-45.

McDonald reviews symptoms of political decay (the Tupamaros, arbitrary and harsh
government, reduced importance of the legislature), analyses the 1971 elections, and
concludes that 'the Uruguayan political system with its checks, balances, controls, and
its extensive structural development, has "stabilized" national government to the point
of paralysis and stagnation'.

284 **Uruguay: a competitive two-party system.**
Ronald H. McDonald. In: *Party systems and elections in Latin America.* Chicago, Illinois: Markham, 1971, p. 198-214.

Three main sections in this piece are: evolution of the modern parties; electoral system and party organization; and a case-study of campaigning and voting in the 1966 elections. The conclusions to the analysis are generally favourable and optimistic: 'the persistence of the two-party competitive system is a credit to the well-informed, responsible electorate, and to the adaptability of the parties . . . The fact that the political culture and representational processes exist within the framework of a two-party system is more or less a historical and legal coincidence, although the institutional framework has provided strength of its own in the process of national integration'. Some may question whether, even in 1966, 'two-party' adequately describes what the author shows to be a multi-faction system; and whether the institutional structure has not had a more determining effect on the system.

285 **Reforma electoral: posible, deseable?** (Electoral reform: possible, desirable?)
Edited by Dieter Nohlen, Juan Rial. Montevideo: Ediciones de la Banda Oriental, 1986. 278p.

In May 1986 the Friedrich Ebert Stiftung Uruguay (FESUR) organized a conference on Uruguay's electoral system – in particular the double simultaneous vote – and whether it might or should be reformed. This volume collects the papers delivered at the meeting, and is particularly valuable for reproducing the discussion which took place. The authors are Dieter Nohlen, Angel Cocchi, Luis González, Jorge Otero Menéndez, Aldo Solari, Mario Daniel Lamas, César Aguiar and Andres Rius, Renan Rodriguez, Oscar Botinelli, Juan Rial, Gonzalo Aguirre, Hugo Batalla, Manuel Flores Silva, and Jorge Batlle.

286 **The Uruguayan election of 1984.**
Francisco E. Panizza. *Electoral Studies*, vol. 4, no. 3 (Dec. 1985), p. 265-71.

This is a succinct and helpful analysis of the 1984 election, which is compared with that of 1971. The author's interpretation of the result is that it represented a vote both for stability (represented by Sanguinetti) and for social change (in the substantial support for the Blanco party and Frente Amplio coalition).

287 **El club político.** (The political club.)
Germán W. Rama. Montevideo: Editorial Arca, 1971. 137p.

During 1967 Rama recorded interviews with a number of directors of political clubs, of which five (three Colorado, two Blanco) are reproduced here, with an extensive introduction. Both parts are of absorbing interest. The clubs (estimated to number 8,000 in 1966) occupy a key place in the Uruguayan political system. In earlier times they played an important role in the socialization and political incorporation of the expanding urban population. From the mid-1950s the clubs became increasingly significant as the mechanism through which electoral clienteles could be maintained, by the distribution of jobs in the bureaucracy, pensions, and other favours. The effect was, however, to impede the politicization of the electorate, and thus to block social and institutional change. The five political autobiographies of the party faithful are fascinating.

288   **The electoral system in Uruguay.**
Phillip (*sic*) B. Taylor.   *Journal of Politics*, vol. 17, no. 1 (Feb. 1955), p. 19-42.

Proportional representation by double simultaneous vote continues to determine the electoral system in Uruguay, so that this article, though written in very different national circumstances and under the constitution of 1952, has far more than historical interest. After discussing the origins and functions of the Electoral Court, Taylor analyses the multiplicity of party fractions but concludes that in spite of the proliferation of candidate lists at elections there are nonetheless only two major parties and the differences between them are not great. The integrity of the system, popular support for it, and the validity of Uruguay's democratic reputation are all affirmed: 'Uruguay seems to have achieved elections as free as any nation in the world'. On the other hand the author's view that the electoral system had not resulted in incompetent or ineffective government would be harder to sustain for the period after 1955.

289   **Interparty co-operation and Uruguay's 1952 constitution.**
Philip B. Taylor, Jr.   *Western Political Quarterly*, vol. 7, no. 3 (Sept. 1954), p. 391-400.

Following an historical introduction, the substance of this thoughtful article is not what the title might suggest, a detailed analysis of the pact between *batllistas* and *herreristas* which paved the way to the new constitution, but instead the likely implications of the constitution for the future of the parties and the conduct of government. On the one hand 'it would appear that Uruguay has re-established an Executive whose capacity for rapid and effective action in a crisis is open to some question'; but on the other, 'a slight impairment of executive efficiency, for the moment, may well be overbalanced by the sense of broadened popular participation in policy decisions'.

290   **Uruguay introduces government by committee.**
Milton I. Vanger.   *American Political Science Review*, vol. 48, no. 2 (June 1954), p. 500-13.

An important analysis of the negotiations between the parties which resulted in the second collegiate constitution of 1952, narrowly approved by plebiscite the previous year. Fundamental to its adoption was the approval of the Blanco leader Luis Alberto de Herrera, a long-time opponent, the motives for whose conversion are discussed. The results of the 1950 elections are also briefly summarized.

Tupamaros

291   **Crisis de los partidos tradicionales y movimiento revolucionario en el Uruguay.** (The crisis of the traditional parties and the revolutionary movement in Uruguay.)
Luis Costa Bonino.   Montevideo: Ediciones de la Banda Oriental, 1986. 87p. bibliog. (Temas del siglo XX, 32).

Costa Bonino presents a retrospective interpretation of the Tupamaros which sees the guerrilla movement as a response to the crisis of '*batllista* Uruguay' and the traditional party system, but a response which found limited acceptance precisely because of the survival of certain old values: a timid nationalism, particularism, 'and above all an unconditional adhesion to the value of security'. This is a helpful introduction to Uruguay's recent past, originally written for a non-Uruguayan readership and therefore less allusive than some Uruguayan work.

292 **Alto el fuego: FF.AA. y Tupamaros.** (Cease fire: the armed forces and the Tupamaros.)
Nelson Caula, Alberto Silva.   Montevideo: Monte Sexto, 1986. 292p. bibliog.

Two journalists attempt to reconstruct what happened in Uruguay in 1972, when they were eighteen and seventeen respectively. That year marked the climax of Tupamaro activity and ended in the defeat of the movement. Nonetheless, the authors argue that there were three levels of collusion between guerrillas and armed forces. The first, agreed at the highest level on both sides, was a truce intended to result in the restoration of internal peace. The second, the result of conversations between the military and Tupamaros in captivity, saw information pass to the military about economic and financial crimes, and about future plans for economic development. The third, not approved by the hierarchy on either side, consisted of information from a disgruntled former Tupamaro leader (Amodio Pérez) about the movement. The three main sections of the book follow these themes. There is a huge amount of information here, much of it in the form of transcriptions of interviews, and the text is enlivened with photographs. However, the material is frequently allusive and assumes considerable knowledge on the part of the reader.

293 **No hope but God.**
Claude Fly.   New York: Hawthorn Books, 1973. 220p.

The author, an agronomist from the United States who had previously worked as a Food and Agriculture Organization (FAO) consultant on the Laguna Merim project, returned to Uruguay in 1970 as an adviser on a soil survey. On 7 August he was captured by the Tupamaros ('goons', 'devils, faceless hoodlums with the horns of Satan'), and remained their prisoner until 5 March 1971. In his mid-60s, Fly unquestionably suffered greatly, and eventually sustained a heart attack which precipitated his release. This account expresses great bitterness not only towards the Tupamaros, for whom he had neither sympathy nor comprehension, but also towards President Pacheco Areco ('obdurate'), who refused to allow anyone to negotiate Fly's release. A strong theme throughout is Fly's religious conviction. His 'Christian Checklist', which he prepared while a captive, occupies pages 149-220. There are a few photographs, and plans of the cells in which he was held.

294 **Uruguay's urban guerrillas.**
Marysa Gerassi.   *New Left Review*, no. 62 (July-Aug. 1970). p. 22-29.

One of the earliest accounts of the Tupamaros in English, this article offers a straightforward account of the origins of the movement, and of their activities up to May 1970 when 'humour, audacity and good planning' were still the primary characteristics of their raids. The author's belief that the Tupamaros had won 'wide sympathy and popularity among the Uruguayan proletariat and petty-bourgeoisie' would have been harder to sustain in the following two years.

295 **The Tupamaro guerrillas: the structure and strategy of the urban guerrilla movement.**
Mario Esther Gilio, with an introduction by Robert J. Alexander and a foreword by Anne Edmondson (translator). New York: Saturday Review Press, 1972. First published in Spanish by Ediciones de la Flor, 1970. 204p. Also published as *The Tupamaros* (London: Secker & Warburg, 1972).

The title of this fascinating book is very misleading, since it has nothing to say about the structure or strategy of the Tupamaros, nor does it set out to analyse any aspect of the movement. It consists mostly of a series of fragmentary interviews taken with anonymous Uruguayans during 1965-70. Those in the first half of the book draw a bleak picture, not normally visible, of the plight of the economically or socially weak. There are also interviews dealing with political attitudes, especially towards the Tupamaros. The second half of the book presents material on the Tupamaros in varying forms, some apparently as interviews with named members of the movement. There are also narrative accounts of Tupamaro operations written in the first person, though it is not clear in what circumstances they were written or by whom. There are interviews with Tupamaros reporting on tortures inflicted on them, and what appear to be dramatic reconstructions of the mass escapes of Tupamaro prisoners which presumably have a different kind of documentary status to the transcribed interviews. The flaw in the book as a record of what happened is not the author's sympathy for the movement but her failure to indicate where the tape-recorder ends and creative writing begins.

296 **People's prison.**
Geoffrey Jackson. London: Faber and Faber, 1973. 222p.

In January 1971 Sir Geoffrey Jackson, then British Ambassador to Uruguay, was kidnapped by the Movimiento de Liberación Nacional (Tupamaros). This remarkable book recounts his experiences as a captive until his release 224 days later. It is primarily a human, witty and moving document, which manages to be both indignant and as much as possible dispassionate. To the extent that it achieves the latter, it offers some evidence about the qualities displayed by individual members of the Tupamaros, and the tensions between them. They included 'some quite charming human beings poised . . . on the brink of transformation into robots'. There are ten photographs, and the texts of interviews conducted with the author when in captivity by Leopoldo Madruga and Maruja Echegoyen. The book was published in New York in 1974 as *Surviving the long night: an autobiographical account of a political kidnapping.*

297 **Guerrilla and terrorist organizations: a world directory and bibliography.**
Edited by Peter Janke, with Richard Sim. Brighton, Sussex: Harvester, 1983. 531p. maps. bibliog.

The section on Uruguay (p. 507-10) contains a brief and sometimes contentious but also precise analysis of the Tupamaros. There is a highly selective but useful annotated bibliography.

298 **Urban guerrilla warfare in Latin America.**
James Kohl, John Litt.   Cambridge, Massachusetts; London: MIT
Press, 1974. 425p. map. bibliog.

The long section on Uruguay (p. 173-309) contains important material on the
Tupamaros. In their introduction the authors (in fact, editors) review the movement's
history, and find that the defection of Amodio Pérez, one of its leaders, was the
principal reason for the army's success against it. In addition to a full chronology,
documents reproduced here include 'Thirty questions to a Tupamaro'; accounts of
operations by María Esther Gilio, Julion Hernández, and Luis Matirena; an interview
with 'Urbano' in the aftermath of the killing of Mitrione; and the Tupamaros'
programme for government.

299 **The Tupamaros: urban guerrillas in Uruguay.**
Alain Labrousse, translated by Dinah Livingstone with an introduction
by Richard Gott.   Harmondsworth, England: Penguin, 1973. First
published in French by Editions du Seuil, 1970. 168p.

This account of the guerrilla movement is sympathetic but contains useful information.
The analysis of the Tupamaros is chronological in form, with a postscript covering
1971-72, in which the movement passed from the zenith of its influence to military
defeat. There are background chapters of a somewhat simplistic nature on national
history, the economic crisis, and the role of the United States in Uruguay. A number
of Tupamaro documents or statements are reproduced in translation.

300 **Hidden terrors.**
A. J. Langguth.   New York: Pantheon Books, 1978. 339p.

On 31 July 1970 Dan Mitrione, an adviser to the Uruguayan police from the US Office
of Public Safety (OPS), and former instructor at the International Police Academy in
Washington DC, was kidnapped by the Tupamaros. Ten days later his body was found,
bound and gagged, with bullet wounds to the head. The figure of Mitrione was
immediately made a symbol, either as an innocent victim of murderous terrorism, or as
a vicious agent of imperialism teaching the techniques of torture. Langguth, who was
Saigon Bureau Chief for the *New York Times* in the mid-1960s, sets out to tell
Mitrione's story on the basis mainly of interviews with his family, colleagues,
employers, and adversaries, as well as published materials. He found that Mitrione
went to Uruguay in 1969 (as earlier to Brazil) because he needed the increased income
to support his large family. Although very many OPS advisers were CIA agents,
Mitrione was not one. He did not instruct in torture techniques but did advocate brutal
procedures, witness and assist in the use of torture, and help to secure more
sophisticated equipment for it. Langguth presents much of the story as dramatic
reconstruction, but there are fourteen pages of references to his sources. The final
hundred pages hold most of the Uruguayan interest. They include a dramatized
transcription from a tape-recording of Mitrione's interrogation (in English) by a
Tupamaro. The tone of the conversation is polite. There is no suggestion that he was
to be killed.

301 **Generals and Tupamaros: the struggle for power in Uruguay 1969-1973.**
Latin America Review of Books.   London; Leeds: Latin American
Newsletter and Books of Leeds, 1974. 77p.

Prefaced by a short but valuable introduction on the Tupamaros by Carlos López
Matteo, this book reproduces the news items chronicling the political crisis which were

published in the weekly newsletter *Latin America* between vol. 3, no. 26 (27 June 1969) and vol 7, no. 32 (10 Aug. 1973). There is much information here for an analysis of the period.

302 **Tupamaros: antología documental.** (The Tupamaros: an anthology of documents.)
Edited by Ernesto Mayans. Cuernavaca, Mexico: Centro Intercultural de Documentatión, 1971. 485p. bibliog. (CIDOC, Cuaderno no. 60).

In spite of its early date, this is one of the best available collections of documents relating to the Tupamaros. It opens with a committed introduction by the editor, and succeeding sections present documents or extracts from publications dealing with the background to Uruguay's crisis; a chronology of Tupamaro activity from May 1962 to March 1971; reactions to the Tupamaros; Tupamaro manifestos; and Tupamaro communiqués.

303 **The literature of terrorism: a selectively annotated bibliography.**
Compiled by Edward F. Mickolus. Westport, Connecticut: Greenwood Press, 1980.

On pages 178-81 forty-four items are listed which deal wholly or primarily with the Tupamaros. A minority are annotated.

304 **Urban guerrillas: the new face of political violence.**
Robert Moss. London: Temple Smith, 1972. 288p. bibliog.

Chapter 10 ('The Tupamaros: masters of the game', p. 210-39) is a useful account and analysis of the movement. Written at the end of 1971, the history is obviously incomplete. Indeed, the author's assessment is that Uruguay is the only Latin America country in which 'urban guerrillas appear to stand a chance of carrying off an armed insurrection'. See the same author's *Uruguay: terrorism versus democracy* (London: Institute for the Study of Conflict, 1971. Conflict Studies no. 14), 10p. map.

305 **Eleuterio Fernández Huidobro.**
Carlos Núñez. *Report on the Americas*, vol. 20, part 5 (1986), p. 43-50.

Fernández Huidobro was a leader of the Movimiento de Liberación Nacional (MLN) – Tupamaros, operating clandestinely from 1967, and was in jail during 1969-71 and 1972-85, mostly in solitary confinement. This interview with him is based on neutral or friendly questions. A number of significant points are made (for example, 'The struggle for what we term national liberation is not, essentially, a struggle for socialism'), though there are also contradictions (in the non-Marxist sense) over whether or not the MLN was dedicated to exclusively military struggle, and over the role of political parties in democracy.

306 **Uruguay's Tupamaros: the urban guerrilla.**
Arturo C. Porzecanski. New York: Praeger, 1973. 80p. bibliog.

This is the best of the 'contemporary' analyses in English of the Tupamaros. Chapters examine the ideology of the movement, its military and political strategies, membership and internal organization, tactics, and government attempts to defeat it. By February 1973, when the Epilogue to the book was written, the armed forces had won that campaign and had laid the foundations for their coup later that year. The author concludes, on the lessons taught by the Tupamaros, that urban guerrillas can attain a position of 'dual power' even in a politically stable country; that anti-guerrilla strategies based on repression have democracy and liberty also as their victims; and that although the movement was defeated, 'ideas can last longer than organizations'.

307 **The urban guerrilla in Latin America: a select bibliography.**
Charles A. Russell, James A. Miller, Robert E. Hildner.' *Latin American Research Review*, vol. 9, no. 1 (Spring 1974), p. 37-79.
The section on Uruguay (p. 70-74) lists twenty-nine items, with brief annotations.

Armed forces and military régime

308 **Armed forces of Latin America: their histories, development, present strength and military potential.**
Adrian J. English. London: Jane's Publishing, 1984. 490p. maps. bibliog.
The chapter on Uruguay (p. 423-40) gives an interesting historical account of the development of the three services, and full details of their equipment (including four photographs). The text notes that the army is one of the very few in Latin America to rely on voluntary recruitment, and that the navy 'remains a modest force of very limited military potential'.

309 **The Uruguayan navy.**
Adrian English. *Navy International* (March 1984), p. 156-59.
English gives details of the navy's ships, aircraft and manpower since its formation. 'Although it is one of the smallest in South America, equipped with largely obsolescent material, [it] is an efficient and highly professional force.' For more recent and fuller information of the navy's current ships and aircraft, see *Búsqueda* (item no. 638), no. 454 (6 Oct. 1988).

310 **Military government and the movement toward democracy in South America.**
Edited by Howard Handelman, Thomas G. Sanders. Bloomington, Indiana: Indiana University Press, 1981. 388p.
The section dealing with Uruguay (p. 215-84) contains two major contributions by Handelman which originally appeared as *Reports* of the American Universities Field Staff: 'Military authoritarianism and political change' is dated June 1978, and 'Economic policy and elite pressures' was prepared in May 1979. The first of these is a general discussion of the origins and conduct of the military régime, free of theory and full of perceptive analysis and revealing anecdote. The tone is not optimistic for an early end of the régime. The second contribution, based on an extensive programme of interviews with interest group representatives and survey data, is perhaps even more valuable. Handelman's conclusion here is that the influence of individual pressure

groups has been reduced but the power of the upper class as a whole relative to other sectors of the population was enhanced under the military régime. Even so, 'government economic policy is dictated more by external market factors and by the demands of the IMF [International Monetary Fund] and World Bank than by domestic economic elites'. A short postscript dated March 1980 (i.e. before the November plebiscite which rejected the military's proposed constitution) is unable to dispel the doubts about the political future.

311   **Military government in Uruguay: prospects for the 1980s.**
Kenneth F. Johnson.   In: *New military politics in Latin America.*
Edited by Robert Wesson. New York: Praeger 1982. Co-published with
Hoover Institution Press, Stanford University, Stanford, California,
p. 117-30. bibliog.

Johnson gives a largely narrative account with little analysis of the decay of Uruguay's democracy. The look forward promised in the title is confined to a short conclusion. Apart from rendering COMASPO (Comisión de Asuntos Políticos) as COMPASO, the author makes the startling assertion that in 1971 'nearly all electoral candidates for the presidency of all major parties, from the extreme left to the extreme right' were military figures; and from this false premise he goes on to state that therefore even by 1971 'the military had come to occupy a dominant and crosscutting role in the Uruguayan political system'. The article concludes with the question whether the military will merely take its turn in using power for its own ends (as the politicians had done), or will break that cycle of corruption. There is important attribution to 'Soldiers, politicians, and reaction: the etiology of military rule in Uruguay', unpublished PhD thesis (q.v.) by Richard Kinney Moore.

312   **Las fuerzas armadas al pueblo oriental.** (The armed forces to the people
of Uruguay.) Vol. I: La subversión (Subversion). Vol. II: El proceso
político (The political process).
Montevideo: Junta de Comandantes en Jefe, República Oriental del
Uruguay, 1976, 1978. 776p., 746p.

'The armed forces have considered it necessary to place before the people of Uruguay a report on the tactics of sedition within its frontiers, which would be both a documented study of its origins, evolution and interconnection with international subversive groups, and the present aims of terrorist activity in the western world.' The result in Volume I is a major compilation of material relating to the armed forces' campaign against the Tupamaros. There is an extensive chronology, and numerous illustrations, some reproducing Tupamaro material in colour. Volume II, which defines the political crisis as 'irresponsible demagoguery' as well as subversion, deals primarily with the course of the military régime after 1973, reproducing and justifying its various repressive measures. Written during the period of the armed forces' greatest self-confidence, it contains important sections on the doctrine of security for national development, and on their disagreement with the puppet President Bordaberry in 1976 which caused his removal. It is therefore an extremely useful, if by its nature deeply unpleasant, source for the study of the régime. There are excellent indexes in Volume II to both volumes (the subject index alone occupying 150 pages).

313 **Uruguay in transition: from civilian to military rule.**
Edy Kaufman. New Brunswick, New Jersey: Transaction Books, 1979. 126p. bibliog.
This is a valuable and well-informed analysis of the military coup and the politics of the military in power. The author worked for a period during the preparation of the book for Amnesty International and testified in Washington in 1976 on the human rights situation in Uruguay. The book combines elements of both political science (though not the dominant 'bureaucratic-authoritarianism' model) and critique of military repression. Chapters are: methodological outline; operational environment, external and internal settings; the decision-making élite; the post-crisis stage; and testing hypotheses (in which twenty-five hypotheses regarding military intervention are briefly assessed against Uruguayan experience). There is an appendix on the sequence of events during 1968-77, and the Blanco party leader, Senator Wilson Ferreira Aldunate, contributes an important foreword.

314 **World armies.**
Edited by John Keegan. London: Macmillan, 1983. 2nd ed. 688p.
The section on Uruguay (p. 643-46) is by the editor and Adrian English. The military coup is unfortunately dated as 1975, but the information is otherwise detailed and appears to be accurate, and the judgments well founded. There are sections on national history and the political role of the armed forces; strength and budget; command and constitutional status; deployment; organization; recruitment; equipment; and rank and dress (wherein is noted that 'there are no military medals or decorations').

315 **Confined to barracks: emergencies and the military in developing societies.**
Aaron S. Klieman. *Comparative Politics*, vol. 12, no. 2 (Jan. 1980), p. 143-63.
On the basis of a comparative analysis of Uruguay, Pakistan and Turkey, the author argues that the most critical phase in the transition from civilian to military rule begins with the decision of civilian government leaders firstly to invoke special emergency powers, and secondly to summon the armed forces to apply those powers.

316 **The rise of military politics in Uruguay.**
Ronald H. McDonald. *Inter-American Economic Affairs*, vol. 28, no. 4 (Spring 1975), p. 25-43.
The article argues that 'the growth of military participation was partially sequential, taking on different national institutions in a constantly escalating struggle' which was successful in its objective of reducing violence but at the price of 'national deinstitutionalization'. How was it that a professionalized, non-politicized military reversed its traditions and seized power in 1973? The author suggests it was because the military were perceived as being above politics, thus having public respect while politicians were mistrusted. This is a contentious view, as is the reference to Uruguay's long 'experiment' with civilian politics.

317 **Uruguay: generals rule.**
Jenny Pearce.   London: Latin America Bureau, 1980. 73p. map.
bibliog. (Latin America Bureau Special Brief).
This useful publication is both a general introduction to Uruguayan politics and a
critical analysis of the military régime. It is full of information, and contains also
extended quotations from members of the régime and its opponents.

318 **The military in South American politics.**
George Philip.   London: Croom Helm, 1985. 394p. bibliog.
The régime in Uruguay is considered in a short but perceptive account (p. 344-55)
which concludes with brief reference to the result of the elections in November 1984.
The author takes the view that 'the armed threat posed by the Tupamaros was
probably not very great'.

319 **Las fuerzas armadas: soldados-políticos garantes de la democracia?** (The
armed forces: soldier-politicians, guarantors of democracy?)
Juan Rial Roade.   Montevideo: Ediciones de la Banda Oriental, 1986.
109p. bibliog.
The early chapters consider the history of civil–military relations in previous decades,
the increasingly professional and political military in the 1950s and 1960s, and
characteristics of the military in power. The second half analyses the issues affecting
the military which threaten the stability of the restored democracy.

320 **Kidnapped in Buenos Aires.**
Enrique Rodríguez Larreta.   *Index on Censorship*, vol. 6, no. 4 (July-
Aug. 1977), p. 22-29.
In July 1976 the author, a journalist with no political involvement, went to Buenos
Aires from Montevideo seeking his son who had been arrested there while in exile.
The author was in turn arrested and tortured, and subsequently moved to Uruguay
where his detention continued until the end of the year. The account of his experience
– related factually and unemotionally – is immensely significant because he gives the
names of the Uruguayan military torturers and the addresses where the acts took
place. Ten years later at least one of the named individuals is openly acknowledged to
have committed acts which violated human rights. The article is preceded by 'In
defence of the word', an account of literary censorship by Eduardo Galeano (p. 15-20),
and a poem by Mario Benedetti. For a list of the twenty-nine articles and features on
Uruguay published by *Index* during 1974-84 (including works by Martínez Moreno and
Onetti), see vol. 14, no. 5 (Oct. 1985), p. 51.

Democratization

321 **Uruguay: the challenge of democratic consolidation.**
Miguel Arregui, Charles Gillespie. In: *Latin America and Caribbean Contemporary Record, vol. V, 1985-6.* Edited by Abraham F. Lowenthal. New York; London: Holmes and Meier, 1988, p. B205-30.

This is a useful and factually supported essay, with many references back to Gillespie's earlier published work. It was written probably during the later months of 1986. The essays on Uruguay in earlier volumes of this publication were contributed by Ronald H. McDonald.

322 **Uruguay: back to Utopia?**
Henry Finch. In: *Third World Affairs 1986.* London: Third World Foundation for Social and Economic Studies, 1986, p. 140-49.

Three months after the restoration of democracy, the article suggests that the new government had early successes, but goes on to analyse the probable sources of instability. As the immediate threat of another military coup recedes, so it becomes more difficult to maintain the framework of agreement achieved during the transition. It also suggests that 'the real threat to democracy lies in the performance of the economy in the medium term'.

323 **Uruguay's return to democracy.**
Charles G. Gillespie. *Bulletin of Latin American Research*, vol. 4, no. 2 (Oct. 1985), p. 99-107.

A useful account of the transition to democracy in 1984-85 which concludes that because its outcome has been a return to the status quo ante, 'the structural weaknesses of the democratic system remain, while the challenges it must face have grown'. The greatest challenge is predicted to be industrial militancy, as trade unions seek to restore the level of real wages after the fall of the previous decade.

324 **Uruguay's transition from collegial military-technocratic rule.**
Charles G. Gillespie. In: *Transitions from authoritarian rule: Latin America.* Edited by Guillermo O'Donnell, Philippe C. Schmitter, and Lawrence Whitehead. Baltimore, Maryland; London: Johns Hopkins University Press, 1986, p. 173-95.

Gillespie again deals with the process of transition, focusing on the negotiations between the parties and the military in 1984, but with more analysis of the crisis of democracy and the nature of the authoritarian régime, and ending with the results of the 1984 elections. He concludes 'by stressing the need to avoid executive-legislative deadlock, a built-in danger of presidential constitutions that has been exacerbated by the arrival of a three-party system. The real political problem would seem to be the absence or weakness of party government in Uruguay'. O'Donnell's introduction to the volume contains errors in relation to the Uruguayan case.

325 **Redemocratization in Uruguay.**
Ronald H. McDonald. In: *Liberalization and redemocratization in Latin America.* Edited by George A. Lopez and Michael Stohl. New York; Westport, Connecticut; London: Greenwood Press, 1987, p. 173-89.

Given the date of publication, it is an unexpected and serious limitation on the usefulness of McDonald's piece that it was apparently written in mid-1984, at a time when the holding of elections in November was still in doubt. The discussion is therefore both historical and general.

326 **Freely and without fear.**
Luis Pérez Aguirre. *Index on Censorship,* vol. 14, no. 5 (Oct. 1985), p. 52-54.

SERPAJ (Service for Peace and Justice), created in 1968, is the principal group defending human rights in Uruguay. Here its president describes its work during the period of transition to democracy. In the same issue there is an interview with the writer and Tupamaro leader Mauricio Rosencoff, on his release from prison (p. 48-50); a short story by Rosencoff (p. 50-51); and a poem by Mario Benedetti (p. 52). On page 51 there is a list of twenty-nine articles and features on Uruguay published by *Index* during 1974-84.

327 **Uruguay after the dictatorship.**
David Ransom. *New Left Review,* no. 163 (May/June 1987), p. 114-20.

Ransom writes as one revisiting the country after fourteen years, but it is not clear in what capacity either visit was made (perhaps tourism or journalism), or why he remained away so long. The context of the article is the Law of December 1986 giving immunity from prosecution to military personnel for human rights offences committed during the period of the régime, within which a general description of the state of the country is given. Unfortunately fatuous statements abound ('for a brief period in the mid-1960s it was the only country in the world officially described as going backwards'; 'Their [the military's] towering achievement was to make of Uruguay a country that can now be described, with reasonable accuracy, by the same tired clichés that have been used over the years to dismiss the experience of an entire continent'), and the absence of sources or references reinforces the feeling that none were consulted.

Breve historia de la dictadura (1973-1985). (A short history of the dictatorship, 1973-1985.)
See item no. 172.

Uruguay's new path: a study in politics during the first *colegiado,* **1919-33.**
See item no. 181.

El impulso y su freno: tres décadas de batllismo y las raíces de la crisis uruguaya. (The thrust and its brake: three decades of *batllismo* and the roots of the Uruguayan crisis.)
See item no. 183.

Politics. Democratization

Reshaping the urban core: the politics of housing in authoritarian Uruguay.
See item no. 480.

Singing in exile.
See item no. 619.

Cinemalore: *State of Siege* as a case study.
See item no. 625.

Constitutions and the Legal System

328 **Constitutions of the countries of the world.**
Edited by Albert P. Blaustein, Gisbert H. Flanz. Dobbs Ferry, New York: Oceana Publications, 1971. [14] vols. bibliog.
'Uruguay', in common with the other countries, was first published separately as a pamphlet (edited by Gisbert H. Flanz and Carol Serpa, April 1971, 67p.), and was subsequently incorporated into volume 13 of the collected pamphlets. The text of the constitution of 1967 is reproduced in the translation of the Pan American Union. In addition there is a nine-page constitutional chronology, as well as a shorter supplement by Martin Weinstein, 'The Uruguayan constitution and the 1971 elections', and an annotated bibliography of twenty items.

329 **A new constitution for Uruguay.**
Bulletin of the International Commission of Jurists, no. 29 (March 1967), p. 37-45.
A brief general review of the constitution of 1967 (which was reinstated at the end of the military dictatorship, in 1985), setting it in the context of the country's constitutional development and the political and economic problems of the time.

330 **A statement of the laws of Uruguay in matters affecting business.**
Horacio Cassinelli Muñoz. Washington, D.C.: Pan American Union, General Secretariat, Organization of American States, 1963. 4th ed. 255p. bibliog.
This volume reviews the substance of Uruguayan law (but does not reproduce any individual statutes) under thirty-nine headings (for example, taxation, labour and social legislation, contracts and obligations, registers). The text is very clear, and where doubt might arise over particular terms the Spanish original is also given.

Constitutions and the Legal System

331 **The administration of justice in Latin America.**
Helen Lord Clagett. New York: Oceana Publications, 1952. 160p.
bibliog.
As Chief of the Latin American Law section of the Law Library of the Library of
Congress, the author was well placed to prepare this short but incisive survey. She
found that 'the systems for administration of justice in the various countries of Latin
America are sufficiently uniform in organization and fundamental principles to warrant
systematic treatment in one volume, yet the variations that occur in the details require
careful examination and comparison'. For that reason she adopted a thematic basis for
the work, with chapters on the relation of the judicial to other powers of government;
judicial systems; jurisdiction; special courts and jurisdiction; jury trials; precedent and
jurisprudencia; and judicial guardianship of the constitution. Although material
specifically on Uruguay is limited, it gains in significance from the comparative basis of
the book.

332 **A guide to the law and legal literature of Uruguay.**
Helen Lord Clagett. New York: Gordon Press, 1979. 128p.
A reprint of the 1947 edition published by the Library of Congress (Latin American
Series, no. 26), this work is a very important reference on the Uruguayan legal system.
It is not at all an arid compilation, but in fact a series of studies on the literature
(almost invariably published in Uruguay) relating to the various branches of the legal
system. The main chapters deal with the civil code; commercial law; judicial system;
court reports; civil procedure; criminal code; criminal procedure; constitutional law;
administrative law; labour legislation; and public and private international law. There
are also helpful sections on bibliographies; collections of laws; legal periodicals; and
the history and philosophy of the law.

333 **Uruguay: farm leases.**
Phanor J. Eder. *American Journal of Comparative Law*, vol. 4, no. 3
(1955), p. 438-39.
Interpreting it an 'another illustration of the progressive social legislation which has
been characteristic of Uruguay in recent decades', Eder comments on the 1954 law
designed to protect farm lessees and sharecroppers.

334 **The commercial, bills of exchange, bankruptcy and maritime laws of
Uruguay.**
Compiled and commented on by Daniel García Acevedo, Adolfo Berro
García, translated by Sydney Leader. In: *The commercial laws of the
world*. Consulting editor: Sir Thomas Edward Scrutton, General editor:
William Bowstead. Vol. 1: *The Argentine Republic and Uruguay*.
London: Sweet and Maxwell, 1911. 183p. bibliog.
This compilation is intended to assist those who through trading contacts required
knowledge of the commercial laws of other countries. 'The work does not present a
mere reprint of the codes or statutes, but in its notes and commentaries summarises
everything necessary to a thorough grasp of the principles of commercial law.' There
are introductory sections on Uruguayan legal history and commercial procedure, and
an index. The text is bilingual throughout.

335 **Uruguay: encouraging return to democracy.**
International Commission of Jurists Review, no. 34 (June 1985), p. 20-27.

The article welcomes the return to democracy, and reviews the (especially legislative) activity of the first months of the new government under twelve headings (amnesty for political prisoners, administration of justice, re-establishment of freedom of expression, restitution of political rights, etc). It concludes that the government's measures 'have surprised by their extent even the most optimistic'. Earlier reports by the International Commission of Jurists (ICJ) critical of the status of human rights under the military régime of 1973-85 appeared in the *Review*, nos 16 (1976), 24 (1980), and 31 (1983).

336 **Uruguay: decree extending territorial waters.**
International Legal Materials: Current Documents, vol. 8, no. 5 (Sept. 1969), p. 1067-72.

By decree dated 16 May 1969 Uruguay extended her territorial waters to twelve miles. Helen Lord Clagett translated the text of the decree which is reproduced here. There is no introduction or annotation.

337 **Report on the situation of human rights in Uruguay.**
Organization of American States, Inter-American Commission on Human Rights (CIDH, OEA/Ser.L/V/II.43, doc.19 corr 1, 31 Jan. 1978). 70p.

After reviewing the evidence of the period since early 1973, the report concludes that 'a regime exists in Uruguay under which rights recognized in the American Declaration of the Rights and Duties of Man have been violated'. This conclusion was reaffirmed in a later report dated October 1979. The situation in the final years of the military régime is assessed in Amnesty International, *Report on human rights violations in Uruguay* (London, Nov. 1983, 34p.).

338 **Constitution of the Republic of Uruguay 1967.**
Washington, D.C.: Pan American Union, General Secretariat, Organization of American States, 1967. 67p.

An English translation of the text of the 1967 constitution which restored the one-person presidency, and created the Central Bank, Social Welfare Bank (Banco de Previsión Social) and Office of Planning and Budget (Oficina de Planeamiento y Presupuesto).

339 **The criminal justice systems of the Latin American nations: a bibliography of the primary and secondary literature.**
Richard Rank. South Hackensack, New Jersey: Fred B. Rothman, 1974. 540p. (Publications of Criminal Law Education and Research Center, New York University, vol. 11).

The Uruguayan section (p. 481-511) of this authoritative but unannotated bibliography consists almost exclusively of works in Spanish. About 500 titles are listed under the principal headings of general works, criminal law, criminal procedure, criminology, and military criminal law.

Constitutions and the Legal System

Labor law and practice in Uruguay.
See item no. 450.

The legal position of the professional football player in Belgium, England and Wales, France, Germany, Italy, the Netherlands, Scotland and Uruguay.
See item no. 630.

Administration

340 **La administración pública en el Uruguay: sugerencias para una reforma de la organización administrativa.** (Public administration in Uruguay: suggestions for a reform of administrative organization.)
John O. Hall. Montevideo: Instituto de Asuntos Interamericanos de los Estados Unidos de América, 1954. 90p.
Hall's analysis of the deficiencies of public administration in Uruguay – nine are indentified – and his proposals for their remedy, have not lost their validity since this report was published, although the structure of the executive arm of government was radically changed in the 1967 constitution. A version of the report is said to exist in English (Montevideo: The Institute of Inter-American Affairs, 1954).

341 **National personnel administration in Uruguay.**
James D. Kitchen. *Inter-American Economic Affairs*, vol. 4, no. 1 (Summer 1950), p. 45-58.
In view of the notoriety which Uruguay's bureaucracy had acquired by the 1960s, for its size, inefficiency and politicization, Kitchen's assessment of it is rather bland and generally positive. After examining personnel agencies, personnel functions and working conditions, he identifies as the principal weaknesses of the system its 'absence of active recruitment, lack of pre-entry and in-service training, insufficient job analysis as the basis of the classification system, over-elaborate tenure safeguards, and low pay'. However, these defects do not prevent the system from meeting its primary responsibility of giving effect to government policy, and morale, honesty and performance are thought to be higher than in other Latin American nations. Interestingly, political qualifications for entry seem to be much less important than in most other Latin American states.

Government and politics of Uruguay.
See item no. 269.

Foreign Relations

General

342 **A defensive alliance for the Americas.**
Baltasar Brum. In: *The Monroe Doctrine: its modern significance.*
Edited with an introduction by Donald Marquand Dozer. New York:
Knopf, 1965, p. 83-86.
This fragment of a speech made by Brum, President of Uruguay, in 1921, urges that
the undertaking made by the United States to the nations of Latin America in the
Monroe Doctrine should be made by all those nations to each other. The Doctrine
would thus be 'Pan-Americanized'.

343 **Latin American foreign policies: an analysis.**
Harold Eugene Davis, Larman C. Wilson. Baltimore; London: Johns
Hopkins University Press, 1975. 470p.
Chapter 13 'Uruguay' (p. 273-93) is contributed by G. Pope Atkins. His observation
that 'little has been written concerning the foreign policy of Uruguay' is still
substantially true, but nonetheless he provides a competent and well-balanced
summary. Foreign policy is shaped by the weaknesses of small size and poor economic
performance, by a nationalism made more prestigious by democratic tradition, and by
geographical location between Argentina and Brazil. Hence the objectives of policy
have been the maintenance of independence, especially from her neighbours and the
United States; the promotion of her own political and social values; and the search for
export markets. The techniques for policy implementation include an active role in
international organizations; the promotion of international law and the principle of
non-intervention; and neutrality in and exploitation of rivalries between her two
neighbours. Review of these general aspects is followed by historical sections in which
the Brum, Guani and Rodríguez Larreta doctrines are discussed, and the traditional
suspicion of Argentina is noted.

344 **'Will there always be a Uruguay?' Interdependence and dependence in**
the inter-American system.
William A. Hazelton. In: *Latin American foreign policies: global and*
regional dimensions. Edited by Elizabeth G. Ferris, Jennie K. Lincoln.
Boulder, Colorado: Westview, 1981, p. 61-78. bibliog.
'To dispel any mistaken impression conveyed by the title, Uruguay's future survival is
neither the exclusive nor the main subject of concern in this discourse. Rather,
Uruguay, like other small nations in South America and the circumCaribbean region,
provides an excellent example of a country that must constantly confront the
conflicting demands of interdependence and dependence.' The author underlines the
point that Uruguay's proximity to Brazil and Argentina is both threat to and guarantee
of sovereignty. He also comments on the paradox of import-substituting industrialization: 'the more a small country like Uruguay tries to enhance its survival by
promoting internal development, the greater the likelihood its national independence
may have to be compromised in the process'.

345 **Boundaries, possessions, and conflicts in South America.**
Gordon Ireland. Cambridge, Massachusetts: Harvard University
Press, 1938. 345p. maps.
The two boundary disputes examined are between Argentina and Uruguay concerning
the River Plate and the island of Martín García in particular (p. 34-39); and between
Brazil and Uruguay in the north (the Yaguarón dispute, p. 130-38). The history of
each is given, and in both cases there are grounds for optimism. The first 'may be
expected to be adjusted in the not very remote future by special agreement'; the
disputed boundary of the second 'as adjusted in detail by the successive treaties
appears to be stable and may be considered definitely settled'. Uruguay's existing
treaty relations with the nine other South American countries are also summarized.

346 **Soviet–Uruguayan relations: yesterday and today.**
K. Khachaturov. *International Affairs* (Sept. 1986), p. 67-74.
Written by the president of the USSR–Uruguay Society of Cultural Relations, this
interesting article was published in Moscow, not in the British journal of the same
name. It reviews past relations between the two countries, and in particular the
resumption of diplomatic relations in 1985 after a gap of twenty-one years. There are
errors, notably that Gabriel Terra was a colonel and that his was a 'military coup
d'état'.

347 **Uruguay and her international relations.**
Pedro Manini Ríos. *Inter-America*, vol. 9, no. 2 (Dec. 1925), p. 141-
48.
Written for *La Nación* of Buenos Aires commemorating Uruguay's centenary, the
article examines in somewhat rhetorical style the origins of the nation and its external
relations, especially with Argentina and Brazil. The piece is especially notable for the
argument that Hispanic Americanism is a 'purely historical concept' that should not be
amplified or given operational effect. The author was Minister of Foreign Affairs
during the period 1923-25.

348 **Latin America and the war.**
Percy Alvin Martin. Baltimore, Maryland: Johns Hopkins Press,
1925. 582p. (The Albert Shaw Lectures on Diplomatic History, 1921).
Chapter 5 (p. 349-82) deals with Uruguay, concentrating on the diplomatic history of
the First World War rather than its commercial and financial aspects. The author
emphasizes the strength of Pan-American feeling which caused Uruguay to lead an
attempt at concerted action by the other republics following the entry of the United
States into the war. Pro-Ally sympathies were strong in 1914 and grew stronger.
Relations with Germany were severed in October 1917.

349 **A bibliography of United States–Latin American relations since 1810: a**
selected list of eleven thousand published references.
Compiled and edited by David F. Trask, Michael C. Meyer, Roger R.
Trask. Lincoln, Nebraska: University of Nebraska Press, 1968. 441p.
The entries to this excellent bibliography are organized by period and theme (chapters
1-12), and by country: the United States and Uruguay (p. 343-45) lists over 60 items,
but without annotations. It should be consulted alongside *Supplement to a bibliography*
of Uruguay–Latin American relations since 1810, compiled and edited by Michael C.
Meyer (Lincoln, Nebraska: University of Nebraska Press, 1979), 193p. Essentially the
same organization is adopted. The section covering bilateral relations with Uruguay
lists thirty items on pages 148-49. There is an author index.

350 **El equilibrio difícil: política exterior del batllismo.** (The difficult
balance: the foreign policy of *batllismo*.)
Dante Turcatti. Montevideo: Editorial Arca, 1981. 124p. bibliog.
Foreign policy in the first three decades of the twentieth century is examined in this
work, whose text is supplemented by a chronology and extracts from key documents of
the period. Chapters examine the second international conference at The Hague,
arbitration in Uruguay's bilateral treaties, incidents with Argentina and Brazil in 1907
and 1909, the First World War, Pan-Americanism, and reactions to United States'
interventionism. The difficult balance of the title is presumably a reference to the
batllistas' traditional support for the United States as counterweight to British
influence, Latin American interventions notwithstanding.

351 **Uruguay and the United Nations.**
Prepared under the auspices of the Uruguayan Institute of International
Law for the Carnegie Endowment for International Peace. New
York: Manhattan Publishing, 1958. 129p.
The manuscript of this important document was prepared by Aureliano Aguirre with
assistance in final editing by Eduardo Jiménez de Aréchaga, the distinguished jurist
and secretary of the Uruguayan Institute of International Law (UIIL). The principal
chapters concern Uruguayan policy on international agreements for collective security
before 1944; the foundation of the United Nations Organization; participation in the
UN; and some brief conclusions. Appendices reproduce statements to the General
Assembly by the chairmen of the Uruguayan delegation in 1956 (on the UN Charter)
and 1957 (on the Hungarian uprising and other matters). The text of this volume is
fully documented and indexed, and it constitutes an important reference for this aspect
of Uruguay's foreign policy.

352   **The meaning of the Monroe Doctrine to the republic of Uruguay.**
J. Varela Acevedo. *Annals of the American Academy of Political and Social Science*, vol. 111 supp. (1924), p. 21-23.

As Uruguayan Minister to the United States, Varela delivered a diplomatic but rather lukewarm address on the Monroe Doctrine to the Academy. 'In the Republic of Uruguay the Monroe Doctrine has done no harm during one hundred years . . . What bloody struggles would have been imposed on us if the Monroe Doctrine had not existed? Nobody knows . . . If the Monroe Doctrine is in future times what it has been in the past, in relation to the Republic of Uruguay, a safeguard, a shield against non-American aggression, long live the Monroe Doctrine.'

353   **The United States and the Southern Cone: Argentina, Chile, and Uruguay.**
Arthur Preston Whitaker.   Cambridge, Massachusetts; London: Harvard University Press, 1976. 464p. maps. bibliog.

The first three parts of this book are primarily a general history of the Southern Cone in the nineteenth century, from the turn of the century to World War II, and from the war to the coups of 1973 and their aftermath. The chapters on Uruguay (p. 41-56, 104-32, 256-87, 347-51) do give some prominence to foreign policy, but especially for the post-war period they have a strong narrative base. In addition there is reference to the interpretations of Uruguayan social scientists and historians. The fourth part, on United States relations with the Southern Cone, analyses the region as a whole, and there is relatively little reference to Uruguay after 1945. The bibliographical notes, which cover history and contemporary affairs very generally, are excellent.

354   **Bibliography of Western European–Latin American relations.**
Ulrike Wolf.   Madrid: Instituto de Relaciones Europeo-Latinoamericanas, 1986. 207p. (Working Paper 1).

There are 1807 entries on relations between the two regions over the last twenty-five years, in a variety of languages but without annotations. Surprisingly, only fourteen refer specifically to Uruguay.

Second World War

355   **Battle of the River Plate.**
Geoffrey Bennett.   London: Ian Allan, 1972. 96p. maps. bibliog. (Sea Battles in Close-up, 4).

A short, illustrated but unoriginal account of the battle which concentrates on technical aspects, including armament.

356   **The battle of the Plate.**
Comdr. A.B. Campbell, R.D., with a foreword by the Rt. Hon. Lord Chatfield.   London: Herbert Jenkins, 1940. 256p.

A colourful, dramatized account of the battle with little in the way of documentation. There are sixteen illustrations.

357 **The battle of the River Plate: an account of events before, during and after the action up to the self-destruction of the** *Admiral Graf Spee.*
London: His Majesty's Stationery Office, 1940. 16p. 3 maps.

A brief, factual account of the action of December 1939, 'compiled in the Admiralty from despatches forwarded by Rear-Admiral Harwood and the Captains of H.M. Ships *Ajax, Achilles* and *Exeter*'. There is no reference to the diplomatic exchanges involving Uruguay. The charts of the naval engagement itself are excellent.

358 **The Nazi octopus in South America.**
Hugo Fernández Artucio. London: Robert Hale, 1943. 248p. maps.

Fernández, a philosophy teacher at the University of Montevideo and a member of the executive council of the Socialist party of Uruguay, had campaigned in the 1930s against the spread of fascism and totalitarianism, including its sympathizers in the régime of Gabriel Terra (1933-38). On the basis of his own investigations and from information provided by an alarmed public, a plot was discovered which centred on a German photographer in Salto, Arnulf Führmann, 'the Hitler agent in whose possession was found the plan for the military occupation of Uruguay'. This Nazi conspiracy was taken very seriously by the government of Uruguay, though Humphreys (*Latin America and the Second World War*, q.v.) refrains from confirming that the conspiracy was real. The details of it, and of the growth of German influence in Uruguay which made it 'the key of the Nazi strategy in the River Plate region', form chapters 1, 4 and 7 of the author's vitriolic denunciation of Nazi Germany.

359 **Good neighbours: Argentina Brazil Chile and seventeen other countries.**
Hubert Herring. New Haven, Connecticut: Yale University Press, 1941. 381p. maps. bibliog.

This short introduction to Uruguay (p. 247-53) does not deal specifically with the Second World War, but it does focus on the country's strong anti-fascist stance (and in doing so whitewashes the régime of Gabriel Terra in the 1930s).

360 **Latin America and the Second World War.**
Robert Arthur Humphreys. London: Athlone Press, 1981-82. vol. 1 (1939-1942) 232p., vol. 2 (1942-1945) 296p.

This authoritative work, based on British and US documentary sources, contemporary Latin American newspapers, and Humphreys's own involvement in Allied war-time policy, contains frequent references to Uruguay *passim*, and more detailed consideration in vol. 1, p. 144-48 and vol. 2, p. 120-26. Material on Uruguay's support for Brazil and the US at the Rio de Janeiro conference in 1942, when Argentina failed to sever relations with the Axis, is particularly interesting. 'No Latin American country had followed a more consistently pro-Allied or anti-Axis policy between 1939 and 1942 than . . . Uruguay'.

361 **The drama of** *Graf Spee* **and the battle of the Plate: a documentary anthology 1914-1964.**
Compiled by Sir Eugen Millington-Drake, with a foreword by Earl Mountbatten of Burma and a preface by Sir Philip Vian. London: Peter Davies, 1964. 510p. maps. bibliog.

The compiler was British Minister in Montevideo during 1934-41, having spent fifteen years in the River Plate since 1914 (in which year he first met Alberto Guani, Uruguayan Minister of Foreign Affairs at the time of the battle). He thus 'took an active part in the extraordinary and unprecedented events during the *Graf Spee*'s four days there'. His book consists of extended quotations from other accounts and reports of the affair, supplemented by his own notes and comments 'especially as regards the Uruguayan background at the time, which accounted for the unflinching attitude of the Government and people'. Amongst the works selected from (and translated) are the account of F. W. Rasenack, a gunnery officer of the pocket battleship, and *Un episodio de la segunda guerra mundial en aguas territoriales de la República Oriental del Uruguay* by Alfredo R. Campos, then Minister of Defence (Montevideo: Biblioteca General Artigas, vol. 5, 1952). Oddly, he also quotes extensively from the semi-fictional *Graf Spee* by Michael Powell, producer of the film 'The Battle of the River Plate' (London: Hodder & Stoughton, 1956). The four days in Montevideo are dealt with on pages 283-358, but the Uruguayan interest is extensive throughout. There is also fascinating material on the reunions of and warm relations between those who survived the battle, in which the compiler played a considerable part. There are thirty-eight plates, numerous charts, diagrams and appendices, and an excellent index. Very strongly recommended.

362   **The battle of the River Plate.**
Dudley Pope, with a foreword by Admiral Sir Edward Parry and a preface by Admiral Sir Charles Woodhouse.   London: William Kimber, 1956. 259p. maps.

Pope gives a lively and well-written account of the battle which concentrates primarily on the menace of the *Graf Spee* to Allied shipping, and the naval engagement itself. Montevideo is reached on page 200. There is a useful account of the diplomatic manoeuvres before the scuttling, using captured German sources in particular, but the Uruguayan dimension receives little emphasis. The decision to scuttle is attributed to Langsdorff himself, rather than (as in some earlier accounts) to orders from Berlin. Both Parry (commanding officer of H.M.S. *Achilles* in the battle) and the author emphasize that Langsdorff's decision to steer for Montevideo, defeat and suicide is very difficult to explain. There are twenty-one plates.

363   **The battle of the River Plate.**
Lord Strabolgi, R. N. London;   Melbourne: Hutchinson, [n.d.].
238p. map.

As a former member of the Admiralty War Staff, Strabolgi gives a detailed and factual account of the battle. The book, probably published in 1940, is by no means exclusively concerned with naval aspects, and reproduces many of the communications between the government of Uruguay and the British and German Legations. United Press and Associated Press reports are also reprinted, alongside those of the German News Agency. Captain Langsdorff of the *Admiral Graf Spee* is represented as a man of spirit, character and humanity, a judgment which has stood the test of time; but the decision to scuttle the ship is here assumed to have been Hitler's. There are ninety-four excellent illustrations.

Uruguay under Juan Idiarte Borda: an American diplomat's observations.
See item no. 160.

Economy

General

364 **Cuatro respuestas a la crisis.** (Four responses to the crisis.)
Danilo Astori, Luis Faroppa, Luis Macadar, Israel Wonsewer.
Montevideo: Ediciones de la Banda Oriental, 1984. 151p. (Temas del
siglo XX, 10).
Four leading Uruguayan economists reply to three questions: what are the origins of
the present economic crisis? how long is it likely to last? what are the ways out of it?

365 **The decline of South America's first welfare state: Uruguay's economic
problems in historical perspective.**
Eric N. Baklanoff. *Revista Brasileira de Economia*, vol. 24 (1970),
p. 166-82.
'My purpose is to enquire into the causes that have contributed to Uruguay's postwar
economic problems . . . Two conclusions emerge from our historical venture: 1.
Uruguay's economic engine has been debilitated by official support of high-cost
industry and its corollary, the neglect of the nation's basic pastoral sector; 2.
additionally, this weakened economy has been overloaded with heavy public subsidies
for state enterprises, the burden of social welfare, and a large and growing
bureaucracy.'

366 **Notes on the pathology of Uruguay's welfare state.**
Eric N. Baklanoff. *Mississippi Valley Journal of Business and
Economics*, vol. 2, no. 2 (Spring 1967), p. 63-69.
A brief polemic which attributes Uruguay's deteriorating economic performance to
industrialization, hence the failure to follow New Zealand's example of pasture
improvement (but compare Lovell S. Jarvis, 'Predicting the diffusion of improved
pastures in Uruguay', item no. 429); and to 'grafting a welfare state onto a semi-
feudal, pastoral-agricultural economy'.

367 **Reseña de la actividad económico-financiera.** (Review of economic and financial activity.)
Montevideo: Banco Central del Uruguay, Departamento de Investigaciones Económicas. annual.

The main sections are: the international context; output and employment; prices, wages, and exchange rates; money and credit; external sector; public finance; and principal financial measures. The analysis is supported by abundant statistics.

368 **La crisis uruguaya y el problema nacional.** (The Uruguayan crisis and the national problem.)
Centro de Investigaciones Económicas (CINVE). Montevideo: Ediciones de la Banda Oriental, 1984. 258p. bibliog.

This volume is a collection of papers of varying length on aspects of the Uruguayan economy, by members or associates of the Centro de Investigaciones Económicas (CINVE). There is a historical overview of the Uruguayan state by José Pedro Barrán and Benjamín Nahum; modernization in the rural sector, by Carlos Paolino, Gabriel Porcile, Rosa Osimani and Sonia Sosa; twenty-five years of economic policy failure, by Nelson Noya, Silvia Laens, Luis Casares and Magdalena Terra; and Uruguay's international situation, by Hugo Davrieux and Fernando Antia. The collection is completed by a wide-ranging discussion of the economic and political crisis in Uruguay by Octavio Rodríguez, Celia Barbato de Silva and Luis Macadar, which builds on earlier analysis by Macadar (*Uruguay 1974-1980: un nuevo ensayo de reajuste económico?* q.v.), and concludes by arguing for a new growth strategy based on agro-industry.

369 **Uruguay: ten years of crisis.**
Comercio Exterior de México, vol. 25, no. 3 (March 1979), p. 105-11.

In English, this detailed and polemical summary of economic and political developments during the period of military rule is a valuable contribution. One of its conclusions – 'What does seem clear is that none of the groups or individuals who today possess any capacity of decision have the slightest chance of carrying out an open and unrestricted testing of the popular will' – was certainly true, yet at the end of the following year the military staged and lost a plebiscite.

370 **Estudio económico del Uruguay: evolución y perspectivas.** (Economic survey of Uruguay: evolution and prospects.)
Comisión de Inversiones y Desarrollo Económico (CIDE). Montevideo: Centro de Estudiantes de Ciencias Económicas y de Administración (CECEA), 1963. 2 vols.

The Comisión de Inversiones y Desarrollo Económico (CIDE) was created in 1960, and with the formation of its Technical Secretariat under Enrique Iglesias the following year it began the task of elaborating basic statistical material and establishing sectoral working groups prior to the preparation of Uruguay's first national development plan (item no. 387, q.v.). At the beginning of the 1960s the country lacked the most fundamental prerequisites of rational policy-making: for example, no population census since 1908, no national income accounts. This publication, which gives a global and sectoral diagnosis of the country's economic problems, was therefore a milestone in the process of defining the nature of Uruguay's crisis, although it is no more than a preliminary report, and is somewhat naive in its structuralist-inspired belief in the possibilities of planning and reform. The two chapters of volume I concern the basic problems of the economy, and its evolution. Volume II examines the financial and external sectors, and isolates the main areas requiring decisions of a political nature. An edition of this report was also published by the Banco de la República.

371 **The Uruguayan economy: its basic nature and current problems.**
Herman E. Daly. *Journal of Inter-American Studies*, vol. 7, no. 3 (July 1965), p. 316-30.

One of the first writings in English on Uruguay's economic crisis of the 1950s and 1960s, this short and vigorous diagnosis examines certain cultural preferences (for lethargy, for consumption rather than production), but finds the explanation for the downturn in the economy instead in economic organization. Uruguay combines an enterprise economy with a large state sector, but lacks a 'disciplining, coordinating force, . . . be it the visible hand of the planner or the invisible hand of the market'.

372 **An historical question and three hypotheses concerning the Uruguayan economy.**
Herman E. Daly. *Inter-American Economic Affairs*, vol. 20, no. 1 (Summer 1966), p. 87-93.

The question is: why did democratic, utopian Uruguay of earlier times become a nation in crisis? The hypotheses offered relate to 'misplaced modernity', and are firstly economic, that Uruguay has reached the limits of its small domestic market and its extensive land-use pattern; secondly political, that in passing very rapidly from feudalism to democratic socialism Uruguay failed to absorb certain characteristic features of capitalism, notably individual initiative and market discipline; thirdly moral, that the edifice of modern Uruguay rests on 'the theological assumption of the perfectability of man'. The article does not develop these ideas.

373 **Uruguay, Paraguay.**
Economist Intelligence Unit, country profile. annual. map. bibliog.

Known until 1986 as the *Annual Supplement*, the main sections of the profile are: government and general; population and employment; national accounts; agriculture; fuel and power; manufacturing industry; transport and communications; finance; foreign trade and payments; and trade and exchange regulations. The information is up-to-date and reliable.

374 **Uruguay, Paraguay.**
Economist Intelligence Unit. 4 issues per year. (Country Report no. 46).

Known until 1986 as the *Quarterly Economic Review*, the country report contains a short 'outlook' and more extended 'review' of the economy in the previous three months, including also political developments. A valuable feature is the amount of information expressed in the form of tables and figures.

375 **A political economy of Uruguay since 1870.**
Martin Henry John Finch. London: Macmillan; New York: St Martin's Press, 1981. 339p. map. bibliog.

A wide-ranging study of Uruguay's economic development in historical perspective. Chapters deal with the ideology of *batllismo*, population and society, the agrarian sector, taxation, exports and the meat industry, imports and industry, public utilities, economc stagnation after 1955, and the military régime after 1973. Described by *Choice* as 'the definitive modern economic history in English of Uruguay', the book has seventy tables. A preliminary, less complete edition in Spanish was published as *Historia Económica del Uruguay Contemporáneo* (Montevideo, Ediciones de la Banda Oriental, 1980).

376 **The economy of Montevideo.**
Russell H. Fitzgibbon. *Inter-American Economic Affairs*, vol. 6, no. 2 (Autumn 1952), p. 70-88.

This article is largely a descriptive account of economic activity in Uruguay, which states (but does not substantiate) the view that 'to say "Uruguay's economic development" is a misnomer – it is Montevideo's. The economic growth of the city has been achieved only at the cost of an extraordinary imbalance. It is an imbalance which is at once economic, social, political, cultural, psychological'. The case for economic imbalance was made forcefully by Julio Martínez Lamas, *Riqueza y pobreza del Uruguay* (q.v.), but Fitzgibbon makes no reference to this classic work and does not set out to analyse the relationship between capital and *campo*.

377 **Uruguay: promise and betrayal.**
Eduardo Galeano. In: *Latin America: reform or revolution?* Edited by James Petras, Maurice Zeitlin. New York: Fawcett World Library, 1968, p. 454-66.

Published during the period in which Uruguay's traditional political tolerance was replaced by bitter confrontation, this angry denunciation of the nation's stasis makes good and bad points with equal vehemence. The promise and betrayal are of bourgeois reformism. The author does well to underline 'the incongruency between trade union and political consciousness'. But what does one make of 'It is not an accident that the famous international resort of Punta del Este is worth more than the entire national industry; nor is it by accident that it is in the same country'?

378 **Private and social rates of return to capital in Uruguay.**
Arnold C. Harberger, Daniel L. Wisecarver. *Economic Development and Cultural Change*, vol. 25, no. 3 (April 1977), p. 411-45.

'The primary purpose of this study is to estimate the historical rate of return to capital in Uruguay', which is judged for the period 1967-71 to be within the range of 4.3 per cent to 6.3 per cent. Private and social rates of return on private-sector investment are also estimated which, although they prove to be rather higher than the estimated range for the global rate of return, do not disturb the conclusion that the return on capital is very low. The authors proceed to use sectoral income estimates to assess the impact of taxation; their conclusion is that although the effect of direct taxes is generally non-discriminatory, when indirect taxes are included there is strong discrimination against agriculture, and in favour of housing, relative to the business sector.

379 **El proceso económico del Uruguay: contribución al estudio de su evolución y perspectivas.** (Economic process in Uruguay: a contribution to the study of its evolution and perspectives.)
Montevideo: Instituto de Economía, Universidad de la República, 1969. 423p.

The political and economic changes which occurred in Uruguay during 1968, in the first year of Pacheco Areco's administration, gave rise to a general view that a phase in the country's development had come to an end. This work, the product of collaboration amongst the researchers of the Institute of Economics, sought to define and interpret the significance of those changes in terms of the country's economic development. The work is organized in three parts: general tendencies in the economy since 1930; the inflationary process since 1954; and the stabilization policies of 1968-69. Publication of the book, implicitly neo-marxian in its theoretical structure, marked an important stage in the radicalization of the social sciences in Uruguay, following the failure of 'developmentalism' earlier in the decade. The problem of Uruguay's underdevelopment was seen as 'the necessary consequence of relations of exploitation between regions, in other words as the product of the nation's situation of dependency . . . the economic process is seen as basically sustained by relations of opposition between the various groups and classes which compose the social structure'. The notion of dependency, which was to dominate analysis of Latin American development in the 1970s, had barely surfaced in 1969.

380 **On the viability of small countries: Uruguay and New Zealand compared.**
John Kirby. *Journal of Interamerican Studies*, vol. 17, no. 3 (Aug. 1975), p. 259-80.

Kirby's article is provocative. He argues from the basic similarities in geography and social development between the two countries, and their parallel economic development until some decades ago, that Uruguay has been a victim of self-deception but should now learn lessons from New Zealand's success. He draws attention to the limited purchasing power of the mass of the rural Uruguayan population, which could potentially increase the size of the domestic market for manufacturing industry, and the low yields per animal and per land unit. Kirby argues that the reasons for the latter are institutional and structural, rather than physical or technological. A more equitable distribution of land, with appropriate financial support by the state, would result in a more responsive and productive agriculture, while its greater capacity to absorb the output of the urban sector would enhance the integration of the economy. Kirby concludes with a challenge: 'real development is a function of political will and leadership'. See also item no. 159: J. P. Barrán and B. Nahum, 'Uruguayan rural history'.

381 **Price expectations and monetary adjustments in Uruguay.**
Ronald S. Koot. *Social and Economic Studies*, vol. 21, no. 4 (1972), p. 474-80. bibliog.

The universality of econometric techniques is well illustrated by this article, which makes substantive statements about the Uruguayan economy without any reference in either text or bibliography to Uruguay itself. The author examined price and money supply data (source unstated) for 1956-68. He concluded that inflation in Uruguay is likely to be self-generating, since 'a rise in prices causes such a reduction in the demand for money that prices rise more than in proportion to the initial rise'; and that

'The simple expectations-adjustment model estimated by two-stage, constrained, non-linear least squares seems applicable to the short-run demand for real cash balances in Uruguay'.

382 **Uruguay 1974-1980: un nuevo ensayo de reajuste económico?** (Uruguay 1974-1980: a new attempt at economic readjustment?)
Luis Macadar.   Montevideo: Ediciones de la Banda Oriental, 1982. 319p. (Estudios CINVE, 1).
The Centro de Investigaciones Económicas (CINVE, Centre for Economic Research), founded in 1975, was the principal independent group conducting research on the Uruguayan economy during the military régime. This analysis of the functioning of the economy during the period of neo-liberal policy introduces the concept of a 'desajuste básico' (basic imbalance) in the economy: an asymmetry between the conditions of capitalist reproduction in the competitive sector of the economy (i.e. livestock production), and the dependence of the rest of the economy on the redistribution of surplus generated in the livestock sector, which resulted in loss of profitability and stagnation in the latter. The attempt to resolve the imbalance after 1974 was no more successful than earlier attempts undertaken since the 1950s.

383 **Riqueza y pobreza del Uruguay: estudio de las causas que retardan el progreso nacional.** (Wealth and poverty in Uruguay: an examination of the factors retarding national development.)
Julio Martínez Lamas.   Montevideo: Palacio del Libro, 1930. 439p.
'The most serious work to be written on the national reality in the first half of the twentieth century.' This remarkable and impressive book, strangely neglected by Uruguayans, argues soberly and analytically that the nation's progress lags behind its own potential and the achievement of other Latin American countries. Montevideo is portrayed as a suction pump, impoverishing the rural sector in order to finance its own industrial and bureaucratic development. The argument was taken up in the 1960s, especially by external observers, to explain Uruguay's crisis; there is a critique of it in M. H. J. Finch, *A political economy of Uruguay since 1870* (q.v., p. 96-105).

384 **The economic decline of Uruguay.**
David C. Redding.   *Inter-American Economic Affairs*, vol. 20, no. 4 (Spring 1967), p. 55-72.
This is a savage critique of policy errors resulting in economic crisis; the promotion of industry instead of livestock exports in defiance of the laws of comparative advantage, unrealistic wage increases, the deterioration of agriculture, an inefficient state sector, and budget deficits traceable to the cost of subsidies. But the argument is weakened by a lack of historical insight: 'In 1950, Uruguayan prosperity rested on a solid foundation of cattle and wool production'.

385 **Uruguay: economic memorandum.**
Washington, D.C.: World Bank, Latin America and the Caribbean Regional Office, 1979. 201p. map.
'World Bank country studies such as this "Economic Memorandum on Uruguay" are prepared primarily for the Bank's own use. Their purpose is to provide the information and analysis the Bank needs for planning its own lending operations and for its discussions on economic development policies with the officials of the country

concerned.' There is a heavy concentration of statistical materials (national accounts, balance of payments, public sector, output, prices and wages, etc); chapters are devoted to recent economic performance, non-traditional exports, agriculture, and growth prospects. Other economic memoranda on Uruguay have been published by the World Bank from time to time.

Economic policy and planning

386 **Política económica y distribución del ingreso en el Uruguay, 1970-1976.**
(Economic policy and income distribution in Uruguay, 1970-1976.)
Alberto Bensión, Jorge Caumont.   Montevideo: Acali, 1979. 213p.
bibliog.

With so few analyses of income distribution available for Uruguay, this publication is particularly welcome. It demonstrates that between 1970 and 1976, the income share of the middle sectors was reduced, to the benefit of in part the poorest 5 per cent, but mainly the top 20 per cent of income receivers, and especially the top 5 per cent. In the functional distribution, labour's income share diminished, while that of capital grew. These changes are related to economic policy during the period, and the work concludes with policy proposals for achieving a more equal distribution.

387 **Plan nacional de desarrollo económico y social, 1965-1974: compendio.**
(National plan of economic and social development, 1965-1974: a compendium.)
Montevideo: Centro de Estudiantes de Ciencias Económicas y Administración (CECEA), 1966. 2 vols. 315p., 485p.

Uruguay's first plan was prepared by the Comisión de Inversiones y Desarrollo Económico, under the direction of its technical secretary Enrique Iglesias, and was published in 1965. This abstract is the most readily available and easily utilized version. The plan itself was structuralist and 'developmentalist' in nature, and followed CIDE's diagnostic report *Estudio económico del Uruguay: evolución y perspectivas* (q.v.). It proposed targets for the ten-year period (including an annual average growth of output per head of 4 per cent), and a three-year indicative plan for private and public investment. More significantly, it also outlined reforms to be achieved in agrarian structure, industrial promotion, taxation, the financial sector, social security, housing, and education. The failure to give substance to these proposals does not in the least detract from the importance of this document. Volume I contains the overall plan proposals, social and demographic aspects, and the sectoral plan for agriculture and livestock. Volume II has the sectoral plans for industry, energy, transport, communications, tourism, education, housing, public health, public administration, taxation, social security, foreign trade, and the banking system.

388 **Políticas para una economía desequilibrada: Uruguay, 1958-1981.**
(Policies for an unbalanced economy: Uruguay, 1958-1981.)
Luis A. Faroppa.   Montevideo: Ediciones de la Banda Oriental, 1984.
108p.

Faroppa argues that the Uruguayan economy is fundamentally unbalanced, having an internationally competitive agrarian sector, and a manufacturing sector which is inefficient at world prices and dependent on the net foreign exchange earnings of the agrarian sector for its growth. He divides the policy response to this imbalance into two phases. The first from 1958 to 1971 was marked by attempts to liberalize the economy while government at the same time sought to control wage and employment levels. The second phase was that of neo-liberalism, which in fact appeared in three distinct guises in three sub-periods: from 1972 to 1974; from 1974 to 1978; and from 1978 to 1981.

389 **Stabilisation policy in Uruguay since the 1950s.**
Martin Henry John Finch.   In: *Inflation and Stabilisation in Latin America.* Edited by Rosemary Thorp and Lawrence Whitehead.
London: Macmillan, 1979, p. 144-80.

Measures were taken on three occasions, in 1959-60, 1968, and 1973-74, seeking to arrest Uruguay's long-run inflation. This analysis argues that inflation can be understood only in terms of the economic and political decline from the mid-1950s, and that 'the stabilisation periods correspond to distinct phases of the crisis, characterised by changes in the structure of the state, by shifting alliances within the capitalist class, by worsening symptoms of economic decline affecting the mass of the population, and by the emergence of new relationships with an evolving international economy'.

390 **The Uruguayan experience with liberalization and stabilization, 1974-1981.**
James Hanson, Jaime de Melo.   *Journal of Interamerican Studies,*
vol. 25, no. 4 (Nov. 1983), p. 477-508. bibliog.

This article reviews economic policy and performance during the first eight years of the military régime, in which the objectives of stabilization (essentially reducing inflationary pressures) and reduced government intervention in the economy were pursued. The authors, World Bank economists, mention in passing the fact of an authoritarian government, but do not appear to regard it as significant to an understanding of the period. Anti-inflation policy was orthodox during 1974-78, but had only limited success. From 1978 until its abandonment in chaos in 1982, the practice of announcing devaluations of the peso months ahead of their implementation was the central instrument of the stabilization effort, but no account is given of how this foreign doctrine was imported into Uruguay, or of its legacy. Liberalization cum stabilization is given the credit for the improved growth performance of the period, which to judge from this account imposed no costs on anyone. By the same authors, making identical points, but with greater technical sophistication and five general lessons instead of only two, is 'External shocks, financial reforms, and stabilization attempts in Uruguay during 1974-83', *World Development,* vol. 13, no. 8 (1985), p. 917-39. This article notes that 'the stabilization episode ended with generalized loan defaults and a banking crisis. In addition, GDP [gross domestic product] fell in 1982 and in 1983, when unemployment reached 15.5%', but does not speculate on any connection between the policy and the aftermath.

391 **La desigualdad como estrategia: la asignación de recursos en el Uruguay neo-liberal.** (Inequality as strategy: resource allocation in neo-liberal Uruguay.)
Alicia Melgar, Fabio Villalobos. Montevideo: Centro Latinoamericano de Economía Humana/Ediciones de la Banda Oriental, 1986. 144p.

During the period of the military dictatorship after 1973, the implementation of neo-liberal policies resulted in falling real wage rates and a sharp increase in income concentration. The authors trace this process and its implications. They note that it had very little effect in raising the rate of domestic saving, the growth of investment in the period being due fundamentally to the public sector. On the other hand income concentration and declining levels of tariff protection had an important effect on the structure of the economy.

392 **Microeconomic adjustments in Uruguay during 1973-81: the interplay of real and financial shocks.**
Jaime de Melo, Ricardo Pascale, James Tybout. *World Development*, vol. 13, no. 8 (1985), p. 995-1015. bibliog.

Using the financial statements of industrial firms, this article analyses the reaction of firms to the liberalization reforms of the military régime. At the macro-economic level 'the Uruguayan economy responded almost miraculously. Output growth jumped, exports sky-rocketed, the financial sector boomed, and new investment accelerated. But, for reasons not completely understood, the economy was once more in crisis in 1982'. There is less euphoria in the analytical section, where three phases are identified: during 1973-75, firms' earnings were low but negative real interest rates allowed them to survive; during 1976-78 higher financial costs were outweighed by greatly improved earnings; but after 1979 financial costs were so high as to swamp earnings.

393 **La política económica en el Uruguay, 1968-1984.** (Economic policy in Uruguay, 1968-1984.)
Jorge Notaro. Montevideo: Ediciones de la Banda Oriental, 1984. 316p.

Notaro's book is an important study of economic policy, in which he identifies five phases. The first, from 1968 to 1972, is dominated by the wage and price freeze decreed in 1968. During the second (1972-73) increased attention was paid to short-term objectives, while the National Development Plan 1973-77 was in course of preparation and approval. Most attention in the book is given to the following three. From July 1974 to October 1978 the central characteristic is 'restructuring interventionism', organized by an economic team led by Végh Villegas. From then until November 1982 is described as 'stabilizing liberalism', a disastrous period whose central device was the programme of pre-announced exchange rates (the *tablita*). From November 1982, when the *tablita* was abandoned, policy was 'interventionism for the survival of finance capital'. In his conclusion the author argues the failure of all these routes, including the attempt to increase the rate of saving by income concentration, and the need to promote a middle way which would combine a more open economy with a healthy interventionism. The text is supplemented by forty-five tables.

394 **Plan nacional de desarrollo, 1973-1977.** (National development plan, 1973-1977.)
Montevideo: Oficina de Planeamiento y Presupuesto, Presidencia de la República, 1977. 2nd ed. 2 vols. 667p., 561p.

Uruguay's second plan was published in April 1973 by Bordaberry's government, a few months before the military coup and at a moment of great political tension. The decision to adopt the plan was taken at a civilian–military conclave in August 1973, and the fact that a second edition was printed in June 1977 indicates the military régime's commitment to it. The plan's diagnosis and proposals are very different from those of its predecessor, and foreshadow the neo-liberal orientation of policy during the régime. Whereas CIDE had regarded inflation as a consequence of economic stagnation and resulting social conflict, this plan emphasized the implications of inflation for economic growth, and saw official bank credit as well as wages as the main inflationary factors. The plan regarded government interventionism in the economy as a fundamental constraint on economic performance and proposed to limit it, elevating market forces and private profitability in its place as determinants of resource allocation. Greater openness to international trade was proposed, with growth to be based on a dynamic export sector. Volume I contains the general plan proposals, public sector investment, and the sectoral plans for agriculture and livestock, and manufacturing industry in general. Volume II indicates the plans for specific industries, construction, energy, tourism, foreign trade, communications, public health, and taxation and public administration.

395 **Economic policy revolution and industrialization in Latin America.**
Pedro C. M. Teichert. Mississippi: University of Mississippi, Bureau of Business Research, 1959. 282p. bibliog.

Until the preparation of national income accounts in Uruguay, as part of the economic planning exercise in the 1960s, quantitative studies of the Uruguayan economy are both few in number (especially in English) and uncertain in quality. Therein lie the strengths and weaknesses of this book, which uses Uruguayan experience as case-study material for the evolution of economic policy towards protection (chapters 4-5, p. 41-56), the role of public sector enterprise (chapter 6, p. 57-76), the evolution of foreign exchange systems (chapter 7, p. 77-91), and the process of industrialization (chapter 11, p. 124-52). There is useful information here, but also naive judgment of the kind that has Uruguay as 'the first country in Latin America to start the economic policy revolution'.

396 **Economía política: teoría y acción.** (Economic policy: theory and action.)
Alejandro Végh Villegas. Montevideo: Ediciones Polo, 1977. 123p.

As Minister of the Economy and Finance between 1974 and 1976, Végh Villegas presided over the design and implementation of neo-liberal economic policy in its relatively pragmatic and constructive phase. Végh expresses himself freely, and this volume, which consists mainly of speeches and interviews given during 1974-77, is particularly interesting. The differences and tensions which existed between Végh and the military component of the post-1973 régime are notorious, and there is evidence of them to be found here.

Economy. Economic policy and planning

Utopia in Uruguay: chapters in the economic history of Uruguay.
See item no. 178.

Military government and the movement toward democracy in South America.
See item no. 310.

Monetarismo en Uruguay: efectos sobre el sector industrial. (Monetarism in Uruguay: its effects on the industrial sector.)
See item no. 413.

Boletín estadístico. (Statistical bulletin.)
See item no. 455.

Formación bruta de capital. (Gross capital formation.)
See item no. 456.

Producto interno bruto trimestral 1975-1981. (Quarterly data on gross domestic product 1975-1981.)
See item no. 457.

International financial statistics yearbook.
See item no. 466.

Statistical yearbook for Latin America and the Caribbean, 1985.
See item no. 469.

National accounts statistics: main aggregates and detailed tables, 1984.
See item no. 474.

Statistical yearbook.
See item no. 475.

Finance and Banking

397 **The tax system of Uruguay.**
Juan Eduardo Azzini, Hugo A. de Marco. *Public Finance*, vol. 11,
no. 2 (1956), p. 112-29.

This is a very detailed analysis of the fiscal and budgetary structure of the country, mostly describing sources of revenue. The importance of indirect taxation in the absence of an income tax is noted, but the authors offer very little judgment or interpretation. There are some data for fiscal year 1953. Azzini became Minister of Finance in the Blanco administration which introduced the Monetary and Exchange Reform Law in 1959.

398 **Domestic and external factors in the determination of the real interest
rate: the case of Uruguay.**
Mario I. Blejer, José Gil Díaz. *Economic Development and Cultural
Change*, vol. 34, no. 3 (April 1986), p. 589-606.

'In this paper, the behavior of the real interest rate in Uruguay is analyzed for the period August 1977–August 1981 . . . Our central conclusion is that, under the circumstances of the country considered, the authorities have little or no control over the real interest rate, which is mainly determined by external factors.' Gil was president of the Central Bank of Uruguay at this time.

399 **La deuda externa y la crisis uruguaya.** (The external debt and the
Uruguayan crisis.)
Fernando Calloia, José I. Gabriel, Mabel Hopenhaym, César
Lavagnino. Montevideo: Ediciones de la Banda Oriental, 1984. 115p.
bibliog. (Temas del siglo XX, 19).

The huge foreign debt borrowed during the neo-liberal years of the military régime is likely to remain a fundamental determinant of economic performance for many years to come. As the authors, members of the Centro Interdisciplinario de Estudios sobre el Desarrollo, Uruguay (CIEDUR), point out, 'Uruguay is today not a country deeply in debt but with a greatly increased stock of physical resources. Uruguay is a poor country which got into debt to make itself even poorer'. The analysis is in six parts: long-run crisis since 1955; the growth of debt in the 1970s; the debt in the crucial years 1979-82; the present agreement with the IMF; short-term prospects; and policy alternatives (in which non-payment is not regarded as a possibility).

400   A note on the pathological growth of the Uruguayan banking sector.
Herman E. Daly.   *Economic Development and Cultural Change*,
vol. 16, no. 1 (Oct. 1967), p. 91-96.

From the late 1950s the banking sector grew very rapidly, in the number of banks and of branch offices. The author relates this to the inflationary process, with banks induced to open new branches as a form of property speculation as well as of non-price competition to capture a share of people's savings. Bank profits were high during this period (though there were also bank failures, not discussed here), but the growth of the financial system was 'cancerous'.

401   **Inversión extranjera en Uruguay.** (Foreign investment in Uruguay.)
Alicia Melgar.   Montevideo: Fundación de Cultura
Universitaria/Centro Latinoamericano de Economía Humana, 1979.
103p. bibliog.

This short book examines the history of foreign investment in Latin America in general and Uruguay in particular, the legal framework for foreign capital, and the amount and character of foreign capital currently in the country. There is a useful list of the fifty largest branches of non-bank international companies, but as the author points out, foreign capital has been interested only in the manufacturing industries in Uruguay which could compete in world markets; currently it is the financial sector which is completely dominant.

402   **The effects of financial liberalization on savings and investment in Uruguay.**
Jaime de Melo, James Tybout.   *Economic Development and Cultural Change*, vol. 34, no. 3 (April 1986), p. 561-87.

The authors examine the de-regulation of the financial system after 1974 to test whether financial liberalization generated efficiency and growth benefits. They conclude that there was some increase in the size of the financial sector ('deepening'), and some improvement in the credit allocation mechanism, as dollar-denominated bank accounts were introduced and interest rate ceilings removed. The general conclusion is that the predicted benefits were present early on, but later deepening was due to macro-economic stabilization policies (and to conditions in Argentina) which left a legacy of severe financial instability at the end of the dictatorship.

403   **The effects of entry regulation on oligopolistic interaction: the Uruguayan banking sector.**
Pablo T. Spiller, Edgardo Favaro.   *Rand Journal of Economics*, vol. 15, no. 2 (Summer 1984), p. 244-54. bibliog.

The authors use the relaxation of entry barriers into the Uruguayan banking sector in the late 1970s, and the reaction of banks already operating in it, to test models of oligopolistic behaviour amongst firms.

404   **Compra de carteras: crisis del sistema bancario uruguayo.** (The purchase of portfolios: the crisis of the Uruguayan banking system.) Luis Stolovich, Juan Manuel Rodríguez, Daniel Olesker, Luis Porto, Guillermo Pomi.   Montevideo: Ediciones de la Banda Oriental, 1986. 188p. (Temas del siglo XX, 37).

In spite of the almost total absence of sources and bibliography, the authors give a factual and highly critical account of the extraordinary events of 1982-83, when the (mostly foreign) commercial banks in Uruguay sold their troubled portfolios to the Central Bank of Uruguay, which received in return fresh credits from abroad. The transaction involved the Central Bank in what was effectively a rescue operation for the banking system amounting to about US$600 million. Amongst the questions raised here is the eventual destination of the collateral for the loans originally made by the banks to the urban and rural private sector, which on default should become the property of the Uruguayan state. There is a great deal of information here, but as the authors point out, the whole dubious business remains shrouded in secrecy.

405   **Uruguay and the proposed Basic Agreement for Inter-American Economic Co-operation.**
Juan Felipe Yriart.   In: *Political, economic, and social problems of the Latin-American nations of southern South America.* New York: Greenwood Press, 1949, p. 17-30. (University of Texas, Institute of Latin-American Studies, Latin-American Studies, 6).

One of a disparate series of lectures given in Austin, Texas, in 1948, this paper covers a number of issues relevant to Uruguay's support for closer inter-American relations, particularly in their economic dimensions, but focuses in particular on the post-war problem of blocked sterling balances. Uruguayan policy on foreign investment is also reviewed. The author was First Secretary in the embassy in Washington.

International financial statistics yearbook.
See item no. 466.

Foreign Trade

406 Uruguay: alternative trade strategies and employment implications.
Alberto Bensión, Jorge Caumont.   In: *Trade and employment in developing countries*. Vol. 1: *Individual studies*. Edited by Anne O. Krueger, Hal B. Lary, Terry Monson, Narongchai Akrasanee. Chicago; London: University of Chicago Press, 1981, p. 499-529. bibliog.

The National Bureau of Economic Research sponsored the research of which this study of trade policy in Uruguay formed part. The authors emphasize the data problem in Uruguay, which required them to focus on policy in 1968 when policy was still directed towards import substitution, rather than the neo-liberal period of the 1970s when policy shifted towards export promotion. The same problem makes precise conclusions difficult. 'The available evidence, however, is all consistent with the hypothesis that the switch to a more export-oriented strategy should result in greater demand for labor.'

407 A brief analysis of recent Uruguayan trade control systems.
Herman E. Daly.   *Economic Development and Cultural Change*, vol. 15, no. 3 (April 1967), p. 286-96.

Daly examines certain economic policy objectives (balance of payments, government revenue, the structure of production and the domestic price level) which may be pursued through controls on foreign trade. He then compares the authoritarian system in force during 1949-59 (characterized by quantitative restrictions and multiple exchange rates) with the price discrimination system introduced by the new Blanco government in 1959 in the Monetary and Exchange Reform Law. The effects of the latter, which enabled the government to exercise indirect control through export taxes and import surcharges, are examined in detail for 1960-62.

408 **The Uruguayan–Argentinian Trade Co-operation Agreement.**
Daniel Ferrere. *Journal of World Trade Law*, vol. 18, no. 4 (July-Aug. 1984), p. 320-34.
The agreement (Convenio Argentino–Uruguayo de Cooperación Económica, CAUCE) was signed in 1974, and has proved very significant in increasing the proportion of Uruguay's foreign trade conducted with her neighbour. This lively and interesting article sets the agreement in the context of earlier trade treaties, including the Latin American Free Trade Association, of which CAUCE was 'a flagrant and open violation'. The author is optimistic that the level of integration between the two countries will increase.

409 **Exchange arrangements and exchange restrictions.**
Washington, D.C.: International Monetary Fund. 1979- . annual.
The section on Uruguay (p. 533-34) of the 1986 report indicates the exchange régime in force at the end of December 1985.

410 **South American markets review 1975-76.**
R. A. Walsh. Epping, Essex: Gower Press/Action for Profit, 1975. 386p. map.
The main sections of the chapter on Uruguay (p. 344-61) are basic data; background; economy; doing business in Uruguay; and major companies. The information is updated to 1972-73.

The politics of regional integration: a study of Uruguay's decision to join LAFTA.
See item no. 259.

A political economy of Uruguay since 1870.
See item no. 375.

International financial statistics yearbook.
See item no. 466.

Statistical yearbook for Latin America and the Caribbean, 1985.
See item no. 469.

International trade statistics yearbook.
See item no. 472.

Industry

General

411 **La industria frente a la competencia extranjera.** (National industry and foreign competition.)
Montevideo: Centro de Investigaciones Económicas (CINVE) – Ediciones de la Banda Oriental, 1987. 288p. bibliog. (Estudios CINVE, 7).

In 1982 the Ministry of Economy and Finance commissioned this major study of the level of effective protection available to manufacturing industry, and the impact on industry of the policy of tariff reductions in the period 1978-82. The results of the research, conducted by a team from CINVE led by Luis Macadar and with five consultants from other countries, were initially retained by the Ministry after completion in 1983, but were later released to form this important publication. Among its most significant conclusions is that price distortions arising from the exchange rate policy of this period were at the root of the financial problems suffered by firms at this time, causing a high rate of bankruptcies.

412 **La industria del cuero: auge y declinación, 1968-81.** (The leather industry: boom and decline, 1968-81.)
Hugo Davrieux.   Montevideo: Ediciones de la Banda Oriental, 1983. 217p. bibliog. (Estudios CINVE, 3).

One of Uruguay's oldest industries experienced very rapid expansion during the 1970s, when leather goods were among the non-traditional exports to benefit from favourable government policy. This study examines trends in the international market, including protectionism in the industrialized countries at the beginning of the 1980s; the reasons for and nature of government support for the industry, in contradiction of its liberal ideology; and the response of the industry to support, in terms of the extent to which it modernized in order to enhance its international competitiveness.

413 **Monetarismo en Uruguay: efectos sobre el sector industrial.**
(Monetarism in Uruguay: its effects on the industrial sector.)
Klaus Esser, Gerhard Almer, Peter Greischel, Edith Kürzinger,
Sonnfried Weber.   Berlin: Instituto Alemán de Desarrollo, 1983.
168p. map. bibliog. (IAD Publication no. 75).
This is an important study of the consequences of the 'neo-liberal' economic model
implemented during the years of the military régime after 1973. The model itself is
analysed in five phases, the fourth of which, the attempt to stabilize the economy
inspired by the 'monetary approach to the balance of payments', was to undo what had
been achieved earlier. The growth of non-traditional manufactured exports, as well as
of new import-substituting industries, is analysed, and there is detailed treatment of
the food, leather, textile and clothing industries. The analysis is supported by
numerous tables.

414 **Breve historia de la industria en el Uruguay.** (Brief history of industry in
Uruguay.)
Raúl Jacob.   Montevideo: Fundación de Cultura Universitaria, 1981.
153p. bibliog.
Packed with information, this general study of the development of industry (not just
manufacturing) is mainly factual in tone and covers the period from colonial times to
1959.

415 **El desarrollo industrial del Uruguay: de la crisis de 1929 a la posguerra.**
(The industrial development of Uruguay: from the 1929 crisis to the
postwar period.)
Julio Millot, Carlos Silva, Lindor Silva.   Montevideo: Instituto de
Economía, Universidad de la República, 1973. 287p. bibliog.
Based on the analysis of primary source materials, the authors show that there was
substantial industrial growth during the period 1930-47, and that this was founded on
industrial expansion even before 1930. In doing so they revise the conventional wisdom
of the time, in Uruguay and elsewhere, that rapid industrialization was a post-war
phenomenon. Changing social structure and its influence on economic policy receive
particular attention. Forty tables support the text.

416 **Industry in Latin America.**
George Wythe, with an introduction by George Duggan.   New York:
Columbia University Press, 1945. 371p.
Industrialization in Uruguay is considered on pages 119-30. There is a useful
descriptive account of the principal industries, though little quantification or detail; and
a discussion of national economic policy which is helpful on import tariff rates, but sees
policy as a 'program of Uruguayan state socialism'. Such themes as the impact of
depression, the Second World War, foreign capital, technology, or the sources of
entrepreneurship, are not adddressed.

Energy

417 **Energy sources and development programs of Uruguay.**
J. Bozzo. In: *Long-term Energy Resources*. Edited by R. F. Meyer.
Boston, Massachusetts: Pitman, 1981, vol. 3, p. 2027-36.
Presented to an international conference, partly sponsored by the United Nations
Institute for Training and Research (UNITAR) in 1979, the paper reviews energy
consumption by type, possibilities for developing renewable and non-renewable energy
sources, and work planned.

418 **Hydropower in Uruguay.**
A. R. Fontal. *International Water Power and Dam Construction*,
vol. 38, no. 6 (June 1986), p. 27-28.
The main conclusion of this review of hydroelectricity potential and installed capacity
is that '76 per cent of the overall theoretical hydroelectric potential of the country is at
present being exploited'. There are four tables summarizing aspects of existing plant
and river basins, two photographs, and a topological map.

419 **Electricity generation planning for Uruguay.**
T. Wyatt. *International Water Power and Dam Construction*, vol. 38,
no. 6 (June 1986), p. 36-42. map.
'In 1980 a study was undertaken to plan expansion of the electricity generation system
in Uruguay. This included identifying schemes for exploiting the remaining hydropower potential. The paper outlines the main activities included in the study and the
results obtained.' Although there is some methodological content, there is also close
attention to energy demand and supply conditions in Uruguay, and the sensitivity of
expansion plans to changes in these conditions. 'Emphasis is placed on the account
taken of reservoir release policy when estimating future system operating costs and
supply reliability.' There are three tables and four figures.

Industrial statistics yearbook.
See item no. 471.

Livestock and Agriculture

420 **La evolución tecnológica de la ganadería uruguaya 1930-1977.** (The technological evolution of the Uruguayan livestock industry, 1930-1977.)
Danilo Astori, with the collaboration of José Alonso, Jorge Coll, Carlos Peixoto. Montevideo: Ediciones de la Banda Oriental, 1979. 471p. bibliog.

The fundamental importance of stagnation in the livestock sector to the performance of the Uruguayan economy as a whole, and the perception that its stagnation is rooted in a technological backwardness, makes this a work of great importance. Astori contrasts different interpretations of the problem from structuralist, dependency, and World Bank perspectives; the availability of technology in genetic improvement, nutrition, health, and management; the adoption of this technology; and the attitude of livestock producers and of the public sector. The bibliography is of technical research published in Uruguay, organized under the four headings, and not of materials relevant to a study of the problem. An appendix lists 116 laws and decrees concerned with the generation and diffusion of livestock technology. The author concludes that technological stagnation is a structural characteristic of the livestock industry in all its aspects. Adoption of improved nutrition technology has proved unprofitable or excessively risky to producers, who in turn have not pressed for increased state resources to be devoted to overcoming the problem. Readers will differ in the extent to which they accept Astori's emphasis on 'the dominating presence of capitalist rationality and the country's relations of dependency to the rest of the world in all the strategic variables of [his] interpretation . . .'.

421 **Uruguayan research on forage problems.**
Alberto Boerger, translated by G. M. Roseveare. *Herbage Reviews*, vol. 8 (Sept.-Dec. 1940), p. 143-66. bibliog.

For over twenty years Boerger, director of the agricultural research station 'La Estanzuela', had supervised studies aimed at improving the yield of the country's grasslands. The fact that this remains a fundamental problem for the livestock industry

125

gives added significance to his efforts. This paper was presented to the Eighth American Scientific Congress in 1940. It consists of a brief review of the nature of the forage problem, and a chronological list of about 300 published works relating to it. Only a few are in English, but the titles of all are given in English. There are no annotations.

422 **The agricultural development of Uruguay: problems of government policy.**
Russell H. Brannon, with a foreword by Lowell S. Hardin.   New York: Praeger, 1968. 366p. maps. bibliog.

This important book is one of the 'benchmark' studies of Latin American agriculture sponsored by the Ford Foundation. Its analysis of the problems of the livestock and arable sectors is set within the context of the evolution of the national economy; and although there is detailed discussion of the technical shortcomings of agriculture, responsibility is firmly laid at the door of government policy. The *batllista* emphasis on the concern for distributive justice, and the period of industrialization by import substitution, resulted in a pattern of disincentives to rural production and investment, in which government pricing and fiscal policy played a major part. The policy conclusions are in sympathy with those of Uruguayan planners at that time, and include a call for 'some restructuring of land ownership'. The analysis is well supported by many tables and figures.

423 **Situación económica y social del Uruguay rural.** (Economic and social situation of rural Uruguay.)
Centro Latinoamericano de Economía Humana (CLEH) – CINAM. Montevideo: Ministerio de Ganadería y Agricultura, 1964. 520p. maps.

The most important result of Uruguay's flirtation with economic planning in the early 1960s was the accumulation of data and diagnosis where ignorance had previously prevailed. The CLEH–CINAM report, prepared under contract to the government, was part of that effort. It is an encyclopaedic survey of the problems of the rural areas, with very complete documentation including over 400 tables, figures and maps. The largest part is devoted to descriptive treatment of economic conditions, the relationship of rural centres to local areas, and population and living standards. The second part offers interpretation of the problems of rural poverty, stagnation of production and backward regions. The final part consists of policy recommendations which are broadly structuralist in character, including the redistribution of land and adoption of the 'family farm' as the basic farm unit. There is some evidence also of inelastic supply responses to price changes. On the other hand, there is little evidence that large-sized farms use land less productively than those of medium size. This report is a mine of information which has not lost its relevance.

424 **Herbage abstracts.**
Commonwealth Bureau of Pastures and Field Crops.   Farnham Royal, Slough: Commonwealth Agricultural Bureaux. monthly.

Prepared by the Grassland Research Institute at Hurley, this work lists and gives abstracts of publications on pasture. Those on Uruguay mostly emanate from the Centro de Investigaciones Agrícolas 'Alberto Boerger' at La Estanzuela.

425 **Soils and fertilizers.**
Commonwealth Bureau of Soils. Farnham Royal, Slough:
Commonwealth Agricultural Bureaux. monthly.

Prepared by the Rothamsted Experimental Station in Hertfordshire, this work lists and gives abstracts of publications on soils and fertilizers, a number of which relate to Uruguay.

426 **The military regime and dominant class interests in Uruguay, 1973-1982.**
Martin Henry John Finch. In: *Generals in retreat: the crisis of military rule in Latin America.* Edited by Philip J. O'Brien, Paul Anthony Cammack. Manchester University Press, 1985, p. 89-114.

The position of the landowning class forms the central theme of this work. The economic strategy implemented by the military régime, based on neo-liberal principles, might have been expected to favour the interests of the landowners who produce efficiently at world prices. However, it was not until 1978 that the régime effectively liberalized the rural sector, but by 1980 the cattle sector was again in crisis. Following sections on the military régime, and on relations between the landowners and the state before 1973, the author offers explanations for the discrimination against the livestock sector during 1974-78, for the change of policy, and for the crisis in the sector after 1980. The conclusion tentatively suggests a degree of continuity between civilian and military régimes in their treatment of the livestock sector, because of its difficulty in forming political alliances with other fractions of the capitalist class.

427 **Livestock in Latin America: status, problems and prospects. Vol. I: Colombia, Mexico, Uruguay and Venezuela.**
New York: United Nations Food and Agriculture Organization, 1962.
94p. (E/CN.12/620; sales no. 61. II.G.7).

Uruguay (p. 49-66) is considered under these headings: available resources; production characteristics; factors limiting production; marketing and consumption of livestock products; and exports of livestock products. The analysis is clear and non-technical. A number of factors are isolated as the cause of the stagnation of production, including the rise in the price of land and other inputs, and the reluctance to invest capital in improvements. Two areas are given priority for change: 'the improvement of the condition and handling of pasture-land and the introduction of rational and modern methods of administration'.

428 **Development projects observed.**
Albert O. Hirschman. Washington, D.C.: Brookings Institution, 1967. 197p.

During 1964-65 the author monitored eleven World Bank development projects, of which the Plan Agropecuario (Livestock and Agriculture Plan) in Uruguay was one. Its principal objective has been the improvement of pasture in the livestock sector, and very important insight into the manner of its implementation is to be found at various places in this work. His judgment on it that 'technical change could come about only if it were accompanied by cultural or social transformation' is surely correct; but his conclusion that 'the solutions that were gradually found . . . have started to make this program into a particularly successful operation' seem rather optimistic twenty years on. See also Lovell S. Jarvis 'Predicting the diffusion of improved pastures in Uruguay' (item no. 429, below).

429 **Predicting the diffusion of improved pastures in Uruguay.**
Lovell S. Jarvis. *American Journal of Agricultural Economics*,
vol. 63, no. 3 (Aug. 1981), p. 495-502. bibliog.

The low nutritional yield of Uruguay's natural pastures has been the major obstacle to increased livestock output for many decades. Since 1961 the Plan Agropecuario (Livestock and Agriculture Plan) with financial support from the World Bank has attempted to overcome this problem by making available to livestock producers an improved pasture technology derived from practice in New Zealand. The author, who has evaluated the results of this programme for the World Bank, finds that under the existing relationship of domestic to international beef prices, the maximum area of pasture which can profitably be improved is 13 per cent of Uruguay's pasture land. Some reasons for this extremely low figure are briefly outlined.

430 **Uruguay's agricultural problems.**
Russell H. Fitzgibbon. *Economic Geography*, vol. 29, no. 3 (July 1953), p. 251-62. map.

Although this is a very useful and informative, if bland, introduction to the rural economy, it was Fitzgibbon's misfortune to be writing just before the full scale of Uruguay's economic difficulties became evident. The 'problems' of the title hardly figure at all: 'basically, Uruguay's livestock industry appears as sound as its democracy' (irony unintended).

431 **The criollo: Spanish cattle in the Americas.**
John E. Rouse. Norman, Oklahoma: University of Oklahoma Press, 1977. 303p. maps. bibliog.

Before Uruguay's cattle herds began to be transformed by the import of (mainly) Hereford breeding stock at the end of the nineteenth century, the cattle which populated the unfenced grasslands were Criollos – descendants of the cattle introduced at the beginning of the seventeenth century which ran wild with very little commercial exploitation for a century. This fascinating volume examines the Criollo in Uruguay (see especially p. 72-73, 94-102) as part of the larger story of the breed throughout the Americas. In Uruguay, 'in the mid-1960's, crossbred criollo could still be seen in herds of less progressive owners, but the pure Criollo had disappeared'. There is a photograph from 1964 of a herd of such crossbreeds.

The agricultural land use regions of Uruguay.
See item no. 85.

The grasslands of Latin America.
See item no. 91.

Morphological, physical and chemical properties of major soils from Calagna in northwestern Uruguay.
See item no. 100.

Noteworthy features of Uruguayan soils.
See item no. 103.

Uruguayan rural history.
See item no. 159.

FAO production yearbook.
See item no. 464.

Technology policy and the state in Uruguay, 1900-1935.
See item no. 508.

Transport

432 **Jane's world railways 1986-87.**
Edited by Geoffrey Freeman Allen. London: Jane's Publishing, 1986. 935p.

AFE (Administración de Ferrocarriles del Estado) is listed on page 841. There are details of its chief officers, traffic for 1981-83 ('recent statistics have not been made available'), recent developments and modernization plans (but no anticipation of the abandonment of passenger services at the start of 1988), motive power and rolling stock, and technical details of the diesel locomotive fleet.

433 **Lloyd's ports of the world 1987.**
Edited by John D. Appleton. London: Lloyd's of London, 1987. 729p.

Location, pilotage, accommodation and facilities are listed (p. 219-20) for Montevideo, Colonia, Fray Bentos, José Ignacio (the off-shore buoy for tankers to discharge oil), Nueva Palmira, and Paysandú.

434 **South Atlantic seaway: an illustrated history of the passenger lines and liners from Europe to Brazil, Uruguay and Argentina.**
Noel R. P. Bonsor. Jersey, Channel Islands: Brookside Publications, 1983. 525p. maps. bibliog.

Seventy-one shipping lines flying eleven flags are included here, with Italian (22), British (17) and French (11) companies dominating the trade. There is a brief outline history of each, but the emphasis throughout is firmly on the ships whose individual histories are given in note form. Vessels carrying at most a dozen passengers are excluded, so there is no recent material on, for example, Houlder Brothers. Only one company remained in the passenger business at the time of publication. There are 150 illustrations, including Royal Mail's *Highland Chieftain* which, within a year of conversion to the whaling depot ship *Calpean Star*, foundered at the entrance to Montevideo in June 1960 and lay partly submerged and in full view of the city for many years.

130

435 **Transport and the economic integration of Latin America.**
Robert T. Brown.   Washington, D.C.: Brookings Institution, 1966.
288p. maps. (Transport Research Program).
Written at a time when regional economic integration was perceived as a general
solution to Latin America's economic problems, this study of the transport
infrastructure of Latin America is immensely valuable. There are chapters on the
geographical description of the regions of Latin America; trade and transport patterns;
resources; population and income; shipping policies; ocean transport; other transport
modes; and transport policy proposals for ocean, river and land in the context of South
American integration. Transport provision for Uruguay is not considered individually.

436 **El automóvil en el Uruguay: los años heróicos, 1900-1930.** (The motor
vehicle in Uruguay: the heroic years, 1900-1930.)
Alvaro Casal Tatlock.   Montevideo: Ediciones de la Banda Oriental,
1981. 62p.
Delightfully produced with many illustrations, some in colour, this is a memoir rather
than serious history of the early years of the motor vehicle in the country.

437 **Airlines of Latin America since 1919.**
Ronald E. G. Davies.   London: Putnam, 1984. 698p. maps. bibliog.
The section on Uruguay (p. 513-22) contains valuable information on the pioneer days
of aviation. Its main concern is with PLUNA (Primeras Líneas Uruguayas de
Navegación Aérea), CAUSA (Compañía Aeronáutica Uruguaya SA), ARCO
(Aerolíneas Colonia SA) and TAMU (Transporte Aéreo Militar Uruguayo), with the
emphasis on routes and aircraft. There are nine photographs. Registration details are
given for all aircraft except the modern jets.

438 **World airline fleets, 1986-7.**
Edited by Gunter G. Endress.   London: Aviation Data Centre, 1986.
332p.
The entry for Uruguay lists (p. 47-48) the five aircraft of PLUNA and the twenty of
TAMU. The latter provides scheduled domestic services.

439 **South American steam.**
Martin Henry John Finch.   Truro, England: D. Bradford Barton,
1974. 96p. map.
The section on Uruguay (p. 86-95) comprises eighteen photographs of Uruguayan
railways, mostly steam locomotives, during the period 1967-73. Captions are briefly
informative on the history of the railways and particularly on the types of locomotives
illustrated.

440 **South American packets: the British packet service to Brazil, the River
Plate, the West Coast (via the Straits of Magellan) and the Falkland
Islands, 1808-80.**
Rev. Jeremy N. T. Howat.   York: Postal History Society in
association with William Sessions Ltd., 1984. 283p. maps.
Combining postal history and maritime history, this is an astonishingly detailed and

thoroughly researched reconstruction of the growth of the mail packet service from British ports to (amongst other destinations) Montevideo. The emphasis is on ship sailings, cancellation marks of British postal agencies (several letter covers are reproduced), rather than (for example) estimating the volume of traffic, but the extensive quotations from diplomatic correspondence are fascinating.

441 Uruguay: revitalizing a neglected system.

International Railway Journal (Oct. 1977), p. 28-30. map.

In view of the shutdown of railway passenger services at the start of 1988, this brief and optimistic account is primarily of historical interest. The expansion and modernization planned for the following five years reflects the strategy of the then military régime to promote infrastructural works. The account is illustrated by eight photographs and basic traffic data for 1973-76.

442 Alive: the story of the Andes survivors.

Piers Paul Read.   London: Secker and Warburg, 1974. 308p.; London; Sydney: Pan Books, 1974. 318p. maps.

On 13 October 1972 an aircraft of the Uruguayan air force carrying forty civilian passengers crashed in the Andes at 4,200m. A search for the aircraft proved fruitless and was officially abandoned after eight days. On 21 December, ten weeks later, two survivors from the crash struggled down from the mountains, and were able to guide Chilean rescuers back to the wreckage and fourteen more survivors. They had lived only by eating the flesh of those killed in the crash. The specifically Uruguayan interest in this extraordinary and universal epic, brilliantly related in an 'authorised' account, lies primarily in the social background, life-styles and aspirations of the passengers. Most of them were members of the Old Christians rugby club and former pupils of an élite private Catholic school run by Irish lay brothers in Carrasco, the wealthiest suburb of Montevideo. There are also references to civilian–military relations on the eve of the 1973 coup.

443 Commercial passenger linkages and the metropolitan nodality of Montevideo.

David E. Snyder.   *Economic Geography*, vol. 38, no. 2 (April 1962), p. 95-112. maps.

'In addition to supplying a description of the extensive passenger transport network connecting Montevideo with diverse points in its domestic hinterland, this paper attempts to formulate answers to several specific questions: What important areal differences in passenger linkages to Montevideo are in evidence? How do different properties of these metropolitan linkages reflect a structure of hierarchical association among Uruguayan urban places? What are the comparative roles of the several types of carriers in providing metropolitan accessibility?' Unfortunately the answers to these questions, couched as they are in a fearsome jargon ('time and money losses are powerful frictional deterrents to movement') and displaying a basic ignorance ('the idle Uruguayan *gaucho*, with his abundant leisure'), are less interesting than they deserve to be.

Labour and Trade Unions

444 **El trabajo informal en Montevideo.** (Informal labour in Montevideo.)
Rosario Aguirre, Agustín Canzani, Augusto Longhi, Constanza
Moreira, Raquel Agazzi, Mercedes Achard. Montevideo: Centro
Interdisciplinario de Estudios sobre el Desarrollo, Uruguay
(CIEDUR)/Ediciones de la Banda Oriental, 1986. 237p. bibliog.
An analysis based on sample survey and other data of informal labour and small
enterprise in the city. A feature is the reproduction of ten interviews with participants
in the informal labour market.

445 **Social and labor problems of Peru and Uruguay: a study in contrasts.**
Mary M. Cannon. Washington, D.C.: Women's Bureau, United
States Department of Labor, 1945. 22p.
The author, Chief of the Inter-American Division, toured the countries and gave her
impressions of them in these two lectures, giving particular stress to the place and
problems of women. There is some perceptive comment, but much more introductory
factual material. Collectors of unlikely comparisons ('Switzerland of South America',
'Athens of the River Plate') may enjoy her suggestion of 'Milwaukee with a Spanish
accent'.

446 **International directory of the trade union movement.**
A. P. Coldrick, Philip Jones. London: Macmillan, 1979. 1365p.
The material on Uruguay is on pages 1155-61, and comprises a short history of the
movement, including its persecution by the military régime holding power at the time
the book was compiled, and the names, addresses and international affiliation of thirty-
nine trade unions as reported in 1976.

447 **Historia del movimiento obrero en el Uruguay: desde sus orígenes hasta 1930.** (The labour movement in Uruguay: from its origins to 1930.)
Germán D'Elía, Armando Miraldi. Montevideo: Ediciones de la Banda Oriental, 1984. 184p. (Temas del siglo XX, 18).

Rather little has been written on the history of the working class in Uruguay, a gap which this book goes some way to filling. Making abundant use of quotations from contemporary newspapers and other sources, the authors trace the origins of the movement; the presidency of Williman (1907-11); the period 1911-13; the effects of the First World War and Russian Revolution; and the 1920s.

448 **Sindicato y sociedad en el Uruguay.** (Trade union and society in Uruguay.)
Alfredo Errandonea, Daniel Costabile. Montevideo: Fundación de Cultura Universitaria, 1969. 227p.

Starting from the hypothesis that the pattern of trade unionism in a society is determined not only by its objectives but also by social structures of production, the authors examine the structure and organization of trade unions in Uruguay; their membership; their tactics, with special reference to disputes occurring in 1922, 1946 and 1963; and the ideological orientations of Uruguayan trade unionism. The analysis is primarily sociological rather than historical.

449 **Labor-industrial conflict and the collapse of Uruguayan democracy.**
Howard Handelman. *Journal of Interamerican Studies*, vol. 23, no. 4 (Nov. 1981), p. 371-94.

This article is essentially an account of the decay of Uruguayan democracy in the late 1960s and early 1970s, and the position of the labour movement in that process. The author argues that declining real wage levels during the 1960s sharpened trade union militancy and class conflict, and that repressive legislation before the coup was aimed as much at organized labour as at the Tupamaro guerrilla movement. The position of labour after the coup in 1973 showed a severe deterioration; for example, employers were not allowed to give wage rises in excess of cost-of-living adjustments before 1976, and had no incentive to do so after that control was lifted. Unfortunately the author gives no systematic information on the behaviour of real wages.

450 **Labor law and practice in Uruguay.**
Robert C. Hayes. Washington, D.C.: U.S. Department of Labor, 1971. 88p. bibliog. map. (BLS Report 392).

Hayes was Labor Officer at the United States embassy in Montevideo during 1957-62, and compiled this report while Chief of the Latin American Branch in the Division of Foreign Labor Conditions at the Bureau of Labor Statistics. The detailed analysis of the report is 'intended to provide background material for U.S. businessmen and others who may be employing local workers abroad, trade union and labor specialists, consulting economists, and students'. Following an introductory section, the remaining parts deal with government and labour; labour and management; and conditions of employment. The analysis is detailed and informative, and is supported by numerous tables. There are appendices on occupational groups in 1963; details of major labour laws; names of trade unions with their estimated memberships in 1971; specimen collective contracts; and wages in industry and commerce in 1960 and 1967-69.

451 **Youth and unemployment in Montevideo.**
Rubén Katzman. *CEPAL Review*, no. 29 (Aug. 1986), p. 119-31.
The pronounced fall in living standards during the 1970s resulted in a sharp increase in the proportion of women and young persons seeking work. The recession since 1981 however reduced youth employment opportunities. As a result the number of students increased, but emigration to neighbouring countries continued to be a solution for many in this situation. This empirical study of these trends also observed gender discrimination in the Montevideo labour market, in spite of which young women have since 1981 increased their participation in the economically active population by a proportionately greater extent than have young men.

452 **The urban informal sector in Uruguay: its internal structure, characteristics, and effects.**
Alejandro Portes, Silvia Blitzer, John Curtis. *World Development*, vol. 14, no. 6 (June 1986), p. 727-41. bibliog.
The product of a collaborative study during 1983-84 by the Department of Sociology of the Johns Hopkins University and the Centro de Informaciónes y Estudios del Uruguay (CIESU), this important study focuses on the role of informal economic activity in Montevideo. Traditionally this has had little importance because of state regulation in the Uruguayan labour market and policies of labour protection. The study found that about 20 per cent of the sample survey of those in employment operated in the informal sector; and that there was a clear distinction between employers and employees in the sector, much of it explained by gender difference. Within the sample as a whole, an unusually high proportion of heads of households had taken advantage of pensions schemes and retired. The most general conclusion is that 'a significant expansion of the urban informal sector took place during the years of the Uruguayan neoliberal experiment'. There are seven tables.

453 **Nuestros sindicatos (1865-1965).** (Our trade unions, 1865-1965.)
Héctor Rodríguez. Montevideo: Centro Estudiantes de Derecho, 1966. 2nd ed. 102p.
A brief outline sketch of the history of the trade union movement, focusing on successive efforts to unify the movement.

454 **Women and work in Uruguay.**
Graciela Taglioretti. Paris: Unesco, 1983. 79p. bibliog.
Forming part of a general programme on the status of women, this excellent case-study notes the striking increase in the participation of women in the labour force in recent years. Rather than a continuation of Uruguay's earlier economic progress and social modernization, the trend in fact indicates the reverse. The analysis includes policy recommendations for supporting the role of women in the labour market, and there is a strong statistical base to the argument. See also 'Organizations for low-income women in Montevideo: reenforcing marginality?' by Suzana Prates, in *Muchachas no more: household workers in Latin America and the Caribbean*, edited by Elsa M. Chaney and Mary Garcia Castro (Philadelphia, Pennsylvania: Temple University Press, forthcoming).

Immigration and settlement in Brazil, Argentina and Uruguay: II.
See item no. 194.

La mujer en el Uruguay: ayer y hoy. (Woman in Uruguay: yesterday and today.)
See item no. 237.

Labor legislation in Uruguay.
See item no. 249.

Social legislation in Uruguay.
See item no. 251.

Uruguay: alternative trade strategies and employment implications.
See item no. 406.

Yearbook of labour statistics.
See item no. 465.

Statistics

455 **Boletín estadístico.** (Statistical bulletin.)
Montevideo: Banco Central del Uruguay, Departamento de
Investigaciones Económicas, Departamento de Estadísticas
Económicas. 1969- . monthly.

For many years appearing irregularly but now monthly, the *Boletín estadístico* (normally available without charge from the Banco Central) is the principal source of monthly financial data. The main sections are: money and credit; the balance of payments and foreign trade; public finance; and prices, wages, and exchange rates. The March, June, September and December issues also have an extensive section updating GDP estimates and output series for the principal sectors of the economy.

456 **Formación bruta de capital.** (Gross capital formation.)
Montevideo: Banco Central del Uruguay, Departamento de
Estadísticas Económicas, Sector Contabilidad Económica, 1986.

This valuable publication presents data on expenditure on gross capital formation, gross fixed capital formation, construction, and machinery and equipment, at current and constant (1978) prices for the period 1970-85. There are also some national income and expenditure series for the same period.

457 **Producto interno bruto trimestral 1975-1981.** (Quarterly data on
gross domestic product, 1975-1981.)
Montevideo: Banco Central del Uruguay, Departamento de
Investigaciones Económicas, 1983.

Presents quarterly data for the principal sectors of the economy at 1978 prices, indicating the coefficients used for seasonal adjustment.

458 **Anuario estadístico del Uruguay.** (Statistical yearbook of Uruguay.)
Montevideo: Dirección General de Estadística y Censos (DGEC).
annual.

This is the main statistical source for most economic, social and climatic series. First published in the 1880s, the yearbook has fluctuated in quality with those for the first four decades of this century (when a detailed summary of foreign trade was included) being particularly valuable. In the 1950s and 1960s it became a victim of bureaucratization and the economic crisis, with fewer series and incomplete publication. Performance remained uneven in the 1970s, but an edition in 1981 covered the period 1970-78, and the 1983 yearbook deals (for most series) with 1979-82. In recent years publication has reverted to its proper annual basis. Coverage includes population, education, cultural activity, health, social security, justice, housing, livestock and agriculture, fishing, industry, commerce, services, transport, communications, postal services, energy, foreign trade, public finance, money and banking, tourism, national income accounts, wages and prices, territorial data and meteorology. In some cases series beginning in 1970 are given. The yearbook is indispensable; long may its regular publication continue.

459 **Boletín mensual.** (Monthly bulletin.)
Montevideo: Dirección General de Estadística y Censos (DGEC).
monthly.

The principal features of this publication, which has appeared regularly since 1981, are monthly data (based on household surveys) of consumer prices, wages, and unemployment.

460 **Encuesta anual de actividad económica del sector industrias manufactureras.** (Annual survey of economic activity in manufacturing industry.)
Montevideo: Dirección General de Estadística y Censos (DGEC).
annual.

This annual survey has been in progress since 1970, and data for 1986 were published in January 1988. It contains data on inputs, output, sales, employment, etc, disaggregated by industrial sector.

461 **Encuesta contínua de hogares, 1987.** (Continuous household survey, 1987.)
Montevideo: Dirección General de Estadística y Censos (DGEC), 1988. 117p.

Presumably published annually, this work gives data on population and economically active population; employment and unemployment; hours worked; and underemployment and income. Disaggregation (where appropriate) is by gender, sector of the economy, type of work, status of employment, age group, and level of education.

462 **Estadísticas vitales, 1985.** (Demographic statistics, 1985.)
Montevideo: Dirección General de Estadística y Censos (DGEC), 1988. 65p.

Presents data on births, deaths, marriage, and divorce. It is not clear how frequent publication is, but this publication has data for the previous ten years, and forms a consistent series with previously published data going back to 1961.

463 **Muestra de anticipación de resultados censales. Censo general: VI de población, IV de viviendas, octubre 1985. Volumen I: cuadros. Volumen II: comentarios.** (Selection of preliminary census findings. VI census of population, IV census of housing, October 1985. Volume I: tables. Volume II: commentary.)

Montevideo: Dirección General de Estadística y Censos (DGEC), 1987. 567p., 77p.

Following brief methodological notes, Volume I presents very detailed tabular information from the 1985 census under the following headings: general characteristics of the population; education; migration; economic characteristics; fertility; households; and housing. Volume II gives a brief descriptive analysis of the results.

464 **FAO production yearbook.**

Rome: Food and Agriculture Organization of the United Nations. annual.

The 1986 yearbook (vol. 40, published 1987) has text in English, Spanish and French. Tables are grouped under the following heads: land; population; indices of agricultural production; crops; livestock numbers and products; food supply; machinery and pesticides; and prices. Most data are for 1979-81 (average), 1984-86.

465 **Yearbook of labour statistics.**

Geneva: International Labour Office. annual.

With text in English, Spanish and French, the yearbook has data on Uruguay grouped under nine main headings: total and economically active population; employment; unemployment; wages; prices, etc. There are no entries for Uruguay under hours of work, industrial disputes, or fatal occupational injuries. Most of the data in the 1986 edition are for 1976-85.

466 **International financial statistics yearbook.**

Washington, D.C.: International Monetary Fund. annual.

This is an authoritative source for data on exchange rates; monetary variables; foreign trade; government finance and national accounts. The data are updated and given for the most recent years on a quarterly basis in the monthly edition of *International financial statistics*. The 1986 yearbook gives the series for 1950/55/58-85.

467 **Uruguay, indicadores básicos.** (Uruguay: basic indicators.)

Alfredo Picerno, Pablo Mieres. Montevideo: Centro Latinoamericano de Economía Humana (CLAEH), 1983. 85p. bibliog.

Tables and diagrams present summary data, in most sections from the early 1960s to the present, in eleven sections. They are: the economy; demography; housing; health; employment; education; the family; religion; the mass media; social welfare; and politics.

468 **Uruguay en cifras.** (Uruguay in figures).

Aldo E. Solari, Néstor Campiglia, Germán Wettstein. Montevideo: Universidad de la República, 1966. 177p.

Based largely on the flow of information which became available as a result of the work of the planning agency CIDE (Comisión de Inversiones y Desarrollo Económico) and the 1963 population census (the first since 1908), this volume has over 100 tables and many graphs organized in six sections: population structure; population distribution; labour and employment; literacy and education; housing; and the economy. Text accompanies the statistical material, offering brief analysis of its significance. There is a general index, as well as lists of tables and figures.

469 **Statistical yearbook for Latin America and the Caribbean, 1985.**
Santiago, Chile: United Nations Economic Commission for Latin America and the Caribbean, 1986. 795p. (LC/G.1420).

The text of this standard reference work is in English and Spanish. Uruguay figures in a large number of series under the general headings of social development and welfare; economic growth; domestic prices; capital formation and financing; external financing; population; national accounts; balance of payments; external debt; external trade; national resources and production; infrastructure; social conditions. Most series cover 1950/60/65/70/75/80-84.

470 **Demographic yearbook.**
New York: United Nations Department of International Economic and Social Affairs, Statistical Office. annual.

The 1986 yearbook (published 1988) is the 38th issue (ST/ESA/STAT/SER.R/16). It contains tables of basic and detailed demographic data, including population structure; natality, nuptiality; divorce; mortality; and international migration.

471 **Industrial statistics yearbook.**
New York: United Nations Department of International Economic and Social Affairs, Statistical Office. annual.

Volume 1 of the 1984 yearbook (ST/ESA/STAT/SER.P/23 [vol.1]), published in 1986, deals with general industrial statistics. Data on Uruguay (p. 589-94) are drawn from the *Encuesta anual de producción* (Annual production survey) of the Dirección General de Estadística y Censos (DGEC), and are prefaced by a brief methodological note. The data cover employment, wages, hours, output, and value added, for forty-five industrial sectors for 1980-84.

472 **International trade statistics yearbook.**
New York: United Nations Department of International Economic and Social Affairs, Statistical Office. annual.

The 1985 yearbook (published 1987, ST/ESA/STAT/SER.G/34) is in two volumes. The first deals with trade by country. Uruguay appears on pages 1013-19, with values of total exports and imports for 1950-85, broken down into broad categories and by trade partner for 1980-84, and by individual commodity for 1981-84. Volume 2 deals with trade by commodity.

473   **National accounts statistics: compendium of income distribution statistics.**
New York: United Nations Department of International Economic and Social Affairs, Statistical Office, 1985. 552p.
(ST/ESA/STAT/SER.M/79).
Uruguay is to be found on pages 525-44. Income distribution in 1983 (in Montevideo) is analysed in seventeen tables. The material is drawn from the *Encuesta nacional de hogares* (National household survey) of the DGEC. There is commentary on the methodology, but not on the results.

474   **National accounts statistics: main aggregates and detailed tables, 1984.**
New York: United Nations, 1986. 1784p. (ST/ESA/STAT/SER.X/8).
Drawn from Central Bank of Uruguay estimates, the material on Uruguay (p. 1702-6) covers 1970/74-84, with a breakdown of gross domestic product and gross capital formation. Note that Uruguay is one of six South American countries which does not appear in the companion volume *National accounts statistics: government accounts and tables, 1983* (ST/ESA/STAT/SER.X/6, published 1986), since it failed to provide material in the form required.

475   **Statistical yearbook.**
New York: United Nations Department of International Economic and Social Affairs, Statistical Office. annual.
The 1983/84 yearbook (ST/ESA/STAT/SER.S/10, published 1986) is the 34th issue of this standard statistical reference work. Data on Uruguay are presented in 177 tables under the headings 'general socio-economic statistics' and 'statistics of basic economic activity'. The period covered varies greatly from table to table: some cover selected years from 1965, others 1980-84.

476   **Unesco statistical yearbook.**
Paris: Unesco. annual.
In English, Spanish and French, this source gives information on population; education; science and technology; culture and communication; printed material; cultural heritage; film and cinema; and broadcasting. The 1986 edition has some series starting in 1975, but most cover a shorter period (to 1984). A condensed version of this work is *Unesco statistical digest 1986.*

477   **Statistical abstract of Latin America.**
Los Angeles, California: University of California Press. 1956- . (UCLA Latin American Center Publications).
New volumes of this work appear in most years. Volume 26 was published in 1988, edited by James W. Wilkie with David E. Lorey and Enrique Ochoa as co-editors. It is a major source of statistical information, which is grouped under these heads: main indicators; geographic and land tenure data; social data; socio-economic data; economic data; international statistics; and political data.

478 **World tables.**
Baltimore, Maryland; London: Johns Hopkins University Press for the
World Bank, 1983. 2 vols.

Produced from the data files of the World Bank, volumes 1 and 2 deal with economic
and social data respectively. Some series give selected years from 1950, and there are
annual data from 1970 or 1975 to 1981.

Uruguay: economic memorandum.
See item no. 385.

Environment and Architecture

479 The changing shape of Latin American architecture: conversations with ten leading architects.
Damián Bayón, Paolo Gasparini, translated by Galen D. Greaser.
Chichester; New York; Brisbane; London: Wiley, 1979. 254p.
The Uruguayan architect Eladio Dieste was interviewed (p. 191-213) for this work which was first published in Spanish under Unesco's auspices. The discussion mostly concerns Latin American rather than specifically Uruguayan issues, but Dieste does defend from the example of his own work the use of brick. There are eighteen photographs, including five of his church at Atlántida (1959) and examples of work by Nelson Bayardo, Mario Payssé Reyes and Antonio Bonet. Also shown is the Bank of Caracas building by the Uruguayan architect José Miguel Galia who lives in Venezuela.

480 Reshaping the urban core: the politics of housing in authoritarian Uruguay.
Lauren A. Benton. *Latin American Research Review*, vol. 21, no. 2 (1986), p. 33-52.
Housing and the housing market in Montevideo have received very little attention in the literature on Uruguay. This article helps to fill the gap by focusing on the effects of the Rents Law of 1974, which, as part of the neo-liberal economic policy of the period, aimed at phasing out rent controls. In previous decades, while middle-class families tended to move out of central Montevideo, there had developed a concentration of low-income tenants living in substandard housing (*conventillos*), especially in the financial centre of the city, the Ciudad Vieja, and in Barrio Sur and Barrio Palermo (the traditional centre of Afro-Uruguayan culture). Deregulation of rents resulted in increased homelessness and overcrowding. From 1978 until the end of the property boom in 1981 a policy of eviction and large-scale demolition was applied, which meant the destruction of much of the physically and culturally historic centre of the city, in return for promoting the physical appearance of Montevideo as a Latin American financial centre. In practice this policy 'created a cityscape dotted with empty lots'.

143

And in spite of the régime's technocratic approach to housing, and the abolition of overt political channels, the tradition of state assistance to the urban poor from before 1973 continued in this period with reluctantly-instituted state resettlement schemes for evicted squatters in response to political pressures.

481 **New directions in Latin American architecture.**
Francisco Bullrich.   London: Studio Vista, 1969. 128p. bibliog.

The Uruguayan architects who figure in this work include Julio Vilamajó ('the most independent personality practising in Latin America during the thirties'), Eladio Dieste, Nelson Bayardo and Mario Payssé Reyes. There are seventeen photographs, including houses by Vilamajó, five of Dieste's Atlántida church, and three of Bayardo's Columbarium (1962) at the Northern Cemetery, Montevideo.

482 **Art in Latin American architecture.**
Paul F. Damaz, with a preface by Oscar Niemeyer.   New York: Reinhold, 1963. 232p. bibliog.

There are brief notes on some leading figures, including Joaquín Torres-García (and a photograph of his Cosmic Monument in Parque Rodó, Montevideo), and Mario Payssé Reyes, whose house (1955) is also shown.

483 **La arquitectura en el Uruguay. Vol. I. Epoca colonial.** (Architecture in Uruguay. Vol. I. Colonial era.)
Juan Giuria.   Montevideo: Universidad de la República, Facultad de Arquitectura, Instituto de Historia de la Arquitectura, 1955. 181p.

Preceded by general notes on the country and a brief chronology for the period 1516-1900, the remainder of this volume consists of a survey of works of architectural importance of the pre-1830 period, supported by 149 photographs, plans and drawings.

484 **Una ciudad sin memoria.** (A city without memory.)
Grupo de Estudios Urbanos.   Montevideo: Ediciones de la Banda Oriental, 1983. 101p.

In his brief introduction, Mariano Arana draws attention to the disastrous effect of the construction boom of recent years on the architecture and environment of the city of Montevideo, particularly the Ciudad Vieja. 'Much of the historic, artistic and cultural heritage of the Nation was left open to the laws of supply and demand in the property market' – a market which is notoriously speculative in character. A particular abuse was the decision of the military régime in 1979 to remove protection, as Historical Monuments, from hundreds of buildings. The list included the Club Uruguay in calle Sarandí designed in the 1880s by Luigi (Luis?) Andreoni. The book consists primarily of a hundred photographs of what has been lost, what has replaced it, and what is now threatened.

485 **Latin American architecture since 1945.**
Henry-Russell Hitchcock.   New York: Simon and Schuster for the Museum of Modern Art, 1955. 203p.

Uruguayan architects whose work is illustrated are Julio Vilamajó (Faculty of Engineering building); Raúl A. Sichero Bouret (apartment building on Rambla); and Guillermo Jones Odriozolo and Antonio Bonet (houses at Punta Ballena).

144

486   **Ideas y formas en la arquitectura nacional.** (Ideas and forms in Uruguayan architecture.)
Aurelio Lucchini.   Montevideo: Editorial 'Nuestra Tierra', 1969. 68p.
bibliog. (Nuestra Tierra 6).
Essentially an introduction to the architecture of the period 1750-1900, there are sixty-two interesting but rather muddy photographs. Figures receiving special attention include Tomás and José Toribio, Carlos Zucchi, Bernardo and Francisco Poncini, Víctor Rabu, Ignacio Pedrálbez, Julián Masquelez, Juan Alberto Capurro, and Luis Andreoni (who has the railway station, Italian hospital and Club Uruguay to his credit).

487   **Parks, plans and people: how South America guards her green legacy.**
Mary Rockefeller, Laurance Rockefeller.   *National Geographic Magazine*, vol. 131, no. 1 (Jan. 1967), p. 74-119. map.
Uruguay figures only briefly in this survey (p. 101-4), but it is noted that there are seven small national parks and a programme of forestation.

Education

488 **The literacy campaign in Uruguay.**
Roberto Abadie Soriano. *Fundamental and Adult Education*, vol. 10, no. 1 (1958), p. 11-15.
In 1954 the government of Uruguay initiated a general literacy campaign. As a preliminary step a census of illiteracy was taken, which found a rate of 3 per cent amongst those aged 15-50. More than half of all illiterates were in fact aged over 50. For the total population, the rate in Montevideo was 2.05 per cent, but at the other extreme the frontier zone in the north had rates of 18-20 per cent. The article goes on to describe the general planning of the campaign, and the assistance given by Unesco.

489 **El sistema educativo uruguayo, 1973-85.** (The Uruguayan educational system, 1973-85.)
Rafael Bayce. Montevideo: Ediciones de la Banda Oriental/Centro de Investigación y Experimentación Pedagógica (CIEP), 1988. 2 vols.
A detailed, factual and quantitative analysis of the system of education during the years of the dictatorship. Volume I looks at various dimensions of the system, including literacy rates, coverage and level of instruction, drop-out rates and repeat-years, using the categories of Montevideo/interior, urban/rural, private/public, male/female. Volume II deepens the analysis, focusing on supply and demand factors in education. A third volume of interpretation and evaluation of inequalities within the system is planned.

490 **Autonomy and student co-government in the University of Uruguay.**
León Cortiñas Pelaez. *Comparative Education Review*, vol. 7, no. 2 (Oct. 1963), p. 166-72.
Translated and condensed from the French original, the article emphasizes the 'almost total absence of ties between the central government and the university administration', and the decisive role of students in the university hierarchy. The autonomy of

the university is examined in three phases: outside (and even contrary to) the constitution of 1830; constitutional autonomy after 1918; and under the 1952 constitution and law of 1958. Student co-government was achieved more slowly and (like university autonomy) was partly reversed by Terra after his coup in 1933. The provisions of the 1958 law are spelled out. The author concludes by noting the limited participation of working-class youth in higher education, and calls for students to use co-government to widen the social base of the university population by provision of scholarships.

491   **Education in Uruguay.**
Frances Graham French.   In: *Report of the commissioner of education for the year 1892-93.* Washington, D.C.: Government Printing Office, 1895. vol. 1, p. 337-55.
This short review of education at the end of the nineteenth century is precise, informative and documented. It has sections on the system of education, statistics, supervision and administration, teachers, courses of study, and supplementary institutions. The system described is essentially that of José Pedro Varela ('considered to be the Horace Mann of Uruguay') in the law of 1877. It is worthy of note that 'Corporal punishment is not allowable under any circumstances'.

492   **The international encyclopedia of higher education.**
Asa F. Knowles (editor-in-chief).   San Francisco, California; London: Jossey-Bass, 1977. 10 vols.
The entry for Uruguay (vol. 9, p. 4313-19) is contributed by Roberto Ibargüen. It reviews the history of education, and the administrative structure of the university following the decrees of 1973 and 1975 of the military régime, which deprived it of its autonomy and placed it under the Ministry of Public Education. There are some remarkable errors, such as 'the constitution of 1967, which followed the overthrow of the government', and a reference to industrial decline after the Second World War.

493   **Education in Latin America: a bibliography.**
Ludwig Lauerhass Jr., Vera Lúcia Oliveira de Araújo Hausse.   Los Angeles, California: University of California, Los Angeles; Boston, Massachusetts: G. K. Hall, 1980. 431p. (UCLA Latin American Center Publications, reference series 9).
The emphasis is on works published during 1945-75, and individual journal articles are not listed. There are 208 titles on aspects of education in Uruguay, almost all in Spanish. There are no annotations, and a single index covers authors and titles.

494   **Latin American university students: a six nation study.**
Arthur Liebman, Kenneth N. Walker, Myron Glazer, with an introduction by Seymour Martin Lipset.   Cambridge, Massachusetts: Harvard University Press, 1972. 296p.
A comparative study of student attitudes and activism, the book is based on questionnaire material dating from 1964-65 (when such research conducted by North Americans was regarded with great suspicion in the region), and the analysis makes reference to events up to the early 1970s. Uruguay is not treated separately from the other countries (Paraguay, Colombia, Mexico, Puerto Rico, Panama), but emerges as

distinctive. Compared with the others (excluding Panama, where students refused to answer questions on political activity), Uruguayan students did not share the prevailing conservatism, were more likely to have participated in strikes and demonstrations, and were less contented with their university experience and employment prospects.

495 La Universidad uruguaya desde el militarismo a la crisis, 1885-1958.
(The University in Uruguay from the period of militarism to the crisis, 1885-1958.)
Juan Oddone, Blanca París.   Montevideo: Departamento de Publicaciones, Universidad de la República, 1971. 4 vols. bibliog.

This account of the evolution of the University, between the end of militarism and the law of 1958 which reorganized its functions and relations with government, is a major work of historical scholarship which is indispensable to an understanding of the intellectual development of the nation. Volumes 1 and 2 (688p.) deal with the University as a whole in chronological sequence (vol. 1), and with the development of individual faculties and schools (vol. 2). Volumes 3 and 4 (498p.) are in effect an extended appendix, reproducing lengthy extracts from documents and divided in the same way as the first two volumes. The archive of the University was of course a principal source, but the full list of bibliography and sources is both valuable and impressive, as is the index to the work (both located at the end of vol. 2).

496 Nonformal education in Latin America; an annotated bibliography.
Susan L. Poston.   Los Angeles, California: University of California, Los Angeles, 1976. 268p. (UCLA Latin American Center Publications).

Nine items on Uruguay are listed, three of them in English.

497 Education in Latin America.
Henry Lester Smith, Harold Littell.   New York: American Book Company, 1934.

The education system of Uruguay is the subject of chapter 8 (p. 163-82). Although inevitably dated in certain respects, the material constitutes a useful if uncritical description.

498 Education, occupation and development.
Aldo Solari, Néstor Campiglia, Susana Prates.   *International Social Science Journal*, vol. 19, no. 3 (1967), p. 404-15.

Employing sample survey data gathered in Montevideo in 1959, three well-known Uruguayan sociologists analyse the relationships between education and economic development and education and occupation level. The main substantive finding in a somewhat inaccessible paper is that whereas in advanced countries the level of education required in the occupational structure as a whole increases over time, in Montevideo a phenomenon of 'super-education' has resulted from economic stagnation. 'In Uruguay, various intermediate-level jobs are done by highly educated people because they have no other openings.' The situation is worsened by the fact that half of university students study law or medicine, far in excess of the capacity of these professions to absorb the graduates.

499 **Equality of opportunities and elitism in the Uruguayan university.**
Aldo Solari, Rolando Franco. *NorthSouth*, vol. 6, part 11 (1981),
p. 1-16.

In a valuable analysis of the nature of the University of the Republic, the authors argue that while it may be regarded as a very democratic institution, in terms of free access, free tuition, and adaptation of the system of study to favour those in remunerated employment, there are limits to this democratization. A disproportionately low percentage of sons and daughters of manual workers enter higher education; the very high dropout rate, especially in first year, is associated with the necessity for poorer students to have a job while studying; and while most courses require six years of study, the average duration of study of those who graduate may be almost ten years. This is also likely to penalize the less well-off students.

500 **Uruguay: análisis crítico de los programas escolares de 1949, 1957 y 1979.** (Uruguay: a critical analysis of school programmes of 1949, 1957 and 1979.)
Miguel Soler Roca.   Barcelona: Imprenta Juvenil, 1984. 213p.

The author taught in the interior of Uruguay from 1943 to 1961, and worked for Unesco thereafter, mostly in Latin America, until 1982. In somewhat discursive style the military dictatorship is condemned for its deleterious effects on the education system.

501 **Nuestro sistema educativo hoy.** (Our education system today.)
Alfredo Traversoni, Diosma Piotti.   Montevideo: Ediciones de la Banda Oriental, 1984. 123p. bibliog.

The authors argue that the current low state of the system can be overcome only with the restoration of democratic institutions. This book is no mere polemic against the attack of the military régime on the former system, however, but a wide-ranging review of the evolution of educational policy in Uruguay since the nineteenth century, and the structure and functioning of educational provision.

502 **The present situation and trends of research in the field of special education. Four studies: Sweden and other Scandinavian countries, Union of Soviet Socialist Republics, United States of America, Uruguay.**
Paris: Unesco, 1973. 306p.

The section on Uruguay (p. 273-94) was prepared by Eloísa García Etchegoyhen de Lorenzo, Head of the Mental Retardation Section of the Inter-American Children's Institute (Instituto Interamericano del Niño) in Montevideo. It reports on research projects relating to the learning problems of children having various kinds of handicap, and there is reference to similar work elsewhere in Latin America. In his introduction to the volume John McKenna comments on the Uruguayan experience. The Uruguay chapter has a short bibliography and list of relevant addresses.

503 **The radicalization of the Uruguayan student movement.**
Mark J. Van Aken.   *The Americas* (Academy of American Franciscan History), vol. 33, no. 1 (1976), p. 109-29.

In the aftermath of a student strike in 1917 the Centro de Estudiantes 'Ariel' ('Ariel' Student Centre) was established. The author traces the radicalization of this movement, finding that its early politicization had much to do with a Blanco party leadership (amongst whom was Carlos Quijano) reacting against the political domination of the Colorado party. The University Reform movement does not appear to have been a critical factor. The 'Ariel' Centre disappeared in the late 1930s, but by then the Federación de Estudiantes Universitarios del Uruguay (FEUU, Federation of University Students of Uruguay), founded in 1929, had inherited its radicalism. 'By the year 1960 the triumph of the radical left was complete.' In a brief and rather superficial account of FEUU in the mid-1960s, the author finds anti-imperialism and the rejection of capitalism to be the dominant features of its ideology.

504 **University reform before Córdoba.**
Mark J. Van Aken. *Hispanic American Historical Review*, vol. 51, no. 3 (Aug. 1971), p. 447-62.
The University Reform movement in Latin America is widely believed to have originated at the University of Córdoba in 1918. The author argues, however, that the students of Montevideo, perhaps inspired by the example of Batlle y Ordóñez in government, had successfully pressed for reforms in the Universidad de la República in 1905-8. More significantly, they convened in Montevideo the first International Congress of American Students in 1908, and 'unquestionably contributed most' to its work. Moreover, 'the students of 1908 anticipated almost the entire reform program set forth by the Argentines ten years later'.

Educational backgrounds of Latin American legislators: a three-country analysis.
See item no. 272.

Youth and unemployment in Montevideo.
See item no. 451.

Unesco statistical yearbook.
See item no. 476.

Ciencia y tecnología en el Uruguay. (Science and technology in Uruguay.)
See item no. 506.

Science and Technology

505 Síntesis histórica de la ingeniería en el Uruguay. (Synthesis of the history of engineering in Uruguay.)
Asociación de Ingenieros del Uruguay. Montevideo, 1949. 322p. maps.

Prepared for the First Panamerican Congress of Engineering held in Rio de Janeiro in 1949, this work contains much information and abundant illustration which is very difficult to trace in any other source. Some chapters dwell unnecessarily on the legal framework, others are extremely technical, but for the most part there is a good account of the development of (mostly civil and electrical) engineering in the country. Amongst the public-sector activities covered are roads, railways, sewage disposal works, the Río Negro hydroelectricity scheme, ANCAP (fuel, alcohol and cement), the telephone system, ports, and airport. Eight private-sector companies are also featured, as well as the Faculty of Engineering at the University.

506 Ciencia y tecnología en el Uruguay. (Science and technology in Uruguay.)
Centro de Investigaciones Económicas (CINVE). Montevideo: Ministerio de Educación y Cultura, 1986. 460p.

At the end of 1986 a symposium on science and technology was held in Montevideo, for which this very important book was prepared. It examines the development and current state of various intellectual disciplines (biology, mathematics, chemistry, economics, sociology, history, political science, psychoanalysis, bio-medicine, engineering, and agrarian science), and analyses aspects of the technology problem in Uruguay. The authors (one of whom, the economist Celia Barbato de Silva, provides the preface) are all leading authorities in their fields. The result is a panoramic view of research activity in contemporary Uruguay.

507 **El problema tecnológico en el Uruguay actual: estudio de casos.** (The problem of technology in contemporary Uruguay: case-studies.) Centro de Investigaciones Económicas (CINVE) – Centro de Informaciones y Estudios del Uruguay (CIESU). Montevideo: Ediciones de la Banda Oriental, 1981. 446p. bibliog.

This volume brings together studies of technology policy and technical change in three industries; the leather industry (Luis Macadar); printing (Luis E. González); and the cattle industry (Celia Barbato de Silva, José Maria Alonso and Carlos Pérez Arrarte). The volume is introduced by an overview of economic policy and technological development in Uruguay in the preceding decade, by Macadar.

508 **Technology policy and the state in Uruguay, 1900-1935.** Henry Finch. In: *Technology transfer and economic development in Latin America, 1850-1930.* Edited by Rory Miller and Henry Finch. University of Liverpool, Institute of Latin American Studies, 1986, p. 37-66. (Working Paper 7).

Examines the *batllista* policy and practice of recruiting foreign experts, principally in agriculture, veterinary science, geology, and chemistry, to establish teaching and research facilities in Uruguay. The initiative produced important results, but ultimately failed to create a national technological capacity.

509 **Historia de la química en el Uruguay 1830-1930.** (History of chemistry in Uruguay, 1830-1930.) Jorge Grünwaldt Ramasso. Montevideo: Instituto Histórico y Geográfico del Uruguay, 1966. 204p. bibliog.

Because of the contemporary phenomenon of 'technological backwardness', it is easy to overlook the importance of scientific teaching and research in Uruguay. Grünwaldt's history is a major contribution to filling that gap. From its primitive beginnings early in the nineteenth century, chemistry had risen to claim one of the first chairs at the new university in Montevideo, in 1855. Considerable attention is paid in the book to chemical research outside the university, especially in Latham Clarke's Instituto de Química Industrial, established in 1912. This account contains a wealth of information and numerous photographs, and the primary sources on which it is based are fully referenced.

Literature

General

510 **Spanish American modernism: a selected bibliography.**
Robert Roland Anderson. Tucson, Arizona: University of Arizona
Press, 1970. 167p.
The bibliography lists 125 references for Julio Herrera y Reissig (p. 86-90), and 281 for
José Enrique Rodó (p. 134-43), mostly to Spanish-language works, and without
annotations.

511 **Diccionario de literatura uruguaya.** (Dictionary of Uruguayan
literature.)
Montevideo: Editorial Arca – Credisol, 1987. 2 vols. bibliog.
More encyclopedia than dictionary, the work consists of biographical and critical essays
on an exhaustive list of literary figures, contributed by fifty-two collaborators whose
efforts were directed by Alberto F. Oreggioni. The project in fact began in 1971, but
was disrupted by the impact of the military dictatorship. Each article makes reference
to the critical literature on its subject, and has a bibliography of the subject's work.
There are photographic illustrations. This is a complete and authoritative guide to
Uruguayan literature.

512 **Doors and mirrors: fiction and poetry from Spanish America 1920-1970.**
Selected and edited by Hortense Carpentier, Janet Brof. New York:
Grossman, 1972. 454p.
There are three items of Uruguayan interest in this volume: the Introduction (p. 3-13)
on fifty years of Latin American writing, by Angel Rama, then professor of literature
at the University of the Republic; and short stories by Felisberto Hernández ('The
crocodile', p. 32-44), and by Juan Carlos Onetti ('A dream come true', p. 190-203).

513 **The literary history of Spanish America.**
Alfred Coester. New York: Macmillan, 1928. 2nd ed. 522p.

Chapter 5 (p. 169-95) surveys the literary history of Uruguay, from the verses of Francisco Acuña de Figueroa to the plays of Samuel Blixen and Víctor Pérez Petit. Two dozen other writers are discussed more or less briefly. In the author's view 'the greatest figure in Uruguayan letters is undoubtedly Alejandro Magariños Cervantes'.

514 **A tentative bibliography of the *belles-lettres* of Uruguay.**
Alfred Coester. Cambridge, Massachusetts: Harvard University Press, 1931. 22p.

The principal works of about 320 authors are listed. There are no annotations or index. The very brief Preface, which admits that 'no claim to completeness is made for our list', suggests that poetry is assiduously practised, whereas the less abundant prose production is compensated for by the eminence of Carlos Reyles and José Enrique Rodó.

515 **Spanish-American women writers: a bibliographical research checklist.**
Lynn Ellen Rice Cortina. New York; London: Garland, 1983. 292p.

There are forty-one Uruguayan women writers listed on pages 245-49. The only information given consists of their dates, titles of their work, and the category (prose, poetry, etc) of their writing.

516 **Handbook of Latin American literature.**
Compiled by David William Foster. New York; London: Garland, 1987. 608p. bibliog.

The chapter on Uruguay in this volume of surveys of national literatures is by William H. Kutra, and occupies pages 529-57. In style it is somewhat overwritten, and its laudable attempt to link literary expression with historical development is only partially successful, but it does draw attention to the wide range of Uruguayan writing. 'Defiance and defensive pride are the two themes that characterize the national literary expression in Uruguay's first century as an independent country . . . In the foreseeable future, Uruguayan literature may continue to thrive, but primarily in foreign lands.'

517 **Modern Latin-American literature.**
Compiled and edited by David William Foster, Virginia Ramos Foster. New York: Frederick Ungar, 1975. 2 vols. 539p., 508p.

'This compilation of international critical commentary' assesses the work of eleven Uruguayan writers by reproducing selections from reviews of their work. They are: Delmira Agustini (v.1, p. 16-20); Enrique Amorim (v.1, p. 42-8); Mario Benedetti (v.1, p. 148-53); Julio Herrera y Reissig (v.1, p. 440-5); Juana de Ibarbourou (v.1, p. 453-7); Carlos Martinez Moreno (v.2, p. 52-5); Juan Carlos Onetti (v.2, p. 134-42); Horacio Quiroga (v.2, p. 202-12); Carlos Reyles (v.2, p. 245-8); José Enrique Rodó (v.2, p. 264-72); and Florencio Sánchez (v.2, p. 327-38).

518 **An introduction to Spanish-American literature.**
Jean Franco.   Cambridge: Cambridge University Press, 1969. 390p.
bibliog.

References to Uruguayan literature occur throughout this work, but especially on pages 63-66 (Alejandro Magariños Cervantes and Eduardo Acevedo Díaz); p. 76-77 (Antonio Lussich); p. 152-54 (Julio Herrera y Reissig and Delmira Agustini); p. 179-81 (Carlos Reyles and Javier de Viana); p. 217-22 (Horacio Quiroga); and p. 329-34 (Juan Carlos Onetti, Mario Benedetti and Carlos Martínez Moreno).

519 **The modern culture of Latin America: society and the artist.**
Jean Franco.   London: Pall Mall Press, 1967. 339p. bibliog.

Of principal interest are chapter 2 'The select minority: arielismo and criollismo, 1900-1918' (p. 40-68), which examines the influence of José Enrique Rodó's *Ariel*; and 'The problem of the small country: the case of Uruguay' (p. 242-46), in which the author perceptively examines why 'of the small countries, Uruguay has been most successful in creating a distinctive culture'.

520 **Index to anthologies of Latin American literature in English translation.**
Edited and compiled by Juan R. Freudenthal, Patricia M.
Freudenthal.   Boston, Massachusetts: G. K. Hall, 1977. 199p. bibliog.

An extremely useful guide to 116 anthologies of Latin American literature in English translation. Thirty-three Uruguayan authors are identified as appearing in one or more; in each case the poem/short story/play is named, as is the translator.

521 **The Afro-Spanish American author: an annotated bibliography of criticism.**
Richard L. Jackson.   New York; London: Garland, 1980. 129p.

There is Uruguayan interest in the section on general studies and anthologies, but the most important references are to the works on or by Pilar Barrios (four) and Virginia Brindis de Salas (four). See also by Richard L. Jackson, *Black writers in Latin America* (Albuquerque, New Mexico: University of New Mexico Press, 1979), 254p.

522 **Spanish-American literature in translation.**
Willis Knapp Jones.   New York: Frederick Ungar, 1966, 1963. 2 vols.
356p., 469p.

Volume 1 of this major anthology (*A selection of prose, poetry, and drama before 1888*) has space only for an extract from Juan Zorrilla de San Martín's *Tabaré*. In volume 2 (*A selection of poetry, fiction, and drama since 1888*) there are poems by Julio Herrera y Reissig, Juana de Ibarbourou, Fernán Silva Valdés and Gastón Figueira; prose extracts from Eduardo Acevedo Díaz, Horacio Quiroga and José Enrique Rodó; and short clips from two plays by Florencio Sánchez. Most of the translations are by the editor.

523 **The Borzoi anthology of Latin American literature.**
Edited by Emir Rodríguez Monegal, with the assistance of Thomas
Colchie. New York: Knopf, 1977. 2 vols. 982p.

This anthology of verse and prose offers extracts from a representative selection of
Uruguayan writers. They include Eduardo Acevedo Díaz (short story), Julio Herrera y
Reissig (two poems), Delmira Agustini (poem), José Enrique Rodó (extract from *The
motives of Proteus*), Javier de Viana, Juan Carlos Onetti, and Carlos Martínez Moreno
(extracts from short stories), and Idea Vilariño (three poems). All the writings are in
English translation only. Notes by the editor (himself Uruguayan) on the writers, a
couple of pages each, are insightful, faintly disrespectful, and models of their kind.

524 **Latin American literature in English translation: an annotated
bibliography.**
Bradley A. Shaw. New York: New York University Press, 1976.
144p. (A Center for Inter-American Relations Book).

Both anthologies and individual works, 414 in total, are listed and annotated in this
volume. They are sub-divided into categories of novel/short story/poetry/drama, and
indexed by author, English title, original title, and country. The annotations are
excellent.

525 **Life and literature of the pampas.**
Edward Larocque Tinker. Gainesville, Florida: University of Florida
Press, 1961. 51p. bibliog. (Latin American Monographs, 15).

An attractive and accessible study, Tinker's essay first appeared in unrevised form as
'The cult of the gaucho and the creation of a literature', *Proceedings of the American
Antiquarian Society*, Oct. 1947. Uruguayan authors discussed include Bartolomé
Hidalgo, Florencio Sánchez, Eduardo Acevedo Díaz, Javier de Viana, Carlos Reyles
and Justino Zavala Muñoz. See also by Tinker *The horsemen of the Americas and the
literature they inspired* (Austin, Texas; London: University of Texas Press, 1967), 2nd
ed. revised, with an introduction by Thomas F. McGann, 150p.

526 **Proceso intelectual del Uruguay: crítica de su literatura.** (Intellectual
evolution of Uruguay: a critical analysis of its literature.)
Alberto Zum Felde. Montevideo: Ediciones del Nuevo Mundo, 1967.
3rd ed. 3 vols.

Since its first edition in 1930, this work has constituted the standard text of Uruguayan
literary criticism. Its three volumes are sub-titled *Del coloniaje al romanticismo* (From
the colonial period to the romantic age), 257p.; *La generación del novecientos* (The
generation of 1900), 351p.; and *La promoción del centenario* (Promoting the centenary
of the nation), 256p. The work was designed as an examination 'of our intellectual
evolution in our first hundred years, of the European and international cultural
influences which influenced its development, especially its literature; and of the
sociological factors – internal and external – which affected its evolution . . .'. Every
major literary figure of the period is discussed and assessed. The main parts of volume
1 concern the colonial and romantic ages, and the era of the Ateneo of the 1880s.
Those analysed include Larrañaga, Bernardo Berro, Andrés Lamas, Varela, Juan
Zorrilla de San Martín, and Acevedo Díaz. Volume 2 deals with the age of positivism
and modernism, with chapters on each of Rodó, Vaz Ferreira, Carlos Reyles, Viana,

Florencio Sánchez, Herrera y Reissig, Agustini, María Eugenia Vaz Ferreira and Quiroga, with abbreviated treatment of lesser figures (including Emilio Frugoni). Volume 3 opens with chapters on post-positivism and post-modernism, and on the decline of the University as the centre of creative literary activity. Numerous poets and fiction writers of the first thirty years of the century are then discussed, with limited up-dating of the original text, but none of the major figures of the post-1930 period are included. In spite of the limitations deriving from its age, this is still an indispensable reference.

Novels and short stories

General

527 **Prize stories from Latin America.**
Garden City, New York: Doubleday, 1963. 398p.
In the late 1950s *Life en Español* held a literary contest for the best Spanish-language short novel. Those entries judged best are published in translation in this volume. Two are Uruguayan: 'The Aborigines' by Carlos Martínez Moreno, translated by David Rubin (p. 65-105) which took second prize; and Juan Carlos Onetti's 'Jacob and the other' translated by Izaak A. Langnas (p. 319-59, Honorable Mention).

528 **Latin American writing today.**
Edited by J. M. Cohen.   Harmondsworth, England: Penguin, 1967. 267p.
This collection contains two short stories by pre-eminent Uruguayan writers, translated into English by Jean Franco. They are 'Dreaded hell' ('El infierno tan temido') by Juan Carlos Onetti (p. 34-48) and 'The Iriartes' ('Los Iriarte') by Mario Benedetti (p. 143-49). In his Introduction the editor contrasts the 'sharply etched realism' of the Uruguayans with other national traditions elsewhere in Latin America.

529 **La narrativa uruguaya: estudio crítico-bibliográfico.** (The Uruguayan narrative: a critical and bibliographical study.)
John E. Englekirk, Margaret M. Ramos.   Berkeley; Los Angeles: University of California Press; London: Cambridge University Press, 1967. 338p. bibliog. (University of California Publications in Modern Philology, vol. 80).
The outstanding feature of this book is a bibliography of 265 Uruguayan novelists and 275 story-writers and their 525 novels and 7000 short stories published since the 1840s. In addition to details of publication, for each work the bibliography records in which of nine major libraries (two in Montevideo, the Biblioteca Nacional in Madrid, and six in the United States) the item is to be found, and where appropriate the assessments of literary commentaries on the work are quoted. The bibliography is preceded by an historical introduction (p. 15-95) on the origin and development of the narrative form in Uruguay. There are bibliographical indexes on anthologies which contain the work of Uruguayan writers, and histories and commentaries on the Uruguayan narrative. There is an index of names but not of titles.

530 **The 20th century Spanish-American novel: a bibliographic guide.**
David William Foster. Metuchen, New Jersey: Scarecrow Press, 1975.
227p.

Sixty-five novelists or short-story writers feature in this compilation of references to their work. Uruguayan writers included are Enrique Amorim (20 items); Carlos Martínez Moreno (8); Juan Carlos Onetti (86); and Carlos Reyles (42). Inevitably almost all references are to Spanish-language works, and there are no annotations. There is an index of the critics.

531 **Short stories in Spanish. Cuentos hispánicos.**
Edited by Jean Franco. Harmondsworth, Middlesex: Penguin, 1966.
204p.

Of the eight stories which appear in both Spanish and English (on facing pages), three are Uruguayan: 'The budget' by Mario Benedetti (p. 28-41, translated by Gerald Brown); 'Welcome, Bob' by Juan Carlos Onetti (p. 84-101, translated by Donald L. Shaw); and 'The pigeon' by Carlos Martínez Moreno (p. 136-65, translated by Giovanni Pontiero). There are biographical notes on the authors, and notes on the Spanish texts.

532 **Women's voices from Latin America: interviews with six contemporary authors.**
Evelyn Picon Garfield. Detroit, Michigan: Wayne State University
Press, 1985. 188p. bibliog.

Uruguayan interest consists of a chapter on Armonía Somers (p. 31-51), and another on Marta Traba (p. 117-40) who, though not Uruguayan, set her novel *Mothers and shadows* (q.v.) in Montevideo.

533 **Trends in the Uruguayan short story in the 1970's.**
H. Ernest Lewald, Doris Stephens. *Inter-American Review of
Bibliography*, vol. 30, no. 4 (1980), p. 387-401.

Supporting their conclusion that 'the Uruguayan story of our decade shows a continued strength and vitality', the authors examine some of the work of Tarik Carson, Ariel Méndez, Carlos Martínez Moreno, Julio Ricci, Enrique Estrázulas, and Miguel Angel Campodónico. Numerous quotations are in Spanish, and are not translated.

534 **The contemporary Uruguayan novel: reflections of a society in crisis.**
Corina S. Mathieu, Victor C. Dahl. *Latin American Literary Review*,
vol. 4, no. 8 (1976), p. 57-66.

Drawing on the work of a range of contemporary novelists, the authors note and illustrate the mounting preoccupation since the 1940s to reflect national realities.

535 **El campo uruguayo a través de tres grandes novelistas: Acevedo Díaz,**
Javier de Viana y Carlos Reyles. (The Uruguayan countryside in the
work of three great novelists: Acevedo Díaz, Javier de Viana and
Carlos Reyles.)
Ildefonso Pereda Valdés. *Journal of Inter-American Studies*, vol. 8,
no. 4 (1966), p. 535-40.
This short passage of literary criticism discusses the background of the *campo*, and the
people who inhabit it, in the work of three of Uruguay's major literary figures. Viana's
realism and interest in the psychology of the *gaucho* is contrasted with the greater
romanticism of Acevedo Díaz, while Reyles is represented as a creator of word-
pictures. 'Countryside' is an inadequate, genteel translation of *campo*, failing to convey
the vast extent of the natural rough grassland, and the primitive isolation and heroic
values of its *gaucho* inhabitants, but there is no better alternative. The English
residents of the River Plate called these pastures the 'camps'.

Enrique Amorim

536 **The horse and his shadow.**
Enrique Amorim, translated into English by Richard L. O'Connell,
James Graham Luján. New York: Scribners, 1943. 252p.
El caballo y su sombra was first published in 1941. Its theme is rural social conflict.

537 **Enrique Amorim: the passion of a Uruguayan.**
K. E. A. Mose. New York: Plaza Mayor Ediciones, 1972. 254p.
bibliog.
Amorim was born in Salto in 1900, and after establishing his reputation in Buenos
Aires in early manhood he returned to Salto in 1930. Identification with the interior of
Uruguay (rather than Montevideo) was reflected in the focus in much of his work on
the countryside. Mose's work stands alone as a full-length study in English of Amorim.
Biography and criticism are taken together. Unfortunately the account employs a
persistent and irritating historic present, so that judgments which at first appear
definitive often apply only to a limited period of Amorim's career. There is interesting
material on his radicalism, and his membership of the Communist Party from 1946.
Indeed, Mose concludes that 'Amorim's social passion explains the flaws in some of his
best work and the flawed rhythm of his development as a writer'. There is an excellent
bibliography, but no index.

538 **Contemporary Uruguay as seen in Amorim's first cycle.**
Harley D. Oberhelman. *Hispania*, vol. 46, no. 2 (May 1963), p. 312-
18.
Oberhelman discusses the quartet of novels generally labelled as Amorim's first cycle:
Tangarupá (1925); *La carreta* (The cart, 1932); *El paisano Aguilar* (Aguilar the
peasant, 1934); and *El caballo y su sombra* (The horse and its shadow, 1941). They
develop the theme of conflicts between man and the spiritually barren natural

159

environment of the Uruguayan interior, and within the rural social system. 'In essence Amorim considers the social and spiritual plight of the gaucho throughout the series.' See also by Oberhelman, 'Enrique Amorim as an interpreter of rural Uruguay', *Books abroad*, vol. 34 (1960), p. 115-18.

Mario Benedetti

539 **The truce.**
Mario Benedetti, translated into English by Benjamin Graham. New York: Harper & Row, 1969. 184p.
Originally published in 1960 under the title *La tregua*.

540 **Mario Benedetti: four stories, four styles.**
Oscar Fernández. *Studies in Short Fiction*, vol. 11, no. [2], p. 283-90.
Fernández takes 'Como siempre' ('As always', 1949), 'La familia Iriarte' ('The Iriarte family', 1959), 'El resto es selva' ('The rest is jungle', 1959) and 'Acaso irreparable' ('Perhaps beyond repair', 1968) as representative of four styles in Benedetti's writing. They are, respectively, the reporter on the urban middle-class office workers, writing in simple and direct language with description and metaphor minimized; a more sensitive, technically more accomplished style; the chronicle or record in the style of newspaper or magazine writing; and writings within the trend of fantastic, time-free tales, 'Kafka à la Borges'.

541 **The *écriture* of social protest in Mario Benedetti's 'El cambiazo'.**
David William Foster. In: *Studies in the contemporary Spanish-American short story*. Columbia, Missouri; London: University of Missouri Press, 1979, p. 102-9.
'Despite the acknowledged importance of Mario Benedetti in the contemporary Latin-American narrative, one is surprised by the relative lack of studies devoted to the Uruguayan's works, particularly his short stories.' This contribution to the redressing of that neglect (chapter 8 of Foster's book) is an accessible study of a powerful story published in 1968. In the Introduction, Foster defines *écriture* as 'the series of structural premises that underlie a literary work as a written text'.

542 **The political act in Mario Benedetti's *Con y sin nostalgia* (With and without nostalgia).**
Bart Lewis. *Latin American Literary Review*, vol. 9, no. 17 (Fall–Winter 1980), p. 28-36.
The dominant theme in this collection of fourteen short stories by Benedetti, published in 1977, is constituted by 'the incursions of the political nightmare into the stiff and defeated lives of a Latin American middle class', whose habitual passivity is challenged by violence, terrorism and repression. Lewis's analysis of these stories (with quotations in English) leads him to conclude that 'Benedetti excels in a literary treatment of the political theme'.

W. H. Hudson

543 **The purple land.**
William Henry Hudson. London: Duckworth, 1926. 8th imp. 355p.
Reissued, with an introductory note by Theodore Roosevelt (1916), by
Creative Arts Book Co., Berkeley, California, 1979.

A classic novel whose success in English in the early decades of the century has been
outlasted by the great affection for it in Uruguay. Originally published in 1885 under
the title *The purple land that England lost*, the 2nd edition (1904) bears the more
descriptive sub-title *Being the narrative of one Richard Lamb's adventures in the Banda
Oriental, in South America, as told by himself*. The picaresque (the description recurs
in almost every commentary on the book) story is set in the late 1860s–early 1870s,
and recounts a series of incidents during the narrator's wanderings in the interior.
There is no consensus as to why *purple*: for some it refers to the quality of the light in
the *campo*, for others to the grasses which grow in the interior; but for most it alludes
to the blood spilled in conflicts for possession of the land.

544 **W. H. Hudson: the colonial's revenge.**
Jason Wilson. *Review 31* (Jan./April 1982), p. 53-59.

Although discussion of *The purple land* occupies only part of this article, it provides a
fascinating insight into Hudson's relationship with the River Plate region, which he left
in 1874, and with the natural world. There is important material on Hudson's attitude
to (and short correspondence with) Charles Darwin. On *The purple land*, 'Hudson's
trick is that he adopts the role of an Englishman becoming conscious of the emptiness
of his own culture'.

Juan Carlos Onetti

545 **Three authors of alienation: Bombal, Onetti, Carpentier.**
Michael Ian Adams. Austin, Texas; London: University of Texas
Press, 1975. 128p. bibliog. (Institute of Latin American Studies, The
University of Texas at Austin, Latin American Monographs, no. 36).

The theme of alienation in the work of Juan Carlos Onetti is examined in chapter 3
(p. 37-80). The novels forming the basis of this analysis are *El pozo*, and *Tan triste
como ella*, with less extensive discussion also of *La vida breve* and *El astillero*. Adams
comments briefly on style, noting the influence of Faulkner, before analysing the
theme of alienation and the fragmented image. Quotations from Onetti are in English.
The author concludes that Onetti employs 'a fragmented imagery to convey the
schizophrenic, or schizoid, extreme of alienation'.

546 **The shorter works of Juan Carlos Onetti.**
John Deredita. *Studies in Short Fiction*, vol. 8, no. 1 (1971), p. 112-
22.

Much of Onetti's writing has consisted of novellas and stories, in which his use of
symbolism and explorations in styles of narration are brought into close focus. This

interesting essay draws on the range of Onetti's short writings. 'Onetti's "subjective something" consists in a pathetic and ironic recognition of human aging and decay, of life as tedious compromise, of the futility and necessity of illusion . . . Certainly his habitat, urban Uruguay and Argentina, has offered a natural setting for pessimism and considerations of marginality.'

547   **Ambiguity in Onetti's 'El Astillero'.**
       Beverly J. Gibbs.   *Hispania*, vol. 56, special issue (April 1973), p. 260-69.

'Onetti's work is marked by a fundamental ambiguity that appears in a variety of guises: as doubt, uncertainty, enigma, vagueness, obscurity, inexplicability, indistinctness, unreality, fantasy.' This key to his work is explored in *El astillero* (The shipyard). The author concludes by suggesting that Onetti's characters (like Larsen in this novel), are 'condemned to a predetermined fate struggle to free themselves. To live, in fact, is to so struggle, is to play a game or invent roles, but doing this is also to deceive one's self in a game already lost'.

548   **Psychopathic point of view: Juan Carlos Onetti's *Los adioses* ('The goodbyes').**
       Joel C. Hancock.   *Latin American Literary Review*, vol. 2, no. 3 (1973), p. 19-29.

Hancock argues that 'point of view' is particularly important to an understanding of the enigmatic *Los adioses*, since 'only through a close analysis of this technique does the reader become aware of the narrator's psychopathic mental condition and its effect on the narration'. He develops an analysis of the novel from this perspective, and concludes by suggesting his own explanation of the outcome of the novel.

549   **Into the mainstream: conversations with Latin-American writers.**
       Luis Harss, Barbara Dohmann.   New York: Harper & Row, 1969.
       385p. (Harper Colophon Books).

'Juan Carlos Onetti, or the shadows on the wall' (p. 173-205) is the Uruguayan conversation. It seems to have begun unpromisingly ('Onetti is a man of few words, most of them mumbled or swallowed entirely. He sits slumped, chain-smoking, hunching his shoulders every now and then, looking miserably uncomfortable'). However, the resulting essay gives a fine insight into the nature of the man and his work. But was his great grandfather *really* O'Nety of Irish descent?

550   **Juan Carlos Onetti.**
       Djelal Kadir.   Boston, Massachusetts: Twayne (G. K. Hall), 1977.
       160p. bibliog. (Twayne's world authors series, 469).

Onetti's work is discussed in this study in terms of characterization, treatment of spatial and temporal dimensions, manner of narration, and construction of plot. There is an overview of his style, and an assessment of continuity in his work. The author concludes with 'an attempt to view Onetti and his aesthetics, especially the aesthetics of the mythical, in the light of more recent fiction and the younger novelists'.

551 **Focus on Juan Carlos Onetti's** *A brief life.*
Edited by Djelal Kadir. *Review 75,* no. 16 (Winter 1975), p. 4-33.
Published to coincide with the appearance in English translation of *La vida breve,* the focus contains a biographical chronology of Onetti by the editor and essays on one of the best known of his novels by Emir Rodríguez Monegal, Hugo J. Verani, John Deredita, Zunilda Gertel, and George Levine, and a poem entitled 'La vida breve' by José Emilio Pacheco.

552 **Reading Onetti: language, narrative and the subject.**
Mark Millington. Liverpool: Francis Cairns, 1985. 345p. bibliog.
(Liverpool Monographs in Hispanic Studies, 5).
In addition to a short introduction, this volume consists of nine chapters, each devoted to an analysis of one of Onetti's novels: *El pozo, Tierra de nadie, Para esta noche, La vida breve, Los adioses, Para una tumba sin nombre, El astillero, Juntacadáveres,* and *Dejemos hablar al viento.* The author quotes abundantly from the novels, but all quotations are provided with a translation into English. This work is not a gentle introduction to Onetti: 'My reading is a certain kind of academic criticism. It draws on stylistics, narratology and some ideas in post-structuralism and Lacanian psychoanalysis. These methodological preferences inform my speculations on the reading of Onetti, and that is reading at all levels, from the micro- to the macro-structural. It seems to me that the least problematical conception of reading is as a pragmatic, dialectical practice, which does not seek for positivistic features of a text, but which examines the interplay of reader and text, the differential processing of the text in reading'.

553 **A brief life.**
Juan Carlos Onetti, translated by Hortense Carpentier. New York: Grossman Publishers (Viking Press), 1976. 292p.
The first Spanish edition of *La vida breve* was published in 1950.

554 **The shipyard.**
Juan Carlos Onetti, translated by Rachel Caffyn. New York: Scribner's, 1968. 190p.
El astillero, among the finest of Onetti's works, was first published in 1961.

555 **The formal expression of meaning in Juan Carlos Onetti's narrative art.**
Yvonne Perier Jones. Cuernavaca, Mexico: Centro Intercultural de Documentación (CIDOC), 1971. 162p. bibliog. (CIDOC, Cuaderno 59).
Onetti's work is here assessed under six principal headings; plot and meta-plot; meaning in structure; philosophical implications; mythic-symbolic elements; imagery of sensory appeal; and techniques in Onetti's poetic reality. The text is in English, but the quotations from Onetti are not translated. The author estimates that the publication of *Tierra de nadie* (1941) 'foreshadowed the coming of age of the novel in Latin America'. A theme of the conclusion is the role of repetition in Onetti, 'representing both the fatalistic cycle of human experience and the technical means by which this experience is projected'.

556 **Onetti and the meaning of fiction: notes on *La muerte y la niña*.**
Arthur Terry. In: *Contemporary Latin American fiction*. Edited by
Salvador Bacarisse. Edinburgh: Scottish Academic Press, 1980, p. 54-
72.
This passage of literary criticism deals with Onetti's novel published in 1973. 'To read
La muerte y la niña with the kind of attention it demands is to recognize that, instead
of "reading the book for the story", we are pursuing the traces of several, sometimes
contradictory, stories, in order to arrive at the sense of a text whose justification, quite
simply, is its own existence . . . To compel us to resist the imposition of a false unity,
by reminding us that the products of language themselves are man-made, not natural,
arrangements is perhaps the most urgent task of contemporary fiction-writers, and it is
one to which Onetti continues to make his own distinctive and splendidly intelligent
contribution.'

Horacio Quiroga

557 **Horacio Quiroga: cuentos escogidos.** (Horacio Quiroga: selected short
stories.)
Edited by Jean Franco. Oxford: Pergamon Press, 1968. 198p. bibliog.
Fourteen of Quiroga's short stories are in this collection. They are in Spanish, but the
editor has provided notes on each to assist the English reader with unfamiliar idioms,
and there is in addition a select Spanish–English word-list which excludes words
normally learned in a two-year Spanish course. The editor's Introduction (p. 1-19) is in
English. While acknowledging that Quiroga is not an elegant writer, she finds that
'both in subject-matter and in technique they reveal a vigorous and refreshing
outlook'. She reviews, amongst others, the themes of human effort, accident and
destiny, death, and man and nature. The stories included are: 'Nuestro primero
cigarro', 'La insolación', 'El alambre de púa', 'Yaguaí', 'Anaconda', 'Los fabricantes
de carbón', 'En la noche', 'Los pescadores de vigas', 'La voluntad', 'El simún', 'A la
deriva', 'El hombre muerto', 'El yaciyateré', and 'Tacuara-Mansión'.

558 **Horacio Quiroga and his exceptional protagonists.**
Charles Param. *Hispania*, vol. 55, no. 3 (Sept. 1972), p. 428-35.
'Perhaps the two most obvious elements in Horacio Quiroga's short stories are a
Nature dangerous to man and a kind of fatalism.' Param analyses eight of Quiroga's
200 stories to make the point that man, not nature, was the true focus of the author's
interest, specifically in his capacity to display courage in struggling against a hostile
natural world.

559 **The Latin American short story: a critical history.**
Edited by Margaret Sayers Peden. Boston, Massachusetts: Twayne,
1983. 160p. bibliog.
Chapters by Naomi Lindstrom, John S. Brushwood, and George R. McMurray analyse
Spanish American writers, among whom Uruguayans figure prominently, none more
so than Horacio Quiroga (p. 69-74).

560   *The decapitated chicken* **and other stories.**
Horacio Quiroga, selected and translated by Margaret Sayers Peden, with an introduction by George D. Schade and illustrations by Ed Lindlof.   Austin, Texas; London: University of Texas Press, 1976. 195p.

Quiroga was born in Salto in 1878, but spent much time in northern Argentina and ended his own life in Buenos Aires in 1937. This collection of twelve of his short stories also includes 'The feather pillow', 'Sunstroke', 'The pursued', 'Drifting', 'A slap in the face', 'In the middle of the night', 'Juan Darién', 'Anaconda', 'The incense tree roof', and 'The son'. The Introduction declares him to be 'generally regarded by the critics as a classic and one of the finest short-story writers Latin America has produced'.

561   **South American jungle tales.**
Horacio Quiroga, translated into English by Arthur Livingston and illustrated by A. L. Ripley.   New York: Duffield, 1922. Reissued London: Methuen, 1923; New York: Dodds-Mead, 1950. 166p.

The eight stories of *Cuentos del la selva* were published in Spanish in 1918. The names of some of the creatures of the jungle have not been translated accurately, and brief notes give the Spanish original. There are four illustrations.

562   **Focus: Horacio Quiroga.**
Review 76, no. 19 (Winter 1976), p. 25-45.

This collection includes a chronology of Quiroga's life and work by Patricia Gülmez, a reprint of 'A literary kin of Kipling and Jack London' by Ernesto Montenegro from *The New York Times Book Review* 1925, a review article by George Garrett of Margaret Sayers Peden (ed.) *The decapitated chicken* (q.v.), 'Some notes on Quiroga's stories' by William Peden, and Quiroga's story 'The flies', translated by M. S. Peden.

563   **Contemporary Spanish-American fiction.**
Jefferson Rea Spell.   Chapel Hill, North Carolina: University of North Carolina Press, 1944. 323p. bibliog.

Chapter 6 (p. 153-78) is devoted to Horacio Quiroga, including an extended section on his remarkable life. The assessment of his genius is qualified. 'His forte does not lie in narration or in the analysis of human character. It is ability to transfer to his pages the atmosphere of Misiones . . .' (the province of Argentina where many of his stories are set).

Carlos Reyles

564   **Popular speech, 'gitanismos,' and bullfighting terms in 'El embrujo de Sevilla'.**
Eunice Joiner Gates.   *Hispania*, vol. 45, no. 3 (Sept. 1962), p. 422-27.

Published in 1922, Carlos Reyles' novel *El embrujo de Sevilla* ('Castanets') employs a difficult language of Andalusian words, gipsy language, and technical terms of bullfighting. Gates lists about 150 words, and gives definitions (in Spanish) appropriate to the novel.

565 **Castanets.**
Carlos Reyles, translated into English by Jacquest Le Clercq.
London; New York: Longmans, Green, 1929. Reprinted New York:
Jacobsen, 1929. 297p.
Reyles' best-known novel, set in Spain, was first published in 1922 as *El embrujo de Sevilla*.

566 **A note on the philosophy of Ramiro de Maeztu and Carlos Reyles.**
David T. Sisto. *Hispania*, vol. 41, no. 4 (Dec. 1958), p. 457-59.
Sisto finds a similarity in the philosophical development of Reyles with the Spaniard Maeztu, from Nietzschean radicalism in his novel *La muerte del cisne* (1910) to a more conservative, patriotic stance in his later years.

Other writers

567 **History and fiction: the powerful art of Eduardo Acevedo Díaz.**
R. Anthony Castagnaro. In: *The early Spanish American novel*.
New York: Las Americas Publishing Co., 1971, p. 182-96.
Of the seven novels of Acevedo Díaz (1851-1921), four (*Ismael, Nativa, Grito de gloria* and *Lanza y sable*) are set in the Independence and immediate post-Independence periods. In them the author composed 'a comprehensive image of the Uruguayan national ethos, and simultaneously created an inspiring literary paradigm for the edification of his countrymen'. With discussion also of *Soledad*, this straightforward and uncomplicated account, chapter VI.E of Castagnaro's book, is a useful introduction to Acevedo Díaz.

568 **Javier de Viana.**
John F. Garganigo. New York: Twayne Publishers, 1972. 185p.
bibliog. (Twayne's world authors series, 226).
Garganigo's account of the work of Viana is valuable as the only full-length study of the writer in English. The organization of the book is unusual, with a Background chapter followed by four others identified only by dates: 1896-1901; 1910-12; 1919; and 1920-25. Each of these analyses the themes of the principal works published in those years, but little attention is paid to Viana's literary style. Viana's interpretation of the *gaucho* figure is inevitably a linking theme throughout the book, but because each work is appraised individually there is some repetition. Thus *machismo* is a subtitle in two successive chapters, the theme explored in relationship to two different works without any cross-referencing. The text is written predominantly in the historic present and some names are mis-spelled, but the index makes it easy to locate Garganigo's discussion of any particular work.

Literature. Novels and short stories

569 A South American trilogy.
Edited by Luis Ramos-García.   Austin, Texas: Studia Hispanica, 1982. 102p.

The Uruguayan interest in the trilogy (p. 47-80) is the short story 'Menos Julia' ('Except Julia') by the Uruguayan writer Felisberto Hernández, which appears in Spanish and in an English translation by Stephanie Merrim. The author is briefly introduced by Carlos Cortínez.

570 Mothers and shadows.
Marta Traba, translated by Jo Labanyi.
London: Readers International, 1986. 178p.

Although the author was born in Buenos Aires, her connections with Uruguay were strong. This novel, first published in Spanish in 1981 under the title *Conversación al sur*, is mainly set in Montevideo, and powerfully evokes the fear and despair that so many lived through during the military dictatorship.

571 The South American sketches of R. B. Cunninghame Graham.
Selected and edited, with an introduction, notes, glossary and bibliography, by John Walker.   Norman, Oklahoma: University of Oklahoma Press, 1978. 292p. bibliog.

Whereas his close friend W. H. Hudson was born in Argentina but died in England, Cunninghame Graham (1852-1936) first visited South America in 1870, and returned to Buenos Aires to die. He was in Uruguay in 1876, ranching and dealing in horses, and the connection remained close enough for the monument to him at his family home in Scotland to be built of Uruguayan stone and unveiled in 1937 in the presence of Alberto Guani (who was Uruguay's Minister of Foreign Relations at the time of the Battle of the River Plate). Cunninghame Graham wrote prolifically, much of it set in South America and reminiscent of Hudson's *The purple land*. Walker has here (p. 153-91) collected four delightful fragments of Uruguayan *gaucho* or rural life, taken from three of Cunninghame Graham's books: *Hope* (1910), *Brought forward* (1916), and *Mirages* (1936).

572 Tabaré: an Indian legend of Uruguay.
Juan Zorrilla de San Martín, translated into English verse by Walter Owen. Translation revised by Frank P. Hebblethwaite, foreword by Enrique Anderson-Imbert and with a note on the literary personality of the translator by Sir Eugen Millington-Drake.   Washington, D.C.: Pan American Union, 1956. 366p. (Unesco Collection of Representative Works: Latin American Series. Published with the cooperation of the Organization of American States).

The best known of Zorrilla de San Martín's poetic works, published in 1888, is here presented with an English verse translation alongside the Spanish. The glossary of indigenous words compiled by the author is expanded by the translator. Owen (1884-1953), a poet in his own right as well as businessman, was Scottish by birth but long resident in Buenos Aires; he earns an introduction by Millington-Drake, at whose suggestion the translation was undertaken.

Poetry

573 **Unstill life: an introduction to the Spanish poetry of Latin America.**
Edited by Mario Benedetti, translated by Darwin J. Flakoll, Claribel
Alegría and illustrated by Antonio Frasconi. New York: Harcourt,
Brace & World, 1969. 127p.

In this handsome illustrated volume, Benedetti's Introduction is brief, and of interest
here mainly for the explanation of the absence of Delmira Agustini (whose themes
may appeal less to the collection's audience of young people) and Julio Herrera y
Reissig (who loses too much in translation). Those Uruguayan poets who do appear
(one poem from each, in Spanish and English translation) are Juana de Ibarbourou,
Juan Cunha and Idea Vilariño. There are short biographical and critical notes on each
poet.

574 **The Penguin book of Latin American verse.**
Edited by Enrique Caracciolo-Trejo, introduced by Henry Gifford.
Harmondsworth, England: Penguin, 1971. 425p.

The section devoted to Uruguay (p. 359-72) contains twelve poems or extracts by Julio
Herrera y Reissig, Emilio Frugoni, Delmira Agustini, Carlos Sabat Ercasty, Emilio
Oribe, and Idea Vilariño. The poems are reproduced in Spanish, and are translated
into plain prose by Michael Gonzalez. There are brief biographical notes on each poet.

575 **Julio Herrera y Reissig and the symbolists.**
Bernard Gicovate. Berkeley; Los Angeles, California: University of
California Press, 1957. 106p. bibliog.

'A technical study of poetry seems to require an excuse in these days . . . The work of
Herrera y Reissig is of interest because of its very eccentricity. Lying somewhat
tangential to the poet's own culture and closely related to another . . .'. Gicovate
analyses his subject in chapters which relate modernism to French poetry, examine
influences in Herrera's work and his early poems, explore the impasse of symbolism,
and finally discuss the poet's diction and experiments in structure. Unfortunately the
verse quotations are not translated.

576 **The modernist trend in Spanish-American poetry: a collection of
representative poems of the modernist movement and the reaction
translated into English verse with a commentary.**
George Dundas Craig. Berkeley, California: University of California
Press, 1934. 347p. bibliog.

The Uruguayan representative of modernism is Julio Herrera y Reissig. Four poems
appear in Spanish and English, and there is a useful analysis of his work (including his
surprising references to Scotland) in the 'Comments' section (p. 301-5).

577   **Our race: modern Afro-Uruguayan poetry.**
Marvin A. Lewis.   In: *Afro-Hispanic poetry 1940-1980: from slavery to
'negritud' in South American verse.* Columbia, Missouri: University of
Missouri Press, 1983, p. 9-45. bibliog.
This significant work is primarily concerned with the most important collections of
poetry by two black Uruguayan poets: *Pregón de Marimorena* (1946) by Virginia
Brindis de Salas, and *Piel negra* (1947) by Pilar Barrios. There are extensive quotations
from the poems, and translations into English. Lewis's analysis of the poems is
'culturalist', seeking to assess self-perceptions of ethnicity and integration in the
cultural expression of a small minority population. To enable him to do so, Lewis has
served a larger purpose by outlining the nature of the Afro-Uruguayan community, its
cultural history, and its position in Uruguayan society. His assessment will upset those
who share the common view of Uruguay as generally free of racial prejudice. Blacks
themselves, numbering about 60,000, are largely hidden in Uruguay, as are their
literary works: 'references to Brindis de Salas and Barrios are not included in any
studies of Uruguayan literature that I have seen by Uruguayans past or present'. This
neglect may indeed be studied: after examining Peru, Ecuador and Colombia in other
chapters, Lewis concludes: 'It is ironic that, so far, the poets who come from countries
with the smallest number of blacks (Uruguay and Peru) are the ones who register the
most vehement protests against racism and discrimination'.

578   **Latin American revolutionary poetry: a bilingual anthology.**
Edited and with an introduction by Robert Márquez.   New York;
London: Monthly Review Press, 1974. 505p.
This is a fine collection of modern poetry 'written against the background of
contemporary Latin American history and the global movement for change'. The
section devoted to Uruguay (p. 448-95) consists of four poems each by Mario
Benedetti and Carlos María Gutiérrez. Spanish original and English translation (by
David Arthur McMurray, Robert Márquez, Flinor Randall, Margaret Randall, and
Robert Cohen) are presented side by side. There are biographical notes on the poets,
and explanations of specific terms in the poems. They evoke a most bitter period in the
nation's history.

579   **Young poetry of the Americas.**
Washington, D.C.: Pan American Union, [n.d.] vol. 1. 116p.
This volume, which was published around 1967, is composed of national anthologies
reprinted from issues of *Americas*. The selection of 'Six Uruguayan poets' is edited by
Saúl Ibargoxen Islas, and contains work by Mario Benedetti, Carlos Brandy, Juan
Cunha, Milton Schinca, Jorge Medina Vidal, and Idea Vilariño.

580   **Modern women poets of South America.**
Sidonia Carmen Rosenbaum.   New York: Hispanic Institute in the
United States, 1945. 273p. bibliog.
It reflects the importance of the tradition of poetry-writing in Uruguay that three of the
seven poets analysed in this work of literary criticism are Uruguayan: María Eugenia
Vaz Ferreira, sister of the philosopher Carlos Vaz Ferreira (p. 49-54); Delmira
Agustini (p. 57-167); and Juana de Ibarbourou (p. 229-56). The position of Agustini is
seen as pivotal; she it was 'who lighted the spark which was to become that oft-times
scintillating but uncontrollable and towering bonfire which is present-day feminine

poetry in Spanish America'. Life, death, love and dreams are the primary themes of her poetry. Apart from the literary analysis, the biographical material on all three figures is revealing of the social and cultural milieu of Montevideo in the early decades of this century. Unfortunately none of the poetry quoted is translated from the Spanish.

581 Contemporary Uruguayan poetry.
Alberto Zum Felde. *Inter-America*, vol. 9, no. 1 (Oct. 1925), p. 62-84.

In an important survey of Uruguayan poetry, Zum Felde argues that there was 'no truly lyrical poetry worthy of consideration other than that of the contemporary period'. The first figure who warrants attention is Julio Herrera y Reissig, 'the pontiff of modernism in Uruguay'. Others discussed include Armando Vasseur, the three great women poets, and fourteen others. The article is followed (p. 85-112) by a selection of thirty-two poems by the authors discussed in Spanish and without translation. See also Alberto Zum Felde, *El proceso intelectual del Uruguay*.

Drama

582 The library.
Carlos Maggi. In: *Voices of change in the Spanish American theater: an anthology*. Edited and translated by William I. Oliver. Austin, Texas; London: University of Texas Press, 1971, p. 105-69.

With so few Uruguayan plays available in translation, this three-act piece (first produced in 1959) is particularly welcome. 'It is a comic assault on the bureaucratic life and the regimented mind of the Latin American middle class', set in the library director's office between 1917/18 and 1932/33.

583 Florencio Sánchez and his social consciousness of the River Plate region.
Manuel D. Ramírez. *Journal of Inter-American Studies*, vol. 8, no. 4 (1966), p. 585-94.

Introducing Sánchez as 'the playwright who has probably done more than any other for the development of the modern Spanish American drama', the author examines seven themes which are central to his work: the lack of will power, alcoholism, the degeneration of the *gaucho*, marriage, illegitimacy and the rights of motherhood, poverty, and racial intolerance.

584 Florencio Sánchez and the Argentine theatre.
Ruth Richardson. New York: Instituto de las Españas en los Estados Unidos, 1933. 243p. bibliog.

Although rather dated, Richardson's study of Florencio Sánchez is very valuable. Sánchez (1875-1910) was born and educated in Uruguay but lived his short life on both sides of the River Plate. His immense contribution to the national theatre of Argentina was such that this development might be called more accurately the formation of

Rioplatense theatre, but the author declines to side with either Argentinians or Uruguayans in the debate. The greater part of this book is taken up with synopses and comments on his twenty plays written during 1903-9, but there are also chapters of biography, on his non-dramatic works, ideology, and contribution to the theatre of the region. A feature of the book are extensive assessments of Sánchez (in English) by Uruguayan critics, including Carlos Roxlo, Eduardo Acevedo Díaz, Emilio Frugoni and Alberto Zum Felde. The author's own assessment is that Sánchez showed to the middle classes 'that it was possible to have a sound, thought-provoking, indigenous theatre', in which the traditional *gaucho* theme was treated with new realism and insight, and themes relevant to an urban immigrant community could now appear.

585 **Representative plays of Florencio Sánchez.**
Florencio Sánchez, edited and translated by Willis Knapp Jones. Revised translation by Glenn Barr, with an introduction by Ruth Richardson. Washington, D.C.: Pan American Union, 1961. 326p. bibliog. (Unesco Collection of Representative Works: Latin American Series).

There are eleven plays in this major collection of Sánchez' work, written between 1903 and 1907. The most substantial (and best or best known) are *My son the lawyer* (M'hijo el dotor); and *The immigrant girl* (La gringa). The others included here are *Midsummer Day parents* (Cédulas de San Juan); *Down the gully* (Barranca abajo); *The newspaper boy* (Canillita); *The healing hand* (Mano santa); *Evicted* (El desalojo); *The tigress* (La tigra); *Phoney money* (Moneda falsa); *The family circle* (En familia); *Our children* (Nuestros hijos).

586 **A great national drama of Uruguay.**
George O. Schanzer. *Modern Language Journal*, vol. 38, no. 5 (May 1954), p. 220-23.

The dramatist Ernesto Herrera (1889-1917) is little known outside Uruguay, overshadowed perhaps by Florencio Sánchez and his cousin Julio Herrera y Reissig. Schanzer's interesting article corrects some previously published biographical details, but is mainly concerned to establish the importance of Herrera's *El león ciego* ('The blind lion'). The play was first performed in 1911, immediately following the last ineffective armed uprising of the *gaucho caudillos* in 1910, and on the eve of Batlle y Ordóñez' second reformist administration. The lion is an ageing *caudillo*, crude and cruel but noble, whose time has passed. The play marks the moment of national transition from primitive to modern.

Philosophy

General

587 **Espiritualismo y positivismo en el Uruguay.** (Spiritualism and positivism in Uruguay.)
Arturo Ardao. Montevideo: Universidad de la República, Departamento de Publicaciones, 1968. 2nd ed. 302p. (Colección Historia y Cultura, 10).

First published in 1940, this standard work examines the penetration of and dissemination from the University in the second half of the nineteenth century of French eclectic spiritualism and English positivism. The significance of the study lies in the fact that the two schools of thought 'shaped the national intelligence and even the moral conscience of the country, in a decisive stage of its development'. The sharp polemic which resulted between the two doctrines thus had profound effects on many aspects of the nation's life. Among the Uruguayan intellectuals of the period discussed in the book are Plácido Ellauri, Angel Floro Costa, José Pedro Varela, Carlos Maria de Pena, Alfredo Vásquez Acevedo, Carlos Vaz Ferreira, and José Enrique Rodó.

588 **A century of Latin-American thought.**
William Rex Crawford. Cambridge, Massachusetts: Harvard University Press, 1961. rev. ed. 322p. bibliog.

Crawford devotes chapter 4 (p. 79-94) to José Enrique Rodó and Carlos Vaz Ferreira. His enthusiasm for Vaz Ferreira ('one of . . . the few genuine philosophers, as distinguished from professors of philosophy, in all Latin America') does not quite extend to Rodó, and generous space is given to the critics of *Ariel*.

589 **Juan Zorrilla de San Martín.**
Gustavo Gallinal. *Inter-America*, vol. 8, no. 2 (Dec. 1924), p. 117-22.

A discursive review of the work and philosophy of Zorrilla de San Martín, inspired by the publication of his *El sermón de la paz* ('The sermon of peace').

590 **The Latin-American mind.**
Leopoldo Zea, translated from the Spanish by James H. Abbott, Lowell Dunham. Norman, Oklahoma: University of Oklahoma Press, 1963. 308p.

Zea wrote *Dos etapas del pensamiento en Hispanoamérica* in 1949. The work is a study of romanticism and positivism; pages 236-54 examine the development of positivism and its opposition in Uruguay, relating the ideas to the country's social and political development. This important essay makes reference to Andrés Lamas, the group of the Ateneo, José Pedro Varela, Carlos María de Pena, and others.

José Enrique Rodó

591   **José Enrique Rodó.**
Justo Manuel Aguiar.   *Inter-America*, vol. 6, no. 2 (Dec. 1922),
p. 113-23.
'Frankly admirative but none the less discerning' is the journal editor's own assessment of this piece. Harder to accept than Aguiar's judgment ('In the whole course of the literary history of America, only the name of José Enrique Rodó has received unanimous recognition') is the inflated rhetorical style in which it is expressed. This is not, however, an empty eulogy.

592   **An introduction for studies on Rodó.**
C. C. Bacheller. *Hispania*, vol. 46, no. 4 (Dec. 1963), p. 764-69.
A very general account of the work and significance of Rodó, considered particularly in the light of early and exaggerated criticisms and plaudits, and more balanced recent assessments. There are quotations from authors of the latter, which are not translated from the Spanish. The author considers *Motivos de Proteo* to be Rodó's 'most thoughtful and mature work'.

593   **Homage to Irving A. Leonard: essays on hispanic art, history and literature.**
Edited by Raquel Chang-Rodríguez, Donald A. Yates.   New York: Editorial Mensaje, under the auspices of the Latin American Studies Center, Michigan State University, 1977. 230p.
This *Festschrift* contains two essays bearing on the significance of Rodó. They are 'Rodó, *Ariel*, and student militants of Uruguay' (p. 153-60) by Mark van Aken; and '*Ariel* on Caliban in both Americas' by Arthur P. Whitaker. The former examines the influence of *Ariel* among radical students in the 1920s, and the filling of the gap left by his 'purely esthetic consideration of life' by notions of imperialism. The latter argues that *Ariel* was aimed at materialism in Latin America as well as in the United States.

594   **Rodó and the United States.**
Ramiro de Maeztu.   *Inter-America*, vol. 9, no. 5 (June 1926), p. 460-64.
The author, a Spaniard, believes that Rodó's attack on the United States in *Ariel* originated in Spain's, defeat in the Spanish-American War of 1898; but also the Rodó failed to understand the religiosity of the United States, where efficiency in work and the pursuit of comfort and success encourage the feeling 'of possessing divine grace, of belonging to the elect, of being predestined to salvation'.

595   **Ariel.**
José Enrique Rodó, edited with an introduction and notes by Gordon Brotherston.   Cambridge: Cambridge University Press, 1967. 106p.
The reputation of Rodó (1871-1917) as one of the outstanding members of the group of intellectuals known as the 'generación de novecientos' (generation of 1900) depends to a great extent on this work (published in 1900). It, in turn, is best known for a passage

which appears to affirm the spiritual superiority of Latin America compared to the utilitarianism of the United States. The editor's excellent introduction in English puts some perspective on that interpretation by noting 'it was chiefly the political situation of the time [two years after the Spanish-American War] and not his own intention which made *Ariel* seem like a piece of propaganda' . . . '*Ariel* is great precisely because it offered inspiration to Latin Americans without recourse to patriotic slogans'. There is also discussion of the influence of French writers on Rodó, of the unresolved dilemma in *Ariel* of Rodó's rejection of both aristocracy and democracy, and of his failure to address the material problems of poverty and exploitation. The text itself is in Spanish, with notes largely restricted to explanation of the references and allusions made by the author. There is an index of names.

596 **Ariel.**
José Enrique Rodó. Translation, reader's reference, and annotated bibliography by Margaret Sayers Peden, foreword by James W. Symington and prologue by Carlos Fuentes. Austin, Texas: University of Texas Press, 1988. 156p. bibliog.

We may accept Fuentes' characterization of this translation – 'superb' – as readily as his perplexed view of the author: 'irritating, insufferable, admirable, stimulating, disappointing Rodó: our Uruguayan uncle, sitting in a corner of our family portrait'. This will be for many years the definitive English edition of *Ariel*, and replaces the previous translation and introductory essay by F. J. Stimson (Boston, Massachusetts; New York: Houghton Mifflin, 1922. 150p). Stimson, an ambassador of the United States to Argentina, sought in his essay to soften the sting of Rodó's comments on the materialism and 'flood of vulgarity' of the US. 'What would Rodó have said, had he lived to see our entrance in the great war for world liberty? And how much would he have altered or added to what he says of the United States in *Ariel*? Much, by very much.' Fuentes asks, by contrast: 'why does the United States exhibit such a disparity between the way it acts internally (democratically) and the way it acts externally (. . .)?'.

597 **The motives of Proteus.**
José Enrique Rodó, translated by Angel Flores and introduced by Havelock Ellis. London: Allen & Unwin, 1929; New York: Brentano's, 1928. 378p. bibliog.

Less frequently referred to but regarded by some as perhaps a more significant work than *Ariel*, *Los motivos de Proteo* first appeared in 1909 and is concerned with conscience and spirituality. It is written in the form of 158 brief sections which bear such titles as 'How chance determines indecisions', 'The lover and the omnipresence of his passion' and 'Art can reflect the individual's complexity only to a certain point'. The introduction was taken from Havelock Ellis's *Philosophy of conflict*.

598 **In quest of identity: patterns in the Spanish American essay of ideas, 1890-1960.**
Martin S. Stabb. Chapel Hill, North Carolina: University of North Carolina Press, 1967. 244p. bibliog.

Chapter 3 ('The revolt against scientism') is substantially devoted to an assessment of José Enrique Rodó as amongst the most influential of the group of Latin American 'new idealists' (*arielistas*) at the beginning of the century. *Ariel* itself and contemporary criticisms of its emphasis on the non-utilitarian are examined, but the main significance of this essay is its tracing of the diffusion of Rodó's ideas throughout Spanish America.

599   **José Enrique Rodó and his idealistic philosophy.**
Arturo Torres-Ríoseco. In: *Aspects of Spanish-American literature.*
Seattle, Washington: University of Washington Press, 1963, p. 31-50.
Two rather odd features of this essay are, firstly, that the author judges *Motivos de Proteo* (The motives of Proteus, 1909) to be Rodó's masterpiece, not *Ariel*; but secondly, almost the entire essay is devoted to analysis of *Ariel*. See also, by the same author, *New world literature: tradition and revolt in Latin America* (Berkeley; Los Angeles, California: University of California Press, 1949), chapter 8 (p. 138-53) for an earlier appraisal of Rodó, in which *Ariel* is described as the masterpiece, not once but twice! Here he suggests that 'above all, we must consider Rodó as a literary critic'.

Carlos Vaz Ferreira

600   **Carlos Vaz Ferreira: Uruguayan philosopher.**
John H. Haddox.   *Journal of Inter-American Studies*, vol. 8, no. 4 (1966), p. 595-600.
This short appraisal of Vaz Ferreira (1872-1959), perhaps Uruguay's most distinguished philospher and thinker, concentrates on an analysis of his *Fermentario* (1938). The two most original aspects of his thought are defined: 'The first of these was the claim that there has been a significant progress in the morality of mankind, a marked ethical advance, over the years, decades, and centuries, and the second was that the authentic moral problem is not so much the traditional problem of evil, but rather . . . "the problem of good" '. The latter arises from the necessity to choose on occasion between irreconcilable goods.

601   **Carlos Vaz Ferreira: a review of his collected works.**
Irving Louis Horowitz.   *Hispanic American Historical Review*, vol. 40, no. 1 (Feb. 1960), p. 63-69.
On the occasion of the publication in Uruguay of Vaz' collected works, this appreciation of his philosophical contributions is sharp and provocative, abounding in acute judgment and generalization. Vaz is credited with giving 'intellectual substance to the forms in which his country went about fashioning the most stable political system in the Continent'. In reviewing his dialectical pluralism, his perception of philosophy as a cultural force, his analysis of moral issues and emphasis on education, Horowitz underlines Vaz' importance without being either patronising or uncritical. Indeed he points out in Vaz a 'distinct inability to overcome the problem which is the bane of Latin American philosophy, mimesis' – especially in respect of nineteenth-century modes of European thought. This article is an essential reference on Vaz.

Negro anthology.
See item no. 202.

The *gaucho*: cattle hunter, cavalryman, ideal of romance.
See item no. 206.

Kidnapped in Buenos Aires.
See item no. 320.

Behind Spanish American footlights.
See item no. 626.

The Arts

Painting and sculpture

602 **Proceso de las artes plásticas del Uruguay: desde la época indígena al momento contemporáneo.** (The evolution of painting and sculpture in Uruguay: from the indigenous period to the present day.)
José Pedro Argul. Montevideo: Barreiro y Ramos, 1975. 3rd ed. 364p.

Argul's book is an excellent introduction to the fine arts in Uruguay, illustrated with ninety reproductions of paintings (some in colour) and twenty-two photographs of sculpture. Twenty-four chapters are devoted to the history of painting; sculpture occupies a further eight. Although there is some emphasis on the major figures of Juan Manuel Blanes, Pedro Figari, Joaquín Torres-García, and José Belloni, a very large number of other artists and sculptors are discussed. The reference in the title to the indigenous period is slightly misleading, since 'the indian has left us little', and seven pages are sufficient for the pre-history of Uruguayan art. Earlier editions appeared in 1958 and 1966.

603 **Torres-García: grid-pattern-sign: Paris – Montevideo, 1924-1944.**
London: Arts Council of Great Britain, 1985. 128p. bibliog.

An exhibition of Torres-García's work toured Europe (including the Hayward Gallery in London) in 1985, and this handsome volume was produced to accompany it. Following three introductory essays by Margit Rowell, Theo van Doesburg and Cecilia Buzio de Torres, there are 121 plates, some in colour, and biographical photographs. There is also a chronology, and a selected list of exhibitions.

604 **Handbook of Latin American art: a bibliographic compilation.**
Edited by Joyce Waddell Bailey. Santa Barbara, California: ABC-Clio Information Services, 1984. 2 vols. (in 3 books).

Volume 1 part 2 deals with South American art of the nineteenth and twentieth centuries, and Uruguayan materials are listed on pages 902-28. Approximately 200 entries deal with architecture, art exhibitions, film, folklore, and general studies of the visual arts, as well as fifty-three individual Uruguayan artists. Most of the items are in Spanish, and there are no annotations.

605 Augusto Torres.
Guido Castillo, edited by Elizabeth K. Fonseca.   New York: Scala Books, with the Archer M. Huntington Art Gallery of the University of Texas at Austin, 1986. 167p.

Less well known than that of his father, Joaquín Torres-García, Augusto Torres' work is superbly presented in this volume. There are 150 illustrations, almost all (except the ink drawings) excellently reproduced in colour. Although Torres was born in Europe and did not live in Montevideo until he was twenty-one (and continued to live elsewhere for extended periods), about half of the paintings in this collection were executed in Montevideo, the majority of them street scenes. The plates are introduced by 'a conversation about painting', between Torres and (presumably) Castillo, and followed by a brief chronology of the painter's life.

606 Art of Latin America since Independence.
Stanton Loomis Catlin, Terence Grieder.   October House, for Yale University Art Gallery and the University of Texas Art Museum, 1966. 246p.

Details of twenty-six Uruguayan artists are given in brief but helpful biographical notes; there are also nine monochrome plates including work by Cuneo and Torres-García

607 Contemporary art in Latin America.
Gilbert Chase.   New York: The Free Press; London: Collier, Macmillan, 1970. 292p. bibliog.

'Uruguay owes its importance in the history of Latin American art above all to two artists, Pedro Figari and Joaquín Torres García', and the section on Uruguay (p. 169-80) deals mainly with them. In particular there is analysis of Torres-García's 'constructive universalism' with specific reference to his Cosmic Monument (1938). Other painters briefly discussed are Luis Solari, José Gamarra, and Carlos Páez Vilaró.

608 Modern Latin American art: a bibliography.
Compiled by James A. Findlay.   Westport, Connecticut: Greenwood Press, 1983. 301p.

There are 59 unannotated references on Uruguayan art, architecture and sculpture.

609 Pedro Figari 1861-1938.
Buenos Aires: Ediciones Galerías Witcomb, 1953. 24p.

This sumptuously produced work has text in Spanish by Oliverio Girondo, Jorge Romero Brest, Julio Rinaldini and Manuel Mujica Lainez. They introduce twenty-five colour reproductions of many of Figari's best-known paintings, including rural as well as urban scenes, and a self-portrait.

610 **Vernacular culture in Uruguayan art: an analysis of the documentary function of the works of: Pedro Figari, Carlos González and Luis Solari.**
Alicia Haber. Miami, Florida: Florida International University, 1982. 31p. bibliog. (Latin American and Caribbean Center, Occasional Paper 2).
Haber argues that all three painters 'unveil elements pertaining specifically to Uruguayan culture . . . they share the wish to preserve the Uruguayan ethos'. She analyses especially Figari's portrayal of 'candombe', rural life in the woodcuts of González, and rural myth and magic in the imaginative art of Solari. There are three monochrome illustrations.

611 **Seis maestros de la pintura uruguaya.** (Six masters of Uruguayan painting.)
Buenos Aires: Museo Nacional de Bellas Artes, 1987. 171p. bibliog.
This beautifully produced book, published to accompany an exhibition of the six in Argentina, is focused on Juan Manuel Blanes, Carlos Federico Sáez, Pedro Figari, Joaquín Torres-García, Rafael Barradas and José Cuneo. There are seventy-nine very good reproductions, many of them in colour, and there are also many photographs of the artists and pages from their letters in facsimile. The bibliography covers work by as well as concerning the six, but it is very extensive and not restricted to works dealing only with them. The principal feature of the book are the fragments of biographical or critical appreciation of the six. For example, there are no fewer than twenty-eight of such abstracts regarding Figari, by such writers as Alberto Zum Felde, Jorge Luis Borges, Lewis Mumford, and Anthony Blunt. There are knowledgeable introductory essays on the six by Angel Kalenberg, and on Uruguayan art by Julio María Sanguinetti (then President of Uruguay).

612 **Uruguay: 12 escultores.** (Uruguay: twelve sculptors.)
Raquel Pereda de Nin. Montevideo: Ministerio de Educación y Cultura, 1976. 289p.
The twelve are José Livi, Domingo Mora, Juan Luis Blanes and Nicanor Blanes, Juan Manuel Ferrari, José Belloni, Pablo Mañé, Severino Pose, Antonio Pena, Bernabé Michelena, Edmundo Prati, and José Luis Zorrilla de San Martín. The extensive essays on the life and work of each are preceded by chapters on the origins and characteristics of Uruguayan sculpture. There are nearly 300 monochrome illustrations of the sculptors and their work, which is predominantly but not exclusively 'monumental'.

613 **Universalismo constructivo: contribución a la unificación del arte y la cultura de América.** (Constructive universalism: a contribution to the unification of the art and culture of America.)
Joaquín Torres-García. Buenos Aires: Editorial Poseidon, 1944. 1011p.
For anyone wanting to examine the work of Torres-García in depth, this is an essential reference. It takes the form of 150 'lessons', illustrated by three colour plates and 253 seemingly simple drawings.

Music

614 La música en el Uruguay. (Music in Uruguay.)
Lauro Ayestarán, with a prologue by Juan E. Pivel Devoto.
Montevideo: Servicio Oficial de Difusión Radio-Eléctrica (SODRE),
1953. vol. 1. 818p.

A work of immense scholarship, Ayesterán's history was never completed. This volume is in two parts. The first, on primitive music, has chapters on indigenous music (especially of the Charrúas) and negro music (that is, *candombe*). Part II deals with 'serious' music up to 1860, including church music, opera and music of the stage, chamber music, and the earliest composers. A concluding miscellany has notes on various items including the national anthem and military music. There is an index of names, and the work is illustrated with over 200 high-quality monochrome plates.

615 La música en el Uruguay. (Music in Uruguay.)
Mirta Amarilla Capi. Montevideo: Prisma, 1983. 79p.

A very general and not very profound account of music in Uruguay, with chapters on the penetration of European music, the national anthem ('a patriotic symbol and one of the loveliest . . . the music has influences from nineteenth century Italian opera'), folklore, and Afro-Uruguayan music. There are photographs and illustrations of music.

616 The life, music, and times of Carlos Gardel.
Simon Collier. Pittsburgh, Pennsylvania: University of Pittsburgh Press, 1986. 340p. bibliog.

Gardel belongs to Montevideo as well as to Buenos Aires, in popular sympathy and acclaim, and because, at the age of thirty, he claimed to have been born in Tacuarembó and therefore to be a Uruguayan national. This book is a rarity, being both scholarly and a lively, absorbing read. Carlos was in fact born Charles, in Toulouse.

617 The orchestral music of Louis Moreau Gottschalk.
William E. Korf. Henryville-Ottawa-Binningen: Institut de Musique Médiévale, 1983. 162p. bibliog. (Musicological Studies, vol. 28).

Gottschalk (1829-69), 'the first internationally acclaimed American concert pianist and composer', is a minor figure in the history of music, but played an important part in the growth of musical appreciation in Uruguay. Exiled from the United States following a scandal, Gottschalk arrived in Montevideo in May 1867 and remained there and in Buenos Aires for two years (not months, p. 49). The Uruguayan musicologist Francisco Curt Lange, who is quoted extensively in this book, has paid tribute to Gottschalk as a musical educator in Uruguay. In addition, in 1868 he wrote his *Montevideo Symphony* (symphony no. 2), a work in seven sections lasting ten minutes, the third section of which is an arrangement of the Uruguayan national anthem. Korf presents interesting material on this remarkable character's experiences in Montevideo, and an analysis of the symphony. There is an excellent bibliography, and a discography. Of his subject Korf writes: 'In his life, he seems always to have had an excess of pianos and women.'

618   **Músicos uruguayos.** (Uruguayan composers.)
      Roberto Lagarmilla.   Montevideo: Editorial Medina, 1970.
      91p. bibliog.
There are very brief notes on thirty-six Uruguayan composers, excluding the areas of traditional folklore and popular music, with a chronology and an index of names.

619   **Singing in exile.**
      Braulio López.   *Index on Censorship*, vol. 7, no. 4 (July-Aug. 1978),
      p. 44-48.
The Olimareños, a group playing their own songs based on the Uruguayan folk song tradition, were formed in the interior town of Treinta y Tres in 1962, and by the beginning of the 1970s had become hugely popular in Montevideo. From 1969 however there were restrictions on their appearances, and in 1974 they were banned altogether by the military régime. Arrest in Buenos Aires and exile followed. This account of the author's experiences is followed by three of his songs (translated into English by Nick Caistor).

620   **Música popular uruguaya, 1973-1982: un fenómeno de comunicación alternativa.** (Popular music in Uruguay, 1973-1982: a phenomenon of alternative communication.)
      Carlos Alberto Martins.   Montevideo: Centro Latinoamericano de Economía Humana/Ediciones de la Banda Oriental, 1986. 118p.
Rather than an analysis of the music itself, this is a sociological account of its growth and significance during the years of the dictatorship.

621   **The new Grove dictionary of music and musicians.**
      Edited by Stanley Sadie.   London: Macmillan, 1980. 20 vols. bibliog.
Without question Grove gives the best introduction in English to Uruguayan music. The entry for 'Uruguay' (vol. 19, p. 471-74) has articles on art music by Gerard Béhague and folk music (including instruments and genres) by Alejandro Ayesterán. Figures not deemed worthy of separate entries are mentioned, including Louis Cluzeau-Mortet and Pedro Ipuche Riva. There are also details of music archives. Other entries include 'Montevideo' by Susana Salgado (it includes no mention of Gottschalk) (vol. 12, p. 535-36); the musicologists Lauro Ayesterán (Béhague, vol. 1, p. 754) and Francisco Curt Lange (Béhague, vol. 10, p. 446-47); and composers Vicente Ascone (John M. Schechter, vol. 1, p. 651), Carlos Estrada (Salgado, vol. 6, p. 263), Eduardo Fabini (Salgado, vol. 6, p. 345), and Héctor Tosar (Salgado, vol. 19, p. 85). All entries include bibliographies of their subjects.
  A new edition of this work was imminent when we had to go to press late in 1988.

622   **The tango: its origins and meaning.**
      Russell O. Salmon.   *Journal of Popular Culture*, vol. 10, no. 4 (1977),
      p. 859-66.
The origins of the tango are traced to the brothels of Buenos Aires and Montevideo in the 1880s, where 'insecurity, rancor and sarcasm were formalized in the new dance'. There are notes on the etymology of 'tango', on its expression of sexual feeling, and on the existentialist nature of its lyrics.

623 **Music of Latin America.**
Nicolas Slonimsky. London: Harrap, 1946. 374p.
The section which deals specifically with Uruguay is on pages 282-87. The author
emphasizes Uruguay's musical dependence on Argentina. 'The only musical form
which may be said to be Uruguay's own product is the Pericón, an old round dance in
triple time.' There are notes on twelve figures, including the foremost composer then
living in Uruguay, Eduardo Fabini; the founders of the modern school of composition
in the country, Carlos Pedrell and Alfonso Broqua; and 'the foremost Latin American
musicologist', Francisco Curt Lange, born in Germany but resident in Uruguay since
1930 and a founder of SODRE (Servicio Oficial de Difusión Radioeléctrica).

Theatre and cinema

624 **Cinema and social change in Latin America: conversations with
filmmakers.**
Edited by Julianne Burton. Austin, Texas: University of Texas Press,
1986. 302p. bibliog.
Two interviews are with Uruguayan film-makers: Mario Handler (p. 13-24), and
Walter Achugar (p. 221-36). Because of the political and cultural repression of the
1970s which forced both men into exile, what they have to say about film-making in
Uruguay is mostly concerned with the two previous decades. Other Uruguayan
directors mentioned are Carlos Maggi, Alberto Mantarás Rogé, Alberto Miller,
Feruccio Musitelli, Walter Tournier, and Ugo Ulive. There are photographs of
Handler and Achugar.

625 **Cinemalore: *State of Siege* as a case study.**
Daniel I. Geffner, James W. Wilkie. *Journal of Latin American Lore*,
vol. 2, no. 2 (Winter 1976), p. 221-38.
The authors 'aspire to de-emphasise the analysis of film as an aesthetic medium and to
stimulate scholarly interest in cinema as a component of social myth'. In that context
they assess the film *State of Siege* (1973) by the Greek film-maker Constantin Costa-
Gavras, which portrayed the Tupamaro guerrilla campaign and indicted US
involvement in state terror in Uruguay. They conclude that the film 'more accurately
reflects Costa-Gavras's own political lore than it does the interrelationship between
Uruguay and the United States'. Two further and opposing contributions to the debate
appear in the same issue of the journal: Mark Falcoff, 'The Uruguay that never was: a
historian looks at Costa-Gavras's *State of Siege*', p. 239-56 (critical of the film's
veracity); and E. Bradford Barton, 'A *State of Siege* that never was', p. 257-63.
Falcoff's piece also appears as 'Uruguay: the Tupamaros on the silver screen' in Mark
Falcoff (ed.) *Small countries, large issues: studies in U.S.–Latin American asymmetries*,
(Washington, D.C.; London: American Enterprise Institute for Public Research,
1984), p. 13-33.

626　**Behind Spanish American footlights.**
Willis Knapp Jones.　Austin, Texas: University of Texas Press, 1966.
609p. bibliog.

The chapters of particular interest in this massive and magisterial survey of the Spanish American theatre are 'Uruguayan drama' (chapter 5, p. 56-75) and 'Florencio Sánchez' (chapter 8, p. 105-16). While questioning whether it is appropriate to consider the theatre of Uruguay apart from that of the River Plate region, the author adopts the periodization suggested by Zum Felde: patriotism and politics (1808-56); romanticism (1856-90); and realism (since 1890). Almost every playwright is briefly considered, and there are interesting observations about the state of Uruguayan theatre in the preceding decade, including the emergence of experimental theatre companies. Florencio Sánchez continues to cast a long shadow; the search for another has delayed the development of other Uruguayan dramatists. Sánchez himself (the only individual playwright to be the subject of a chapter) is deemed 'not a great dramatist in comparison with masters of literary style who have influenced writers outside their countries . . . But his good qualities made his theatre an artistic inheritance'.

Folklore

627　**El gaucho.** (The *gaucho*.)
Fernando O. Assuncão, illustrated by Federico Reilly. Montevideo: Dirección General de Extensión Universitaria, 1978. 457p. bibliog.

A well-documented and beautifully illustrated sociocultural analysis of the *gaucho* and his environment, from colonial times to the present day.

628　**The *Candombe*, a dramatic dance from Afro-Uruguayan folklore.**
Paulo de Carvalho Neto.　*Ethnomusicology*, vol. 6, no. 3 (Sept. 1962), p. 164-74. bibliog.

Based on field-work begun in 1952, this essay argues that the *Candombe* has the same origins as the 'Congo' or 'Congada' in Brazil, and that the dramatic dance represents a survival of historic struggles amongst tribes in Africa. However, in recent times the *Candombe* has taken to the streets during carnival, being absorbed by the 'Lubola masquerade'. Its adoption by tenement dwellers with other cultural backgrounds has ensured the survival of the *Candombe*, but only at the cost of losing its true origin and significance. These hypotheses, expressed in rather poorly translated English, are illustrated by photographs of two of the principal characters in the dance, 'El Gramillero' and 'El Escobero', and a fragment of music dating from about 1870.

El legado de los inmigrantes. (The legacy of the immigrants.)
See item no. 197.

Florencio Sánchez and the Argentine theatre.
See item no. 584.

Sport and Recreation

629 **Historia del deporte en el Uruguay (1830-1900).** (The history of sport in Uruguay, 1830-1900.)
José L. Buzzetti, Eduardo Gutiérrez Cortinas. Montevideo: Castro y Cia., 1965. 97p.

Although many sporting activities are discussed, the establishment of football (soccer) is inevitably very prominent. British influence and British players in the earliest clubs, including the Central Uruguay Railway Cricket Club (later Peñarol) and Montevideo Cricket Club, and the growing determination in the 1890s to beat the British which led to the formation in 1899 of the Club Nacional de Football, are all featured.

630 **The legal position of the professional football player in Belgium, England and Wales, France, Germany, Italy, the Netherlands, Scotland and Uruguay.**
J. L. Janssen van Raay. Leyden, The Netherlands: A. W. Sijthoff, 1967. 40p.

The section on Uruguay (p. 37-38) has brief information on organizations; aspects of civil law; disciplinary law; social position (i.e. social security, holidays, medical assistance, etc); and financial position. Although the pamphlet bears the sub-title 'a comparative study' there are in fact no cross-national comparisons.

631 **The rise and demise of sport: a reflection of Uruguayan society.**
March L. Krotee. *Annals of the American Academy of Political and Social Science*, vol. 445 (Sept. 1979), p. 141-54.

'This paper will examine the prominence of the sport of soccer in Uruguay and its interrelationship with the rise and decline of twentieth-century Uruguayan socio-cultural development. The basic premise is that sport and in particular soccer serves as a sociocultural indicator of the patterns of Uruguayan society and mirrors the existing societal condition.' Krotee's argument does not depend on one being the cause of the other, but rather that the sociocultural and sporting processes are symbiotic, both

184

reaching peaks in the late 1920s and early 1950s. The sociocultural criteria are undefined and the idea is rather glib; less contentious is the introductory material on the development of football (soccer) in Uruguay, especially the contribution of British players to it. The author's idea that the Colorados and Blancos produced rival clubs is novel, though it is true that Colorados tend to support Peñarol while Blancos gravitate towards Nacional.

632   **Fútbol: mito y realidad.** (Football: myth and reality.)
Franklin Morales.   Montevideo: Editorial 'Nuestra Tierra', 1969. 64p. bibliog. (Nuestra Tierra 22).

In spite of its important place in the lives of many Uruguayans, there has been little serious analysis of football. This short study examines the sociology of Uruguayan football, including both players and spectators. It avoids clichés, and presents data (on attendances, number of registered players, etc) extending back to 1945 and beyond. The many photographs are interesting and unexpected: the only star player to appear is Pedro Rocha as a member of an under-12s team.

633   **Uruguayan paper money.**
Dale Allan Seppa.   Chicago, Illinois: Obol International, 1974. 60p.

An illustrated catalogue of the banknotes of Uruguay.

Museums and Archives

634 **Latin America in basic historical collections: a working guide.**
Russell H. Bartley, Stuart L. Wagner. Stanford, California:
Hoover Institution Press, 1972. 217p. bibliog. (Hoover Institution
Bibliographical Series, no. 51).
Contains a brief account of archival holdings in the Archivo General de la Nación
(AGN), mainly of the colonial and Independence periods; and the Instituto Nacional
de Investigaciones y Archivos Litcrarios dcl Uruguay, which has family papers, drafts
of literary works and correspondence of outstanding literary figures.

635 **The Archivo General de la Nación of Uruguay.**
John Hoyt Williams. *The Americas*, vol. 36, no. 2 (Oct. 1979),
p. 257-68.
The AGN is the principal public archive in Uruguay. This article has brief notes on
using the archive, but is primarily concerned to indicate its contents. The archive is
organized in four sections. The first, covering the holdings of the former Archivo
General Administrativo, has most of the official government records of the eighteenth
and nineteenth centuries. The second has bound volumes published between 1755 and
1869, and the papers of a number of prominent individuals (including Andrés Lamas,
Eduardo Acevedo, and others) formerly held by the Archivo y Museo Histórico
Nacional. The third has papers deposited by nine of the principal government
ministries and three government agencies (all of which are listed, with the category of
document and the years covered). The fourth, the 'private archives', consists of papers
relating to a large number of individuals who held public office of some kind. The
article is as specific as possible about the contents of the archive (for example, eighty
individuals are named in section four, with the dates covered by the papers), and is
thus an immensely valuable work of reference.

Unesco statistical yearbook.
See item no. 476.

186

Mass Media

636 **Navegar es necesario: Quijano y el seminario 'Marcha'.** (To voyage is necessary: Quijano and the weekly journal 'Marcha'.)
Hugo R. Alfaro. Montevideo: Ediciones de la Banda Oriental, 1984. 122p.

When it was closed down by the military régime in November 1974, *Marcha* had published 1676 editions since its foundation by Carlos Quijano in 1939. By the end it was printing 30,000 copies, and had established an international reputation and circulation. Throughout its history, and in spite of the prestigious names of those who wrote for it, the identification of *Marcha* with Quijano remained total. In 1975 he was forced to seek exile in Mexico, where he died in 1984 as he made preparations for his return to Montevideo. This volume consists of a personal note by the author, a short account of Quijano's ideology, a review of those who wrote for *Marcha* and its orientation ('nationalist inasmuch as anti-imperialist, social democrat inasmuch as socialist'), and a selection of editorials (by Quijano) from its last four years. *Marcha*'s legend 'Navigare necesse. Vivere non necesse' is perhaps easier to translate into Spanish than English. See also Gerardo Caetano and José Pedro Rilla, *El joven Quijano 1900-1933* (The young Quijano 1900-1933) (Montevideo: Ediciones de la Banda Oriental, 1986. 237p.).

637 **Latin American media: guidance and censorship.**
Marvin Alisky. Ames, Iowa: Iowa State University Press, 1981. 265p. bibliog.

There is some useful material on the suppression of press freedom (although Pacheco's action in closing *El Sol* and *Epoca* in 1967 is ignored), but in general this account of the recent history of the media in Uruguay (p. 192-200) is superficial and inconclusive.

638 **Búsqueda.**
Búsqueda began in 1971 as a monthly journal publishing mainly on contemporary economic issues from a liberal (free-market) perspective. Ten years later it began weekly publication, focusing on political developments much more than previously.

Although its editorial posture has not changed, it has acquired a reputation even among its ideological opponents for full, dispassionate and informative reporting. It is the closest that Uruguay has, or has ever had, to a journal of record. Its 450th issue was published in September 1988. Its main sections are: political information; national information; economic information; and national indicators. There are smaller sections devoted to opinion and analysis; business; sport (mainly tennis); international information; books; culture; and letters to the editor.

639 **Medios masivos de comunicación.** (Mass communication media.)
Roque Faraone. Montevideo: Editorial 'Nuestra Tierra', 1969. 60p.
(Nuestra Tierra 25).

A challenging discussion of the media as they existed during the presidency of Pacheco Areco. The work is well illustrated with photographs and reproductions.

640 **La prensa de Montevideo: estudio sobre algunas de sus características.**
(The press of Montevideo: a study of some of its characteristics.)
Roque Faraone. Montevideo: Facultad de Derecho y Ciencias
Sociales, 1960. 203p.

Although inevitably dated in certain respects, this intensive and very detailed study of nine daily newspapers is nonetheless instructive. The publications of a week in May 1957 were analysed for content, and comparison was made with four 'international' newspapers.

641 **The press of Uruguay: historical setting, political shadings.**
Russell H. Fitzgibbon. *Journalism Quarterly*, vol. 29 (1952), p. 437-
46.

Although much of the information is dated (and the number of papers is now much reduced), the structure of the newspaper industry remains very broadly as Fitzgibbon described it: Uruguay's press is dominated by Montevideo papers, each with a well-defined political affiliation and function, but no editorial giants. This article estimates the circulation for the leading eight papers, which in total was a massive 390,000. 'The quality of local news reporting is not especially notable in Montevideo.' There are brief notes on the provincial press, radio, and the prospects for television.

642 **Mass media: la guía, 1988.** (Mass media: the guide, 1988.)
Montevideo: Instituto de Comunicación y Desarrollo (ICD), 1987.
248p.

This is an indispensable directory to the mass media in Uruguay. Its principal chapters deal with the press, radio, television, journals (national, foreign and distributors), cinema, video distributors, information services, advertising and publicity agencies, marketing agencies, research centres, libraries and archives, information technology companies, and state and public communication agencies. The information is reasonably complete in coverage, and gives (as appropriate) names, addresses, phone numbers, where and how printed, circulation, political orientation or affiliation, and much else besides.

643 **Southern cone report.**
Latin American Newsletters. ten issues per year. (Latin American regional reports).
An excellent source of reporting in depth and background information on current political issues.

644 **Latin American weekly report.**
Latin American Newsletters. weekly.
Provides probably the best specialist English-language news service.

645 **World radio TV handbook.**
Edited by Andrew G. Sennitt.   New York; London: Billboard.
annual. map.
The 1987 edition (vol. 41) lists 81 radio stations in Uruguay (p. 360-61), with the call-sign, transmitting frequency and strength, hours of transmission, address, and name of director for each. There are also details of three national radio authorities. Twenty-one TV stations are listed on page 424. All South American radio stations are listed by frequency on pages 485-510 (medium wave) and pages 513-40 (short wave).

646 **Directory of international broadcasting.**
Edited by Christopher Surgenor.   London: BSO Publications, 1983.
401p.
The Uruguay entry (p. 79-80) gives name and address of 75 radio stations (20 in Montevideo) and 25 television stations (6 in Montevideo).

Directories

647 **South America, Central America and the Caribbean 1988.**
London: Europa Publications, 1987. 2nd ed. 683p. map. bibliog.
The section on Uruguay (p. 639-58) contains short essays on national history and the economy by Henry Finch (revised for this edition by Helen Schooley); a statistical survey; and a directory detailing members of the government, ministries, political organisations, diplomatic representation in Uruguay, churches, the media, finance, trade and industry, trade unions and tourism. Addresses and many telephone numbers are given.

648 **The world of learning.**
London: Europa Publications. annual.
The 1988 edition (the 38th, 1925p.) lists Uruguay on p. 1762-64. There are details (in most cases address, purpose and publications) of the Academía Nacional de Letras (National Academy of Literature); 26 learned societies; 18 research institutes; 12 libraries; and 9 museums. The University and six colleges are listed. A serious omission from the listing of research institutes is the group of social science research centres, especially Centro Interdisciplinario de Estudios sobre el Desarrollo, Uruguay (CIEDUR); Centro de Informaciones y Estudios del Uruguay (CIESU); Centro de Investigaciones Económicas (CINVE); and Centro Latinoamericano de Economía Humana (CLAEH).

649 **Diccionario uruguayo de biografías, 1810-1940.** (Uruguayan dictionary of biography, 1810-1940.)
José M. Fernández Saldaña. Montevideo: Editorial Amerindia, 1945. 1366p.
The dictionary gives biographical information on about 800 significant historical figures. The criteria for inclusion are unfortunately not stated by the author, who began work on the project in 1910. It is nonetheless indispensable as a guide to historical figures.

650 **Who's who in Latin America: Part V. Argentina, Paraguay, and Uruguay.**
Edited by Ronald Hilton. Stanford, California: Stanford University Press; Chicago, Illinois: A. N. Marquis; London: Geoffrey Cumberlege; London: Oxford University Press, 1950. 3rd ed. 258p.
Over 250 individuals are listed for Uruguay on pages 219-58 of this valuable source. Personal details, family, career, memberships, publications, and domestic and professional addresses, are the principal categories of information given.

651 **Encyclopedia of the Third World.**
George Thomas Kurian. London: Mansell Publishing, 1982. rev. ed. maps.
The entry for Uruguay is on pages 1876-92 of Vol. III. It presents much summary information relating to geography, politics, history, the economy, education, the media, etc. Data arc mostly given for the late 1970s.

652 **Quién es quién en el Uruguay.** (Who's who in Uruguay.)
Montevideo: Central de Publicaciones, Panamérica Uruguaya, 1980. 688p.
The first part of this illustrated directory deals with individuals from the worlds of business, industry, journalism, the arts, the church, education, etc. The second part gives information on companies and other institutions.

653 **Uruguayans of to-day.**
William Belmont Parker. London; New York: Hispanic Society of America, 1921. 575p. (Hispanic Notes and Monographs, no. 7).
Brief biographical essays of 208 eminent Uruguayans, with photographic portraits of ninety-five. In his foreword the author points out the presence of 'a large number of lawyers and physicians, government officials, diplomats, soldiers, and teachers, and but a comparatively small number of those engaged in industry and commerce'. Why? 'The way to the high places in government, which are the general goal of ambition, so often lies through the professions.'

654 **The statesman's year-book: statistical and historical annual of the states of the world.**
Edited by John Paxton. London: Macmillan. annual.
The 1986-87 edition (the 23rd, 1685p.) covers Uruguay on p. 1563-67 under these headings: history (five lines); area and population (by departments and their capitals); climate; constitution and government (principal ministers listed); defence (including equipment); international relations (apparently negligible); economy; energy and natural resources; industry and trade; communications; justice, religion, education and welfare; and diplomatic representation (with USA and UK). The information appears to be accurate but is thin.

655 **Uruguayos contemporáneos: nuevo diccionario de datos biográficos y bibliográficos.** (Contemporary Uruguayans: new dictionary of biographical and bibliographical information.)
Arturo Scarone. Montevideo: Barreiro y Ramos, 1937. 610p.
Includes more than 1300 leading individuals of the nineteenth and twentieth centuries in politics, business and the professions.

656 **The international year book and statesmen's who's who.**
East Grinstead, Sussex: Thomas Skinner Directories. 1953- . annual.
The entry for Uruguay (p. 679-81) in the 1987 (35th) edition has brief material on the constitution and government; legal system; area and population; currency; principal banks; production, industry and commerce (with data to 1985); and newspapers.

657 **Historical dictionary of Uruguay.**
Jean L. Willis, foreword by A. Curtis Wilgus. Metuchen, New Jersey: Scarecrow Press, 1974. 275p. bibliog. (Latin American Historical Dictionaries, no. 11).
'A succinct account of prominent persons, places, and events of Uruguay's past; important geographical place names and occurrences of contemporary Uruguay are also included.' The result is an unpretentious rag-bag of entries with no sub-divisions, a potentially useful if arbitrary annotated list of names and titles to be encountered in the country. A random page has entries for a contemporary politician, two protagonists of the Independence period, a bird, the main hospital, holidays with pay, the Montevideo race-track, and Holy Week.

658 **Latin America and Caribbean review.**
Saffron Walden, England: World of Information. annual.
This is a useful guide designed primarily for business use. It leads with an assessment of the current political and economic situation (by Michael Rose since 1984), and has sections on useful addresses (including seven hotels in Montevideo), banks, diplomatic representation, climate, entry requirements, travel, telecommunications, media, working hours and holidays, and principal economic indicators for the last three years. The 1988 edition (the 9th) was published in 1987; Uruguay appears on pages 118-21.

Mass media: la guía, 1988. (Mass media: the guide, 1988.)
See item no. 642.

Bibliographies

659 Latin America and the Caribbean: a bibliographical guide to works in English.
S. A. Bayitch. Coral Gables, Florida: University of Miami Press; Dobbs Ferry, New York: Oceana Publications, 1967. 943p. (University of Miami School of Law, Interamerican Legal Studies, vol. 10).

This is a new expanded version of the compiler's 1961 bibliography on Latin America. The foreword admits a bias towards the inclusion of items dealing with economic, legal and political matters, while others such as arts and sciences have been left to other bibliographies. There are thematic and country sections, which for Uruguay includes about 350 items and occupies pages 766-77. There are no annotations, nor are the identities of publishers revealed, though the comparatively unhelpful place of publication is given.

660 Anuario bibliográfico uruguayo. (Bibliographical yearbook of Uruguay.)
Montevideo: Biblioteca Nacional. annual.

Uruguay's national bibliography was published in 1946-49 and resumed in 1968. Books and pamphlets are arranged by subject. There is an index of authors. For an extensive assessment of its strengths and weaknesses see G. E. Gorman and J. J. Mills, *Guide to current national bibliographies in the Third World* (London: Hans Zell, 1987), 2nd ed., p. 340-43.

661 A bibliography of Latin American bibliographies.
Arthur Eric Gropp. Metuchen, New Jersey: Scarecrow Press, 1968. 515p.

This volume updates Cecil Knight Jones, *Bibliography of Latin American Bibliographies* (Washington, D.C.: Library of Congress, 1942), and contains 7210 monograph items containing bibliographical material published by the end of 1964. The items are organized thematically, and the index is extensive. The work has itself

193

been updated with the publication by Scarecrow Press of three supplementary volumes: Arthur Eric Gropp, *A Bibliography of Latin American Bibliographies* (1971) refers to 1416 monograph items published during 1965-69; Daniel Raposo Cordeiro, *A Bibliography of Latin American Bibliographies: Social Sciences and Humanities* (1979) has details of 1750 bibliographical publications appearing in monograph (1969-74) or periodical (1966-74) form; and Haydée Piedracueva, *A Bibliography of Latin American Bibliographies: Social Sciences and Humanities* (1982) lists a further 2122 items (monographs and periodicals) published during 1975-79. There are no annotations in any of these volumes.

662 **A bibliography of Latin American bibliographies published in periodicals.**
Arthur Eric Gropp. Metuchen, New Jersey: Scarecrow Press, 1976.
2 vols. 1031p.

Contains 9715 unannotated references to bibliographical material published in periodicals up to 1965. The work is updated by two volumes mentioned in the annotation to item no. 661 (q.v.).

663 **Bibliographic guide to Latin American studies.**
Boston, Massachusetts: G.K. Hall. annual

This work, publication of which probably began in 1978, provides an encyclopaedic, unselective list of new publications in the preceding year. It is based on works catalogued by the Latin American Collection at the University of Texas at Austin, supplemented by the Library of Congress. There are no annotations. Each volume is organized as a single alphabetical series which includes both authors and themes. The material on Uruguay consists overwhelmingly of works published in Uruguay. The user seeking gold will also encounter a great deal of base rock; but this bibliography enormously simplifies the task of finding items whose publication might otherwise go almost unnoticed outside the country.

664 **Handbook of Latin American studies.**
Edited by Dolores Moyano Martin. Austin, Texas: University of Texas Press. 1935- . annual.

Alternate years of this standard bibliographical guide to Latin American studies are devoted either, like no. 47 (1985), to the social sciences, or, like no. 48 (1986), to the humanities. The former has sections devoted to anthropology, economics, education, geography, government and politics, international relations, and sociology; the latter covers art, film, history, language, literature, music, and philosophy. The *Handbook* describes itself as 'a selective and annotated guide to recent publications', and is 'prepared by a number of scholars for the Hispanic Division of the Library of Congress'. The present editor has served since no. 38 (1976). A feature of the *Handbook* are the introductory notes (on, for example, 'economics: Uruguay') by named North American scholars which precede the annotated bibliographical entries in each section. Both English- and Spanish-language books and articles are included, with introductions and annotations in English or Spanish depending apparently on the preferred language of the individual scholar. As an indicator of its Uruguayan coverage, no. 47 has 23 items on the economics of the country, 10 on education, 2 on geography, 8 on cartography, 7 on government and politics, and 16 on sociology.

665 **Index to Spanish American collective biography. Vol. 4 – the River Plate countries.**
Sara de Mundo Lo. Boston, Massachusetts: G. K. Hall, 1985. 388p.
'The purpose of this work is to provide access to information about the lives of individuals associated with Spanish America, its culture, and its institutions, as recorded in a variety of sources'. References on Uruguay occupy pages 177-204, in sections specific to the armed forces, art, biography, education, genealogy, history, journalism, law, history, medicine, music, performing arts, political parties, printing, pseudonyms, religion, science, sports, and women. In total there are 173 entries, all annotated, which list (where feasible) the biographees, and indicate in which North American libraries the work is to be found. There are four indexes: of authors, short titles, geographical, and biographees. References to works in both Spanish (mostly) and English are included.

666 **Latin American serial documents: a holdings list. Vol. 11: Uruguay.**
Compiled by Rosa Quintero Mesa. Ann Arbor, Michigan: University Microfilms, Xerox Education Group, 1973. 169p. (Latin American Serial Documents, vol. 11).
Lists Uruguayan serial documents and where they are available in libraries in the United States and Canada.

667 **Latin America: a guide to illustrations.**
Alva Curtis Wilgus. Metuchen, New Jersey: Scarecrow Press, 1981. 250p.
This is a guide to illustrations of Latin America which have appeared in some 500 publications written in English and (almost exclusively) published in the United States. The work is divided into five historical periods, each of which is divided thematically and, for the national period, by country. In addition pictures of over 2500 individuals are listed. For all of these categories, the bibliographical reference of the illustration is given. In view of the scale of this undertaking, it is hardly necessary for the editor to admit that it is not comprehensive, but it is not hard to think of items which might have been included. The section on Uruguay (national period) is on pages 146-48, and the main headings (each sub- and sub-sub-divided) are environment; political; cities; society; culture; religion; economy; transportation; and miscellaneous.

Accounts of nineteenth-century South America: an annotated check-list of works by British and United States observers.
See item no. 26.

Travel accounts and descriptions of Latin America and the Caribbean, 1800-1920; a select bibliography.
See item no. 27.

Selective annotated bibliography on the climates of Paraguay, Uruguay and Argentina.
See item no. 90.

Urbanization in twentieth century Latin America: a working bibliography.
See item no. 93.

Bibliographies

Bibliography and index of geology.
See item no. 94.

Bibliografía sobre geología y paleontología del Uruguay. (Bibliography of the geology and palaeontology of Uruguay.)
See item no. 99.

Bibliography of economic geology of South America.
See item no. 102.

Research tools for Latin American historians.
See item no. 134.

Contribution to a bibliography on Artigas and the beginnings of Uruguay, 1810-1820.
See item no. 150.

Race and ethnic relations in Latin America and the Caribbean: an historical dictionary and bibliography.
See item no. 205.

The *gaucho*: cattle hunter, cavalryman, ideal of romance.
See item no. 206.

The Spanish of Argentina and Uruguay: an annotated bibliography for 1940-1978.
See item no. 213.

Protestantism in Latin America: a bibliographical guide.
See item no. 232.

Latin American politics: a historical bibliography.
See item no. 253.

The literature of terrorism: a selectively annotated bibliography.
See item no. 303.

The urban guerrilla in Latin America: a select bibliography.
See item no. 307.

The criminal justice systems of the Latin American nations: a bibliography of the primary and secondary literature.
See item no. 339.

A bibliography of United States–Latin American relations since 1810: a selected list of eleven thousand published references.
See item no. 349.

Bibliography of Western European–Latin American relations.
See item no. 354.

Uruguayan research on forage problems.
See item no. 421.

Herbage abstracts.
See item no. 424.

Soils and fertilizers.
See item no. 425.

Education in Latin America: a bibliography.
See item no. 493.

Nonformal education in Latin America; an annotated bibliography.
See item no. 496.

Spanish American modernism: a selected bibliography.
See item no. 510.

A tentative bibliography of the *belles-lettres* of Uruguay.
See item no. 514.

Spanish-American women writers: a bibliographical research checklist.
See item no. 515.

Index to anthologies of Latin American literature in English translation.
See item no. 520.

The Afro-Spanish American author: an annotated bibliography of criticism.
See item no. 521.

Latin American literature in English translation: an annotated bibliography.
See item no. 524.

La narrativa uruguaya: estudio crítico-bibliográfico. (The Uruguayan narrative: a critical and bibliographical study.)
See item no. 529.

The 20th century Spanish-American novel: a bibliographic guide.
See item no. 530.

Handbook of Latin American art: a bibliographic compilation.
See item no. 604.

Modern Latin American art: a bibliography.
See item no. 608.

Indexes

There follow three separate indexes: authors (personal and corporate); titles; and subjects. Title entries are italicized and refer either to the main titles or to other works cited in the annotation (but not to theses). The numbers refer to bibliographic entry rather than page numbers. Individual index entries are arranged in alphabetical sequence.

Index of Authors

In addition to authors, the index includes compilers, editors, illustrators and translators, as well as contributors of prefaces and introductions. Authors of theses are not indexed.

Index of Titles

The definite or indefinite article has been omitted from most English-language titles where this is the first word in the title. For those which retain it, and for all Spanish-language titles beginning with the definite or indefinite article, the work is indexed according to the second word.

215

218

Index of Subjects

229

Map of Uruguay

This map shows the more important towns and other features.